22201

22201

THE COMPLETE BOOK OF
MATCH FISHING

● *A good way to prevent spare pole sections from slipping into the water is to lay them inside the keepnet mouth*

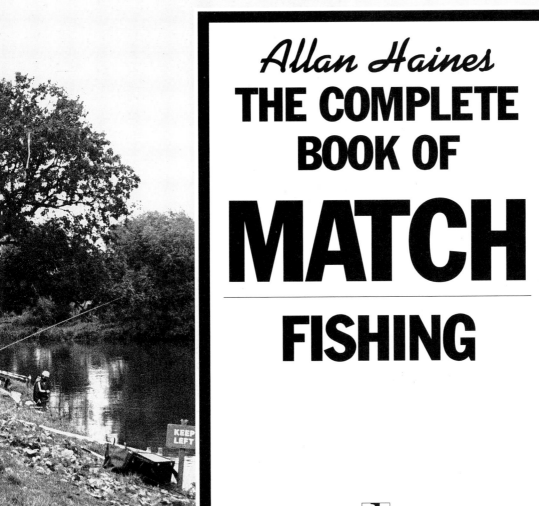

Allan Haines

THE COMPLETE
BOOK OF
MATCH
FISHING

David & Charles

DAVID & CHARLES' FISHING TITLES

THE ANGLING TIMES BOOK OF COARSE FISHING · Allan Haines and Mac Campbell
BIG FISH FROM FAMOUS WATERS · Compiled by Chris Turnbull
CATCHING BIG TENCH · Len Arbery
THE COMPLETE BOOK OF FLOAT FISHING · Allan Haines
FROM WATER TO NET · John Bailey
THE GREAT ANGLERS · John Bailey
THE GREAT SALMON BEATS · Crawford Little
SUCCESS WITH BIG TENCH · Chris Turnbull
SUCCESS WITH SALMON · Crawford Little
SUCCESS WITH TROUT · John Dawson, Martin Cairncross and Chris Ogborne
TALES FROM THE WATER'S EDGE · Tom Quinn

British Library Cataloguing in Publication Data

Haines, Allan
  The complete book of match fishing.
  I. Title
  799.1

ISBN 0-7153-9908-X

Typeset by ICON, Exeter
Designed by Martin Harris
Printed in Great Britain by The Bath Press, Avon
for David & Charles plc
Brunel House Newton Abbot Devon

● *(pp2–3) Who said match fishing isn't a spectator
sport? This crowd turned up to watch a world
championship on the Warwickshire Avon*

Contents

Introduction

Angling came on the scene very early in my life in the most simple of ways. A bamboo cane and the proverbial bent pin was the only tackle to hand and there were precious few fish silly enough to fall for my clumsy attempts at fooling them.

This new-found pastime slowly chipped away at my mind, taking over from the many other important facets of a young boy's lifestyle. Saturday trips to the football match were passed over in favour of even more, long and usually fishless, hours by the riverside. Pocket money went on maggots instead of sweets and every waking hour was spent dreaming of the next trip to the river.

Looking back, it was a tough apprenticeship and many of my friends tired of it and turned towards new horizons. For me the bug had bitten more deeply.

Pocket money was tight and tackle limited, usually handed down, given as birthday and Christmas presents, or, when necessary, earned in exchange for errands. It was not tackle, however, that was lacking, but skill and knowledge. Thankfully my fortunes changed and I was helped and advised well by adult anglers around me. Before I reached my teens a top local matchman told me that if I persevered I might one day fish for my home town in a national championship.

I did persevere and those words came true a few years later and to this day often flash through my mind.

My story is similar to those of so many others in match fishing today. Given the determination, it is that sort of sport. There are no barriers or reasons why the top can't be reached, no matter how humble the beginnings. Success recognises no qualifications other than hard work and a will to win.

Today's match angler has it easy. Good tackle and bait is readily available. Matches are plentiful and there's a fair amount of advice available to those willing to search it out.

Match fishing has played a major part in my life and work. It has brought me pleasure, excitement and above all helped me to make many good friends. If this book lets you share those experiences it will have done its job well.

Part I

Tackle, Preparation and Planning

It is a complicated recipe that goes towards making a successful match angler. This first section explains the many processes that ensure all the ingredients are prepared and brought together efficiently.

1
Getting started

Match fishing is a demanding sport. It takes dedication, time, effort, attention to detail and, at the highest levels, considerable cash outlay. The rewards can be great but if you are going into the game to get rich it would be best to forget the idea right now and take up golf.

There are big prizes to be won. But offset all the other factors against them, and it's easy to see that it's some other driving force which motivates thousands of match anglers every weekend of the season. That motivation is the need for competition rather than the spoils victory may bring. Of course prizes are essential and without them much of the intensity would perhaps be lost. At club level, from which every match angler should start out on the long road to the top, prize money and trophies will probably do little more than cover the day's total outlay. But that is where a match-angling apprenticeship must be served. There are no short cuts. No easy ways. No magic formula to reduce the learning time.

Even before venturing into the world of club match angling you will no doubt have spent several seasons at least, as a 'pleasure' angler. Maybe the term 'pleasure' is wrong to describe the angler who fishes for nothing more than the sport. For match fishing is a 'pleasure' too. It's far more demanding, but just as a professional footballer loves his game, so does the match angler. Those days as a 'pleasure' angler will be the basis on which to formulate the next stage. The principles will be the same but they are going to need fine tuning and adapting to suit the cut and thrust of the competition scene.

So what's the difference between the two sports? For a start the fishing will be harder. Matches are usually fished during the more sociable hours of the day, which are also the times when sport is often slow. Then you draw a swim. It may well be the worst on the water and certainly not one that you would have chosen to fish. But fish it you must, and to catch even a few small fish may be all you can hope for. Finally you will not be alone. Right next to you, just fifteen or twenty yards away, on either side, there will be other anglers, your rivals who will be trying to catch more than you and, if possible, at the same time stop you catching. Yes, match fishing is a tough old game!

So before starting out on this long apprenticeship road it is worth considering what makes a match angler.

Possibly one of the best comparisons is to a Grand Prix motor racing driver. Good eyesight, fast reactions, dedication, attention to detail and above all good preparation.

Eyesight and reactions – except for getting some good glasses – you can do little about. But, just as with the driver, the other attributes can be worked at. The dedication comes from a deep desire to be the best. Attention to detail may mean practice sessions. It may include producing special floats to cope with a new venue. It can mean passing up a night out with the lads, even missing some fishing.

Next is the actual preparation. That involves hours servicing tackle: again, just as the driver wants his car in top condition, so you want your tackle to be right up to scratch. A line that's past its best or a rod with a cracked ring, a bait catapult with perished elastic – just a few of the many things which can cost you dearly in the heat of battle. Bait is going to need time too. Here again you want the best available. The maggots you purchase will need time spent in cleaning and preparing, for here is the real match fishing edge. Your bait must arrive at the waterside in just that little bit better condition than everyone else's.

Practice sessions on a hard water may be no comparison to the pleasurable experience of a day at a

● *The sort of occasion that makes it all worthwhile. International fly fisherman Bob Church (left) presents me with the BBC 2 Television 'Hooked' trophy*

prolific one. All the same you will need to spend time in such a fashion if success is to follow.

So you see, match fishing is not all glamour and trophies. Yet the feeling of knowing you have done everything to lower the odds against you is a great start and armed with the confidence it brings you will at least start every match in the right frame of mind.

Of course there are those who just don't bother. They fish with tackle that is scruffy, worn out and neglected. Their bait is dirty and past its best yet they still win. Perhaps they are naturals, maybe a bit lucky; either way they will, in the long term, suffer for their attitude.

Having tried hard to emphasise the importance of good equipment it must be said that it isn't flashy tackle that wins matches. The fish don't care whether you are sitting on a folding stool or a very expensive continental seat-box. The tackle that matters is the stuff that actually does the catching, the rod, the reel, the line, hook and bait. The rest is fine tuning. What is important is skill, knowledge and confidence. Those,

backed with sound and functional tackle, make the real winning combination.

Now is the time to consider what you want from match fishing. It may be the companionship of a works or pub club and the chance to join their regular outings. If that's the level at which your match fishing is to begin and end there is nothing wrong with it. You are set for many happy years in pleasant company.

On the other hand, you may be more ambitious and eventually feel the need to sample the harsh world of open events. This is the top league of large matches where big money is to be won.

Success may come and if it does you will draw the attention of teams looking to strengthen their squads. Now the real dedication begins. You join a successful team or match group and the pressure is on. You are no longer fishing for yourself. Now you are carrying the responsibility of not letting your side down. Every match is now that bit harder. It's also a lot of fun and for many the ultimate match fishing experience.

At the highest level of team competition are the

● *Under the eye of the camera I try to concentrate. The big fellow with the cap is former England world cup footballer Jack Charlton*

national championships, the big sponsored knockout events and even the world championship itself. In match fishing you decide how far you want to go.

The good thing about match fishing is that it does offer everyone the chance to shine and to progress right to the top. If you are good enough you will get an England cap. There are no barriers other than the ones you erect yourself. If you fish nothing but club matches that's where your career is going to stop.

A good match angler is an all-rounder. An angler who can fish a stick float on a running river, tackle a wide, windswept water with a waggler, be confident with a leger; a master of the pole and all its facets.

Few are equally adept at them all and as your match fishing develops so a pattern will emerge. Maybe the

waggler will be your particular speciality, or perhaps the leger. The danger now is to fish only those events which suit your style. In the early seasons that's fine but take care not to become just another 'one-method match angler'.

While it will be nice to win regularly on the same waters, things will eventually change and you'll be left with no other string to your bow. Sure, carry on winning, but take time to polish up the other methods too. That way the winning spell will continue for much longer.

The secret of the correct learning curve is to work at each method, overlapping them so that they begin to come together in a manageable sequence. Chasing all over the place, fishing one method and one water today and two completely different sets tomorrow is going to leave you a Jack of all Trades but master of none. Take the first steps with care, progress slowly and learn the craft well. Patience is possibly the one quality we have as yet overlooked.

The tackle

Match tackle needs to be the best you can afford. It will be subjected to a lot of wear and tear, and buying cheap will eventually prove costly.

As match fishing takes its hold so the tackle collection will grow too. So this first introduction is going to deal with the basic but complete kit that will see you through a couple of seasons. You will of course add to it to meet the special needs of your own match circuit.

Float fishing is likely to take up much of your time so a couple of good float rods are the first consideration. Modern materials mean the 13-foot rod will be fine. While there are some superb 12-footers around, I can see no real use for a rod of this length. The weight saving is minimal and the loss of that last foot is nothing more than a disadvantage. If the 13-foot rod in a range feels sloppy compared with the equivalent 12-foot model then chances are it's not a good rod anyway.

• A rod handle should feel comfortable; too slim or too fat and it will make the finger ache. Check also for length. Ideally the handle should protrude 2 or 3in beyond the elbow when gripped over the reel.

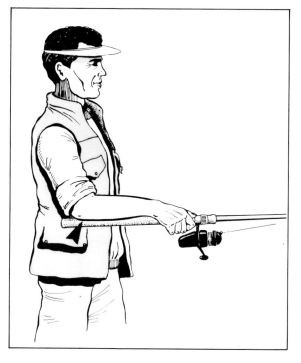

So: a pair of 13-footers with sensible actions. Here you may eventually want to acquire rods with sharp tip actions for close-in stick-float fishing and models with slightly softer characteristics for the waggler. If the budget says just two rods to suit all methods then they must be models that fall somewhere between the two actions. The action needs to be fairly fast and the middle and butt sections on the stiff side. Weight, or at least balance, is critical. You are going to be holding the rod for five hours at a time. If it's badly balanced you will not stay the course. Weight can be added inside the handle to correct bad balance but with so many good rods to choose from it is a modification that's easy to avoid.

Materials such as boron and kevlar have made very big impacts on the match rod scene. Both provide strength and stiffness even if at the expense of a little extra weight. The choice is a personal one but there is nothing wrong with a good quality, high-modulus carbon.

Having found the right action and length to suit your needs, check that the overall profile is slim, the handle is not too long – the ideal length should protrude beyond your elbow when the reel is in the right balancing position and the hand is wrapped around the stem.

Cork is a nice handle material. It wears well, can be cleaned easily and has a warm feel to it in the colder months. It's worth checking that the diameter is right for your hand size. A slim profile that fits comfortably into the palm is what you need.

Rod rings are again a matter of choice. Good quality stainless or hard chrome stand-off patterns are light and will not make the rod feel sloppy. The drawback is that they eventually wear out and need to be replaced. Ceramic-lined ones don't wear but they are usually a little heavier. Single-legged or three-legged types go some way to eliminating this slight drawback. The single-legged ones are also claimed to have a reduced effect on the rod's action but generally this is splitting hairs and the difference is negligible.

Legering is also going to be a part of your match attack so a quivertip rod and maybe a slightly heavier one for feeder work are going to be needed. Go for a bit of length. The old style of a 9-footer does have its drawbacks. A 10½-footer is a much better choice and one of 11 feet would not go amiss on many waters. Choice is wide but a quivertip with a range of interchangeable tips will cover most needs. The action should be such that you can fish with small hooks and fine lines without breaking off. This means a softish, but not sloppy, feel to the top section.

The feeder rod needs some backbone, making it capable of throwing a feeder of perhaps a couple of ounces or more.

Now comes the most expensive item in your kit – a pole – costing anything from £250 to upwards of £1,000. You get what you pay for.

Go for the longest you can afford. One of 11 metres is a good buy and like the float rods it should be slim, light and correctly balanced. The action needs to be very stiff. One which flops around will be unmanageable in anything more than a gentle breeze and in any case bites will be missed and tangles frequent.

The main pole is going to be fitted with an internal elastic system and will be used with a short line for most of the time. But a second pole – or at least a spare set of top sections – will be needed for a whip. This pole will be used with a fine 'quivertip' top and a

● *The most expensive piece of tackle will be a good pole. Go for the longest you can afford but expect to pay anything up to £1,000 for a decent one*

line of the same length as the pole. For speed work when fish can be swung to hand the whip is a superior tool. It works for tiny fish but is equally at home in dealing with weighty chub or other match winners.

A good starting length when selecting a whip is 6 or 7 metres, but often it will be fished at shorter lengths.

Reels

It's no good buying a good rod then ruining the whole thing by sticking a cheap reel on the handle. Weight is a consideration and the engineering will need to be good too. Carbon bodies are all the rage and they certainly help reduce the overall weight. A high gear-ratio will obviously save valuable seconds on each retrieve. These add up to several minutes extra fishing time during the course of a match but beware of the ultra-fast models, for unless used with care they tend to cause twist in the hook length. The high gearing also makes them feel a little stiff – like riding a bike in top gear. A good guide would be a ratio of around 5 to 1.

Spool depth should not be deep. A capacity of 100 metres of 2lb to 3lb line is going to see most service.

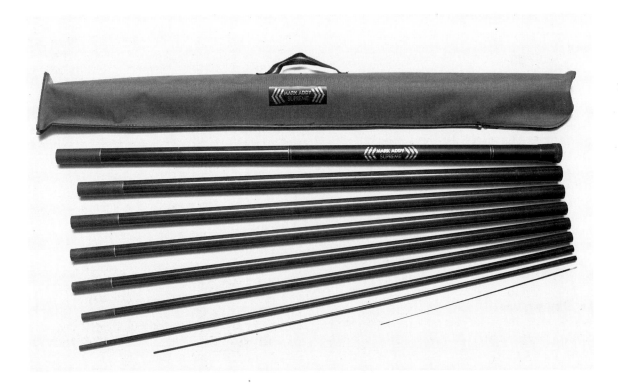

● *A superb example of a modern match reel. The spool is wide and a two-speed oscillating system ensures good line lay*

You'll need several spools and ideally a pair of the chosen model.

Other deeper spools may be needed for heavy feeder fishing when lines of 6lb may be needed.

Closed-face reels do have their good points and on running water chances are you will find a use for one, but for most of the time a good fixed spool is going to be fine. Automatic bale-arms are good – the old Mitchell Match is still going strong after more than a quarter of a century – and they do save time. Here again there are no strict rules. You will have to decide for yourself which suits you best.

As a guide, though, select a pair of reels that are fuctional and don't have lots of protruding bits and pieces which may foul line. Skirted spools prevent tangles forming behind the spool. It's a good idea too to find a model with a wide spool so that fine line does not bed into itself. The wider the spool, the fewer

turns of line there will be stacked on top of one another. Casting will be smoother too as a result.

All the more expensive reels now have 'pop off' spools. These are preferable because they can be changed quickly and, should line get around the back, they can be taken off without having bits left lying around while the problem is solved. A check worth making is that the release button on the spool's front does not protrude in a manner which could result in

● *Watch out for reel spools with protruding release buttons (right). Either grind them down (left) or choose a different model.*

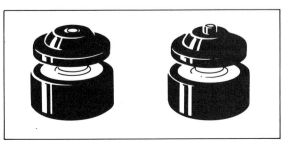

loose line picking up and being wound around it. That was a problem on early Mitchells which was later rectified by reducing the button profile.

A lot of development has gone into reel clutch and drag design. The results are good and many reels with rear drag knobs can be set very accurately to give off line at the desired tension. Yet oddly enough you will find most experienced match anglers tighten their drags right down, preferring instead to play a fish off the handle.

Lines

Having selected suitable rods and reels we need to consider line to match them. Here is where personal choice figures yet again. There are many different brands of line, although they all originate from just a handful of companies worldwide.

There are lines which are pre-stretched, offering fine diameters in relation to their breaking strain. You pay however in that such lines are less tolerant than others and can result in 'cracking off' on the strike unless handled with care.

Then there are sinking and floating lines. Often these are identical in chemical composition but the sinking version will have had the surface shine removed prior to spooling. Some anglers go to great lengths to match the type of line to their method, which is, generally speaking, a sinking line for waggler work and a floater for stick-float fishing. Personally I have found little need for this because a floater can be made to sink with a little treatment, rubbing down with a ball of fuller's earth powder mixed with washing-up liquid to form a putty-like texture. The fuller's earth removes the shine and the washing-up liquid de-greases and helps the line cut beneath the water's surface tension.

If you want a line to float it's a case of rubbing it gently with a suitable floatant such as those used by fly fishers.

Price is no guide to line quality either. My own choice is still one of the cheaper brands and over the years I have had no complaints. If you are really puzzled ask your local dealer for advice, or better still seek help on the local match scene. Anglers will talk for hours about line. All you then have to do is make your own mind up and try a few.

Breaking-strain will of course depend on the waters you expect to fish. A canal may need a line of 1lb or so,

Knot sense

There is no point going to great lengths to build up a reel spool correctly with line if the whole effect is going to be ruined by a poorly tied knot.

A roughly tied, bulky knot will not only be liable to breakage but also results in a bump on the bottom of the spool. This makes the line lie unevenly, which ultimately hinders smooth casting. Watch out too for loose ends left sitcking up from the knot. These catch on the coils of line lying over them and again can prevent a nice flow off the spool.

The knot in the diagram is easy to tie, is not bulky and above all is secure. Although security may not seem particularly important because the whole line rarely comes off the spool, there is always the danger that a reel may fall into the river, and the line is the only means of rescue. If the knot fails then it's goodbye reel.

When tying a spool knot always ease it right to the back of the spool where it can sit well away from the majority of line coils.

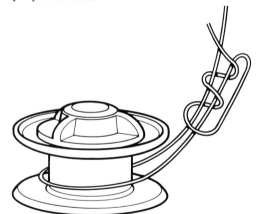

● *This simple knot will not only keep line secure on the reel but will also ensure there is no bulk to hinder casting.*

while a river noted for big fish may demand 3lb or more. The answer is to load up your spare spools with line that will cope with all eventualities. For float fishing, lines of 1.7lb to 2.6lb will cover most waters. For legering a 2.6lb and maybe a 3.2lb will suffice. Feeder fising is another matter, however. For while the leger lines will cope with small and medium feeders the really big 'jam jar' jobs used on rivers such as the Trent will call for something in the 5lb to 6lb region.

Having decided on the lines, you'll need to be sure to replace them regularly. A line used for match fishing is subjected to a lot of use in a very short time. Line is cheap, losing fish is expensive. Check carefully and discard any line that may be suspect. And when you discard it, do so safely by cutting it into small pieces and burning it. That way it will not get left around to harm wildlife.

Hooks

As with line, there are many differing ideas on the subject. Some match anglers demand long shank patterns, others a crystal bend, a barbless or micro-

barb style. Like so much in angling it's all down to confidence in what you are using.

There are many different makes from which to choose. 'Chemically sharpened' is a term you'll see around a lot. All it means is that the hook is de-scaled during its manufacture by the use of chemicals. This treatment produces a superior point and one which is free from tiny burrs.

No matter which pattern you decide upon it must be

● *The easiest and safest way to tie a spade-end hook. Make between twelve and fourteen turns around the shank and always finish with line coming off from the point side of the spade.*

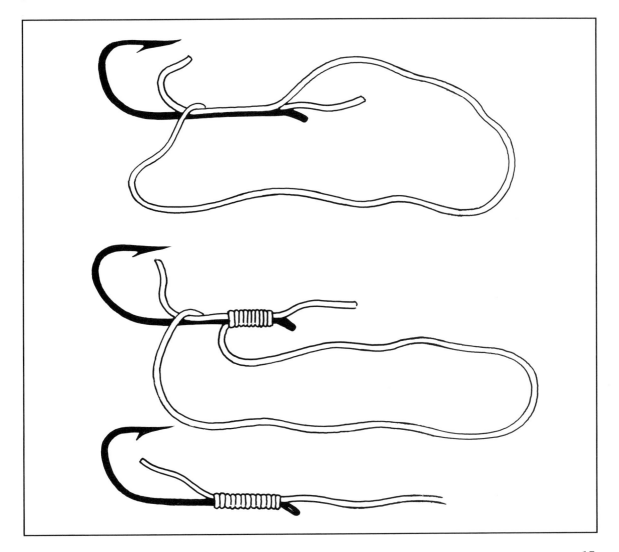

sharp. Chances are you will be tying your own – although there are now some good commercially tied ones available – and if so be sure to select ones with small spade ends and made in a wire as fine as the fishing you will be doing allows. Hooks with big spades will cause the bait to spin on the retrieve. You can of course stone them down to a sensible size but with so many good patterns to choose from it really is time wasted.

Micro-barbs are very popular and rightly so. These tiny barbs enable a hook to be struck home easily, and while they keep the fish on, they can be removed quickly and easily without causing any harm to the fish. Barbless styles also have their uses but before going too far down that route it's worthwhile trying some in practice to see if they suit you.

By tying your own hooks you have the advantage of being able to decide on not only the pattern of hook but also the brand of line and breaking-strain you want. You can decide on the length of line you want to attach, too. Mine are around two feet long for rod and line

fishing and about nine inches for pole work. The shorter pole length is because weight is often needed much closer to the hook than with running tackle and it is best attached to the line rather than the hook length.

Actual tying can be done in several ways. You may find one of the commercially available hook tiers suits you. Certainly many top match anglers simply tie on a length of finer line to their reel line and attach a hook on the bank. This, with practice, can be just as quick as taking a ready-tied one from a packet and attaching in the normal fashion. My own preference is for a hand-tied and pre-packeted hook which I can prepare in the warmth and comfort of my house rather than on a wet and cold February river bank.

With the method I use a length of line is measured off to a pre-determined length – such as the width of an

● *Two ways of attaching hook lengths to main line. The blood knot and three-turn water knot make neat and secure joins. An alternative is a loop and half-blood knot.*

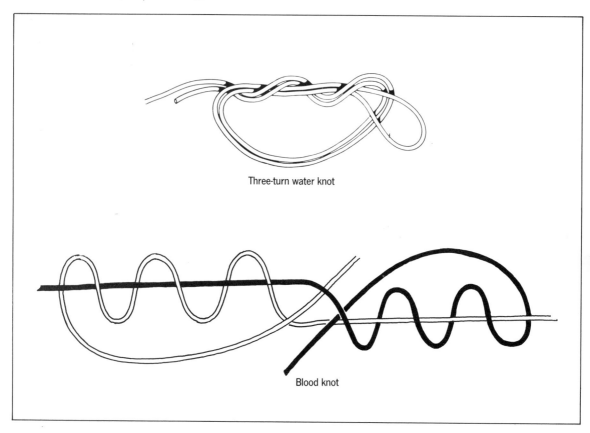

Three-turn water knot

Blood knot

open copy of *Angling Times* – and the knot secured. It's easy to do after you've spent some time at it. Give the knot about twelve to fourteen turns around the shank and be sure when it's finished that the line comes away on the point side of the spade. Mine also have a small loop tied at the other end for use when attaching to the main reel line.

There are several schools of thought on how the hook is attached to the reel line. You can tie a small loop in the reel line, pass the hook loop through it and then the hook through the reel line loop. This has worked well for me over the years, but many anglers rightly claim that it is rather bulky and demands two knots where one would be better. If you agree then you'll have to master the full Blood Knot or at least a Water Knot. Alternatively, just have a loop in the hook length and then tie a Half Blood in the reel line. All these methods work, it's just a case of deciding which you want to adopt.

My own hooks are tied, coiled around three fingers, starting from the hook and finishing with the loop end being tucked inside the coils. The whole lot then goes inside a 2¼in square photographic negative bag. The size and breaking-strain of line is then written on the outside of the packet, along with any other information I may need, such as 'barbless', 'caster' etc.

It goes without saying that hooks need to be kept dry. I find this is best achieved by storing them in a plastic hook wallet, the contents of which I discard every close season and start again. It may sound wasteful but a hook that's been rusting away quietly over the months can be costly in a big match.

Shots

Since the banning of lead shot we have been faced with using alternative materials and of these some form of tungsten shot has proved to be the most acceptable. Because you have been fishing as a pleasure angler you will already know the law, which generally speaking prohibits lead shot over 0.06g – that's a number 8. Styl weights are restricted to those below the same weight, which is considered to be a size 12.

In the early days of the lead ban we faced all sorts of problems, and in some cases saw some rather poor quality alternatives. Thankfully all that is behind us and the survivors are, in the main, at least of an acceptable standard.

Brands such as Dinsmores, Thamesley and Anchor all work well, and provided you don't slide them about

on the line they will do a good job. Pinch them on with your fingers. There is no need to use your teeth as we did with lead. To do so will result in either a broken tooth or a broken line, maybe even both. And if just pinched on, they can be eased open for safe movement.

In the case of tungsten olivettes, watch out for sharp-edged bores. Use those with a fine piece of silicone tubing inside or only the ones with well-finished edges.

Shot dispensers save on spillage and can cut down on time lost during a match. The single-shot tubs that dispense one at a time are also worth considering, but can be slow when a lot of small sizes are needed to re-tackle a broken or tangled rig.

● *A single shot dispenser – safe but not particularly fast*

Keepnets

Keepnets are essential for match fishing, and while they may not seem a very technical item they are worth looking at with match fishing in mind.

For a start they should have a good, very fine mesh of a knotless material capable of withstanding a lot of use. Actual shape isn't too important except that the length needs to be sufficient to handle high banks and swims which are shallow for some way out. Eight feet is possibly the minimum for general use, although a canal net may be considerably smaller.

The top rings must be large. You will be swinging

fish in to hand, unhooking them and placing them into the net without having to look where you're aiming. The bigger the mouth the less chance you have of missing it. If the top ring folds down in some way all the better because it makes transportation so much easier. Another refinement that will pay for itself well is some form of tilt mechanism so that the top can be set at just the right angle to suit the swim and surrounding terrain.

So far we have considered the basic needs of rod, reel, line, hook, shot and net. There are of course many other items of tackle that need to be assembled before you are a complete match angler, but we'll deal with these in the chapters which follow.

The big danger faced in the first few seasons is one of constantly adding tackle, to the point where you need a pack horse to get it all to the water's edge. But as a rule match anglers go for big tackle-boxes, massive holdalls and a sizeable net and bait-bag, so if you're buying, bear in mind the fact that it is easy to outgrow your first purchases unless you plan ahead. After all, just because it's big you don't have to fill it!

Tackle for the job

Match anglers are great inventors, and many of the items seen on tackle-shop shelves have been developed from ideas that were first conceived around the circuits by some enterprising angler.

The need for good rods and reels is obvious enough, but there is much more tackle that makes life easier and helps maintain concentration for the full duration of a hard match.

Float boxes

Without doubt the most personal piece of equipment is the match angler's float box. Inside are all sorts of strange modifications, not least of which will be odd pieces of quill fashioned to do a particular float-fishing task. They, like so much of the contents, may not look brilliant, but if they work then they justify the space taken up.

Contents must be kept in some sort of order. It is no good having all this specialist tackle if it takes time to rummage through the debris to find it. So the first resolution to make is one which promises regular sort-out and tidy-up sessions. The floats themselves need

housing in some way which suits you best. It may be a series of foam strips into which slots have been cut. These certainly protect delicate patterns and make them easy to locate.

A sectioned box is better if vast numbers are being carried around. Each section can be used for a particular pattern: sticks, wire-stemmed sticks, wagglers, insert wagglers etc.

But it is really the other items carried as accessories which stamp your own style on the collection. In mine you'll find several spare reel-spools, each loaded with line in breaking-strains of 2lb, 2.6lb, 3.2lb and possibly another of 5lb or 6lb for big feeder work.

Inside the spool skirts each is marked with the line strain it holds. A bottle of Tipp-Ex correcting fluid is great for this task and some can be carried too for changing float-tip colours. A bottle of the white fluid and a selection of waterproof felt-tipped pens are almost standard kit. Use the Tipp-Ex as a base colour, over which the other colours are applied.

Plummets – always several – are needed. Float adaptors, strips of silicone rubber tubing for float rings and of course some disgorgers are among the most obvious inclusions.

A small penknife, a few cable ties – they are the plastic strips used to fasten catapult elastic to the cup and frame. Some spare elastics are added, along with a razor blade, some small scissors and a roll of adhesive tape, which are going to come in handy too at some stage.

Items such as sticky tape seem to remain unused for months, but leave them out and you can bet you'll need some on the very next outing.

Although my hooks are tied at home there will still be a few boxes of untied ones and some suitable line in my kit ... just in case. If you use a tier then one of those needs to go in too.

Line degreaser and floatant is going to be needed regularly.

Add a good hook-wallet to house a wide selection of different sizes, patterns and breaking strains of hook length. Permits and rod licences can also go in there where they will remain dry.

● *The continental-type tackle box is becoming very popular and its internal layout helps keep everything tidy; but check the weight, as some are very heavy*

Tackle boxes

The actual tackle/seat box needs to be large but within the realms of common sense. Big boxes encourage more tackle, and even bigger boxes seem to attract even more tackle. Over the months the box will get heavier, so spend time sorting out the stuff that's not going to be needed on the forthcoming match. I once overlooked this part of my preparation prior to a canal match. Result was three slipped discs in my back, a lot of pain and no small amount of financial loss. The cause was an overloaded box. No, I didn't need the carrier bag full of swimfeeders I had carried across a ploughed field and along the canal bank for over a mile! I knew they wouldn't be needed but had taken my tackle as it was and not bothered to prepare properly. It is a chore having to offload every time you change type of venue, but it is something that is never again going to be skipped in my preparation.

The development and increasing popularity of the continental-style boxes with removable trays has helped reduce the time needed to add or remove kit. These superb – if rather expensive – boxes permit individual trays to be used for different waters. For example, one tray can be fitted out with the canal floats and pole rigs, while another may be all big-river wagglers and feeder tackle. Get organised and you only need to take the correct trays to each event.

Inside my normal, trayless box there is a large, wide, shallow bowl. This is for groundbait mixing, but in the meantime it serves as a good receptacle for items such as reels, rod rests, catapults, a small spade and anything else which can be fitted in.

A couple of pieces of towel will come in handy and

● *The easiest way to end up with back trouble is to carry a box with the strap too long (right). Set it so the box sits high up across your shoulder blades (left).*

prevent hands getting too wet and slippery. A bait apron goes in so that I can fish in the standing position without having to stoop down to rebait or feed. A cushion keeps my nether regions comfortable, and inside the box it makes good padding to prevent the contents getting banged around too much. A cushion may sound a bit of an unnecessary luxury but if you're comfortable you'll fish much better.

Also on the comfort side, it is worth considering a pair of legs for the front of your box. You could of course fit four, but banks generally slope towards the water, so one in each of the two front corners of your box will usually do the job. They must be adjustable and not prone to jamming when full of mud. Go for the lightest ones too.

Higher up the comfort scale comes a full platform. These are not cheap but they do make difficult pegs that much easier. For pole fishing they are a really good investment. You just cannot use a pole properly if your box is anything but level.

● *A good platform is a sensible investment. This angler has made a difficult bank easier by using it as a bait and tackle tray*

Before we leave the seat box and its contents it is worth checking the strap and getting it adjusted correctly. Far too many anglers run the risk of injury by having a strap set too long. Get yours adjusted so the box sits high on your back, resting over the shoulder blades. With the strap running across your chest rather than on just one shoulder you also reduce the risk of twisting your spine sideways. With the box correctly set up and the rod holdall slung across the chest from the other side and carried in front of you, everything will feel well-balanced.

● *Balance your luggage so there is less risk of walking with the spine twisted. By crossing over the box and holdall straps weight is evenly distributed.*

Trolleys

These are useful but need selecting with care. Firstly they must be light, for you are sure to have to carry one at some stage. They must be strong too and the wheelbase needs to be as wide as possible. Too narrow and the load will roll over at every bump in the bank. Go for big wheels as they cope better with rough terrain. The wide-rimmed ones are particularly good, offering both stability and some resistance to digging-in over soft ground.

The rack on which your box sits while being transported needs to be such that the box fits snugly. Ideally there will be room too for a tackle bag to be strapped in front or at least on top of the box.

Check that ground clearance is such that the slightest hump doesn't cause a problem. Many trolleys look fine in the shop but can be a real pain on the bank.

It helps also if the trolley folds flat for easy packing into the car boot. Here removable wheels are a real bonus, especially on matches where you may have to travel to your peg by coach.

A personal preference is towards trolleys that do not require pieces of metal to be fixed to my box. Adding such structures means I'm carrying unnecessary weight every time the trolley can't be used.

Luggage

Tackle bags, like boxes, get bigger every season. Fine, but you still have to carry 'em when they're full. Select one with a section for a keepnet and one for the bait boxes. Anything more is going to get filled with something. Not much to watch for in the way of design, but a good bag will have sensible carrying handles that don't cut into the palms of your hand. Take time to check what you are buying. One that is too deep may well scrape along the ground if you are short of stature.

Most bags are dark-coloured and, as a result, tend to attract the sun and can get very hot. Leave them exposed for long and any bait will die very quickly.

Cool boxes

With bait still in mind it's a good idea to keep an insulated cool box handy for transporting bait to distant matches. One of these boxes well-packed with bait and a few ice packs lodged between the contents will ensure maggots and casters stay cool overnight. A good tip here when hempseed is to be taken along is to freeze the bagged seed and then use it as cool packs to supplement conventional ice packs.

We all fuss far too much about how our bait is going to travel. If you clean and prepare bait correctly it will be fine if you use a cool box: pack it, seal it and leave it that way. Don't open it to check. All that will do is let some of the cool air out and some warmth in.

If you are in the habit of taking a lot of bait or having to travel to your fishing, a small riddle is a must as part of your bankside kit. Armed thus you can run off casters or replace any tainted bran or other medium in which maggots may have sweated up during transit.

Bait dispensers

Several forms of bait dispenser are available, either as trays that attach to the seat box, or as free-standing models screwed to a bank stick.

A basic frame to take three or four bait boxes will do the job, but you may wish to go for one of the table types which provide space for disgorger, plummet and other small items.

Catapults

Several are required to feed both loose offerings and, if any distance is involved, cereal groundbait.

Different models will be needed to cope with a variety of waters. For canals and narrow venues where it may be a case of feeding just a few squatts, pinkies etc out a few yards, go for a small one with fairly weak elastic. I have seen canal regulars with home-made catapults with minute pouches and pole elastic as the power source. These are perfect for bloodworm or squatts. If a powerful catapult is used for short-range feeding it will result in the feed leaving the pouch much too fast, causing it to spread over a wide area. The pouch, too, needs to be small to help with accuracy.

A larger, more powerful catapult is called for to feed maggots and casters at some range. Again, the slower the elastic the better will be the accuracy. My own preference is for a full pouch on all my catapults but I know a lot of anglers who swear by the flat, mesh types.

For groundbait a 'Whopper Dropper' is the tool. These big 'pults will project a ball of feed beyond casting range. The cup is a plastic moulding that doesn't fold over the groundbait and cause it to break up. They are great but it does take time to get any degree of accuracy. Practise whenever possible, if only to use up some bait at the end of a session.

Rod holdalls

Protection for your rods will be in the form of a holdall. Although an expensive one will not add a single fish to your tally it will still be a good investment in guarding against costly damage. In match circles, rods get thrown around a lot. They may be dropped accidentally while unloading the coach or car, or suffer from being at the bottom of the pile that always seems to form in the team transport.

Go for one that will have room enough for at least half a dozen rods and a pole or two, each housed in a plastic tube. Watch out for too much length, which can make fitting it into the car a problem. A separate section for brolly and bank sticks is also a good feature.

The shoulder strap should be wide and well padded. If possible find a model with a hand grip. Fancy additions such as locks are a bit pointless because a thief will take the whole lot anyway.

As to holdall design, there are several options. But those which can either be unrolled or are fitted with a full-length zip down the main section are preferable because they allow quick access and eliminate the need to empty all the contents in one go.

Nets

Keepnets should be of a very fine mesh and have plenty of length. Both these features are as important as the wide mouth that's essential for speed fishing. Go too for an adjustable attachment which permits the top to be set at any angle. With one of these, the need for a rod rest can often be eliminated. And in any case they are handy when faced with a difficult bank.

An interesting development has been the nylon material-bottomed nets which hold the catch in almost complete darkness. These have the advantage of keeping fish calm, are good in terms of protection and help to keep away the unwelcome attention of predators, such as pike, which can otherwise be attracted to your swim by a net of fish.

Some nets are fitted with one ring of a slightly different size to the rest. This ring, some three or four from the bottom, is then used to fold the net inside itself and enable fish to be emptied into the scales without having to slide down the full length of the net. It's a good idea that protects fish from accidental damage caused by a long slide over the mesh.

Nets which have openings at the bottom, either by means of zips or elaborate fastenings are, in my opinion, risky. Forget to close the zip or fastening at the end of the weigh-in and you run the risk of fishing the next match in vain . . . yes, I've done it!

A couple of landing nets will be needed to deal effectively with waters of varying characteristics. A big net can be a disadvantage at times and it will pay to have a couple of different sizes to hand. On a chub, barbel or bream water the need for a big net is obvious enough. But you won't really want a huge one when all that's likely to be netted are roach of a few ounces. Should there be the chance of both large and small species then set up two nets, one for each eventuality.

Pan bottom nets are fine and certainly they are quick to use. Watch out, though, when fishing from a high bank. A shallow pan net may not hold a netted fish safely when steeply angled. Conventional shapes can be used effectively, but make sure they are not too deep, otherwise you are going to get a lot of shot tangles in the mesh.

Fine micromesh helps reduce the risk of shots or a leger falling through and tangling, but on fast rivers the pressure of water pushing on it can make control almost impossible. A compromise is to use a micromesh bottom with larger side mesh. Better still, go for an overall larger mesh and take the risk of a tangle or two.

The landing-net pole will probably be a carbon or fibre-glass one, extending anything up to 12 feet. Long handles are fine but don't be tempted to lift big fish with them. To do so will end in breakage.

A tip here is to check that the thread actually fits your net. They are supposed to be standard ⅜in BSF but in this age of metrication a few are sneaking through that don't fit old net frames.

Accessories

For legering, a target board is needed. Some are very small, others large. They all do the same job in providing a marker which makes any movement of the quiver or swingtip easier to spot. Clear plastic ones enable a swingtip to hang behind or in front of the board, whichever side gives the most protection from wind interference. Others are of black, matt-finish plastic with some form of white marking, either a white cross or a series of parallel stripes.

Rod rests come in all sorts of shapes and sizes. There are designs for legering, feeder work, float fishing and pole use. For the float a wide-topped one is best, so that the rod can be dropped onto it without the need for accurate location. Pattern is not important but it should be free from anything that might catch loose line. Adjustable heads look a good idea, but few

work well for long, and the extra engineering involved usually results in line getting snagged sooner or later.

Leger rests need to hold the rod steady and are therefore narrower than those for float work but again need to be snag free.

Multi-V heads do give a choice of how the rod can be positioned and they do allow fine adjustments to be made to the rod angle. With all leger rests it is essential that the line remains free beneath the rod. You will need to take up slack to set the tip correctly and this will be difficult if the line is trapped between rod and rest.

Pole fishing needs special rests, ideally a pair which are attached to the side of the seat box. My favourite

● *A simple target board makes bite detection much easier by giving shelter to the rod tip and providing a sight on which to line up the quiver or swingtip*

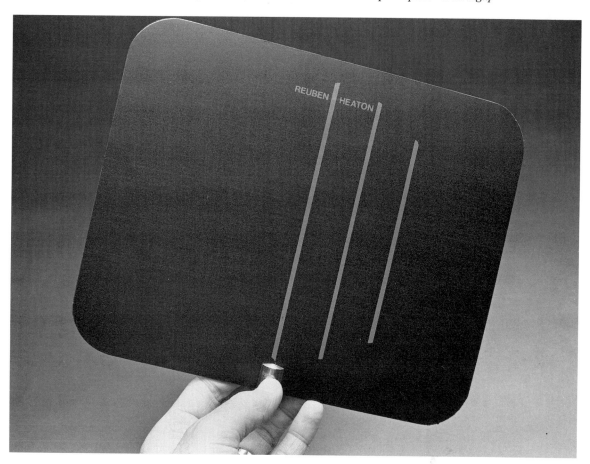

is the Taper Trak model, which is easy to set and can be adjusted for height very accurately with the pole in position.

A pole roller over which the rear end of a long pole can slide when being broken down is also a sensible buy. Both the paint-roller style and the rubber ones are good.

● *Fingerless gloves are not everyone's idea of perfection but they can be useful on a bad day*

Comfort

A waterproof suit in some form is essential. The one-piece type is popular with match anglers but for all-season use jacket and over-trousers are more versatile. Whichever you choose be sure to get one with a good hood.

Waders are also standard gear and they do help keep legs warm and dry. But they are heavy too. I have found the ones with nylon upper sections to be excellent. They are much lighter than rubber, fold down very small and feel just like a wellington boot to walk in.

As a match angler you are going to be faced with the worst of the winter weather, and your personal comfort is just as important as the other tackle you

use. A comfortable angler is an efficient one. You can't concentrate for long if hands and feet are frozen and your body is shaking with cold.

Modern materials mean that thermal clothing is light and very effective. Wear a full thermal shirt next to your skin. Over it, go for several thin layers rather than a single thick one. Each layer will trap air between the garments and add to the overall weatherproofing. Complete the insulation with a windproof outer garment.

Feet can get very cold in traditional waders or wellingtons. A pair of 'moon boots' with thick and well insulated soles is a good alternative.

Gloves are not very practical but some anglers do manage to fish with fingerless types. Keep wrists warm and the hands stay comfortable too.

Wear a hat, for most body-heat loss is from the head. If you have a hooded jacket, fine; but even those will stay more snug with some other headgear beneath.

There are those macho-image anglers who never carry a brolly. And while I agree that it is extra weight to carry, it also protects not only the angler but also his bait from the effects of both rain and hot sun.

A pair of polarising glasses is a very good investment, not only as protection for the eyes from surface glare but to give a clearer picture' of what's beneath the water surface. An eyeshade helps to cut down distracting light from above. A further bonus is that a shade enhances the polarising effect of the glasses.

Well, there are just a few ideas to work on. There are many other items of tackle which will no doubt be added. The difficulty is sorting out 'those that are nothing more than gimmicks. Carry only the tackle you really need and know works well.

● *A good roller makes handling a long pole easier and ensures smoother operation and fewer lost fish*

2
Finding a club

Small clubs are where match fishing apprenticeships are served, and for many anglers they are the level at which competition begins and ends. There is nothing wrong with staying a club angler, and if that is the route you choose then you can look forward to a lot of happy hours among friends.

Finding the right sort of club will, however, take a little effort, for as with all types of organisation there are good and bad. You will need to find one which caters best for your needs.

As a newcomer to match fishing getting in at the right level of competition where you have a reasonable chance of at least some success, is essential. At the same time the club must have enough good anglers for you to be able to learn both directly from them and by being able to compare their performances against your own.

If you are a more experienced angler then maybe a club higher up the scale will be what you want. But even then it is a good idea to search out a club which offers good value for your membership fee.

Clubs come in several forms, the most common of which is the 'pub club'. There are works clubs which are restricted to employees or perhaps employees and a limited number of 'guest' members. These are useful clubs to join because they often get some form of support from the parent company.

Next come the open clubs, 'open' meaning there is no limit or restriction on who can join. These may of course attract the more talented angler, but on the credit side they often offer water which is limited to members only.

Even larger are the associations, parent organisations which, as the name suggests, are large bodies incorporating affiliation membership for local clubs. Membership of these associations can number into thousands, and because of the numbers involved it is this type of body that will control much of the locality's waters. So when considering which will be your first

club it's worthwhile checking to see if it is affiliated. For this type of club usually has a healthy match-fixture list on well-run waters.

A pub club may operate in one of two ways: it may accept any application for membership, or it may require new members to be nominated by an existing member or undergo some form of selection process. This is not a bad idea as it is a means of keeping membership at the right level and undesirable elements out.

A good pub club will have a membership of at least fifty, thus ensuring a match turnout of twenty-five to thirty with a sprinkling of reasonable anglers, and if possible it will have either some water of its own or at least access through affilation to a larger body.

It goes without saying that a fixture list is needed. It doesn't, however, need to contain dozens of matches. In fact too many will only lead to temptation and missed practice sessions. A match every three weeks or so throughout the summer and autumn will be fine for a start, and in winter maybe one a month is the right level.

The matches should be properly booked affairs, not cowboy jobs where the venue is decided over a few beers late on Saturday evening.

Structure of the club needs to be clear: the presence of a secretary, treasurer, chairman and a committee usually suggests everything is run reasonably efficiently. If there is a club membership card containing rules and fixture information, so much the better.

If you think you know of a good club, begin checking it out by asking around the local match circuit. Maybe a stroll along the river while a match is in progress will give you a good 'feel' for the overall atmosphere. And if nothing else you will see what sort of turnout there is and the general standard of angling ability.

Assuming that all looks well, then take a little time to consider the fixture list. If the matches are fairly local and perhaps include the same venues several times a season that's fine, as these will help you judge your performances and progress. Matches away from your patch are nice for a change and later on will help add to experience, but don't run before you can walk. Master the local scene first and then branch out to pastures new. The first few seasons are for learning.

Next find out how much it costs to join – although this is not likely to vary much between clubs in the area. Of more importance is the match structure. At club level there will be either a set entry fee and then optional pools – a sweepstake which, as the name suggests, is optional – or an 'all-in' entry fee.

The beauty of optional pools is that it gives the individual a choice of various levels of financial commitment. For example a match entry of, say, £2 and then a choice of optional pools of £1 and £2 would give you the opportunity of entering either the match or the match and the £1 pool only, the match and £2

● *The draw at a small club match is a casual affair, but still get there early or you might risk missing the pools*

pool, or of course all three for £5. For a start you may wish to enter just one of the pools, depending on your level of confidence and the standard of the opposition. But in most cases a fiver is going to be the maximum the average pub club will be charging, and chances are it will be a lot less.

The 'all-in' system is becoming more popular on the open circuit, and in many respects, while it takes away the individual choice, it does guarantee a stable cash pool and makes overall organisation more straightforward. It also means the result will take less time to work out.

Other ideas which go towards making a good club are special matches such as handicaps. In these each angler is given a percentage start which is added to his actual catch. This means the best anglers are handicapped as 'scratch' and get no percentage added, while a novice may be given 100 per cent, meaning a 2lb catch will count as 4lb. There are different ways of allocating handicaps but they are all similar in principle.

Pairs events, where anglers are paired off by means of a draw and their total weights combined, are also great fun. They are ideal for learning, too, because you may find yourself paired with a very good angler who, because you are his partner, may wish to offer some good advice.

Inter-club matches are popular among small clubs. The bonus is that the entry is usually double the normal turnout and it will put you up against a different set of anglers – yet another stage in the learning curve.

So having found a suitable club the next step is to get to know some of the other members. If the club is pub-based it will just be a case of going along. There may even be a certain night of the week when a group meets up.

On match days, turn up well before draw time so that you are one of the first to arrive. That way it will be easy to get chatting to the other early arrivals before the rush starts. Tell them you're a new member and that match fishing is also something with which you are just getting involved. Match anglers are a friendly lot and they will be as interested in you as you are in them.

Don't be too pushy but don't stand back either. The best anglers will be prepared to help but it is you who must make the first moves. Go up and ask advice about the peg you have drawn or how the water is fishing. True, you may be unlucky and be given inaccurate information; but over the coming weeks you will soon learn which people to listen to and which to avoid.

Once the match is underway you will of course be on your own. But before and after try to store everything you're told and then sift through it later.

If the rules allow it, go along with the scales and take note of what was caught and where. Here a diary will come in handy for future reference. A good way to become involved is to offer to assist with the weigh-in. It will help you remember names and also enables you to see at first hand what was caught where.

At the scales there is always a lot of chatter and in the excitement a lot of information can be exchanged.

The golden rule is: always weigh in. You may not have caught a lot, but club matches can be deceiving, and often a low weight will make the frame. Even if

yours doesn't there is no harm done, and if nothing else you will be able to see how your performances are comparing in relation to anglers around you.

Keep a diary, log down the matches you fished, the peg, conditions, how you fished, what you caught and how. Note too any mistakes you made and anything else that may be significant about the peg. Write down the winning weights, where and, if possible, how they were caught. Build up a complete picture and over a season or so you will be compiling a valuable guide to a lot of venues. Trying to commit everything to memory just doesn't work. And in any case it is nice to look back over the years and re-live some of the more memorable events.

Another good reason for always weighing in is that many clubs operate a club championship table based on where you finish in every match. Just weighing in

every time will earn a few points and over a season they can add up to a fair performance, increasing your satisfaction and also giving you a target at which to aim when next season comes around.

If you do not figure in the leading weights, don't rush off as soon as you've been weighed in. Stay for the results and use the time to ask others how they fished. Be prepared to offer something in return. It may be just a case of buying a beer or two in the early days and then later being willing to share your own knowledge and experiences. It's this free exchange that makes club fishing both friendly and a good place to learn the trade.

The whole idea of joining a club is to find competition of the right standard and to use the other members to help you progress. Get involved, go along to all the functions off the bankside, talk a little, listen a lot and

above all don't be afraid to ask. Every angler had to start somewhere.

Having said that getting involved is a good idea, be careful not to overstep the mark and become roped into an official position too soon. Playing a part is fine and a very commendable thing to do. But during the first couple of seasons at least, you will be busy enough sorting out your own problems without having to attend committee meetings. Offer help by all means but keep it at a level which doesn't interfere with your fishing. There will be plenty of time later on to do your bit officially if you so wish.

Open matches

Open events are a completely different ball game to the club scene. Here you are fishing against more anglers – and usually of a better class.

Not all open-match anglers are efficient and some are nothing short of poor. These are those who did well as pleasure anglers and then dived in at the deep end. As stated earlier, these short cuts just don't work, or at least very rarely.

In the club match you needed to fish a method that would beat maybe thirty anglers spread over 600 yards of river or lakeside. In an open the opposition may be upwards of 100 and even into the 400–500 bracket. It's obvious that different tactics are going to be needed to match the greater odds.

In the club field you will know more or less what is being caught and how to plan your own match accordingly. On the open scene the expanse is so great there is always a possibility that big weights are being taken a mile or more away from your peg.

You can of course fish opens just to win the section you have drawn. This can be a section of ten, twenty, thirty or more pegs and if so, club tactics may be employed. But it is a wasteful way to fish and the target, at least wherever you get a half-reasonable draw, should be to win or get a high overall placing. The section is a safety net to cover your costs if all else is failing.

The amount of time taken up by fishing an open is also going to be much greater than at club level. The

● *A club match underway. The methods might vary a lot from peg to peg, and the results may not always be good, but weigh in just the same so that you earn club points*

● (Left) Boston's Roy Jarvis knows all about both the club and open circuit. During the peak of his open career he went on to become national champion before reverting to the club scene where he enjoyed further, if less spectacular, success

● (Right) Former world champion Kevin Ashurst certainly believes in keeping faith with tried and tested floats. These, including the ancient porcupine quill, are his favourite ten patterns

● (Below) Even the very best need to put in practice. England international Denis White gets down to the task of sorting out a tricky swim

period from draw to fishing time may be two hours or more, to enable anglers who draw distant swims to make it in time for the starting whistle. Actual fishing times may also be later than those of the club match in order to make travelling from some distance away more practical.

Cost is going to escalate too. Bait requirements will almost certainly be higher, entry tickets and pools more expensive. Then there is travel, food and maybe even a bet with the bookie of the day to consider. After all, it is no good going in against the best if you don't fancy your chances enough to have a flutter. Even the best don't win many opens in the course of a season so you have to collect on the few that do pay off.

Another drawback is that because of the match size it stands to reason that there will be a lot of poor pegs and even poor sections included. Draw one of these and you really are fishing to make the numbers up, or at best collect a section prize.

The big match scene is exciting but don't get carried away, they are much more of a lottery than you may think at first sight.

Finding suitable matches is not a problem. Tackle shops, local press and the match guides of the weekly angling papers will supply all the information needed.

When the big day arrives, try to get to match headquarters in good time. Chances are it will appear a shambles, with anglers everywhere and an apparent lack of organisation. The first job is to find out where the organiser is, and where to pay into the pools if they were not entered in advance or included in the entry fee.

It really is amazing how some matches regularly attract big fields yet still fail to cater for them off the bankside. Go prepared to cope with lack of parking, direction signs, even maps of the water and how to get to the sections. Leave it late and you could be in trouble.

Take a pen too. You will need to fill in your pools card and possibly the draw card and other entry formalities which may be in operation.

One other small problem you will almost certainly encounter is the dreaded scales duty. It is a growing trend to include scales duties in the draw bag. This

• *Is there enough? The arrival of the scales marks the moment of truth for every match angler*

usually means certain draw cards will be designated to weigh in. If you draw one you report to the organiser who will load you down with scales or weight board – or, even worse, both – and issue instructions as to the area you are to weigh and be responsible for. It's worth checking at this stage whether you are expected to start and stop the actual match on your section. If so, a time check might be a good idea.

The duty is easy enough and, if nothing else, it will ensure that you stay the distance even if nothing is being caught. On return to headquarters, your task over, you may have your entry fee returned as payment for the job. Some do, some don't, there are no hard and fast rules laid down.

Watch out for rules differing from those employed by your club. There may be certain bait bans in operation, against bloodworm and joker, for example. Pike and zander may or may not count. A small number of waters also operate cereal groundbait bans from time to time. Usually such restrictions are advertised on the ticket, but if in doubt, make certain before you fish.

Actual fishing is going to be considerably more positive than it is at club level, for unless there is a team event everyone will be fishing for a win. That means going for a weight that tops the lot. No time for scratching together a few pounds. This is instant death or glory stuff. You fish hard to win.

There is no reward for getting an average weight and finishing twentieth. You may as well catch nothing. What you need to know, of course, is how much that winning catch is likely to be.

Only a good knowledge of the venue and the anglers taking part is going to tell you the answer, so here again it is easy to see why open matches are so different.

Go with winning in mind. Fish that way and don't be distracted. If, well into the match, you know your plan has failed miserably, you have several options: pack up and go home; pack up and walk the bank in the hope of learning something from the other anglers; or stick at your swim and use it as a practice session, trying a method which isn't going to win you anything today but which might be right for the next outing.

Of those options only the first is out of the question. To go home is just wasting what's left of the day. You have paid out good money to be on the bank so use the exercise in the best possible way by adopting one of the other alternatives.

● *You'll need a positive approach and catches like this if you are to succeed on the open match scene*

3

Target weights and practice

Winning matches is not just about preparing tackle and fishing well on the day. It's also about making decisions on how the water is going to be attacked in order to catch more than anyone else.

On a hard canal a winning catch may be pulled together by scratching around for a pound or so of small fish. Apply those same tactics on a prolific water and you will end up at the scales with little more than a red face to show for your efforts.

What is needed before preparing for any match is a target weight at which to aim. In club matches it is usually much easier to forecast a top weight than in a big match numbering hundreds. But even with a large field it should be possible to get somewhere close to a sensible figure.

Starting to build a picture takes some effort. Watch both local and national papers' match reports for the venue over the weeks running up to your match. Make notes of what has been caught, who caught it, how, and if possible from which pegs. Keep an eye on the weather, too, because a sudden change in conditions may alter everything at the very last moment and the whole plan may need a rapid re-think.

At club level the overall standard of angler is likely to be lower than in the bigger opens. Therefore the winning weight is going to be correspondingly reduced. Take all these elements into account when deciding on how much you are going to need to win.

If the water is nearby, try to get along to see at first hand what is being caught. Talk to pleasure anglers; most are happy to tell of their successes.

All this is of course geared to winning outright. Team fishing is a totally different ball game and is something to consider under the appropriate heading later on. As an individual you are only concerned with winning, or at least making the top end of the frame.

The telephone is a great aid in sorting a water out. At first, finding the right people to help may be a bit of a problem, but at least locally you are sure to know someone who can get you started. A quick call seeking advice usually brings some response and, if nothing else, the person you have called may be able to put you on to another contact. That's the way match fishing is, a continual swapping of information and a search for every little clue.

But once you have obtained the information and fished the match, take time to call back and thank the people who helped and let them know how you fared. You might just need to go back to them in the future.

As your phone links become established, expect incoming calls too. Handle these fairly, be helpful and you'll be amazed at the response you get in return, especially from the very best anglers. Never, ever try to mislead anyone, for you will quickly become an outcast. Match fishing can be hard enough without making enemies who will stitch you up sooner or later.

While searching out information it will be easy to discover the winning weights, but it is also important to see how the overall picture looks. Backing weights that just missed out on the day may suggest there are other ways to win. A few chub spread throughout a section dominated by roach could indicate that there was a chance of a good chub catch if someone had been brave enough to fish for them right from the off.

Now, with some knowledge of what to expect, try to get in practice on the water. This may of course not be possible in the case of distant venues. But even in such cases it may pay to visit a similar water to

● *These may not look much like match fish but they did come from the famous North Bank stretch of the River Nene. Captor was Cambridge angler Dick Toates who took them while practising for a Winter League match. The carp weighed 13lb and 6½lb!*

sharpen up on the likely methods. It may be just a case of distance casting to check out your accuracy, or perhaps getting some speed into a bleak-fishing session.

The whole object is to become as familiar as possible with what you are going to attempt on match day. How many fish you catch doesn't matter at this stage.

Ideally get in a few visits to the match stretch, but if you do go don't leave it until the day before the match. Hammering a peg too close to the event is unfair to someone who may draw the swim in the event. This once happened to me in a very big and valuable invitation match on the River Severn. On the evening

prior to the match I had watched two fellow competitors pleasure fishing on the venue and catching a lot of chub. To my horror I drew on one of the pegs next morning and went on to struggle for a few pounds. The angler next door suffered a similar fate. These could well have been winning pegs had they not been fished so hard only hours earlier.

Another great danger is fishing the wrong pegs. Thankfully many match venues are now permanently pegged, but if you have any doubts at all about the exact location of the match stretch, ring the organisers and double-check. Practice is a costly business in terms of both time and cash. It is certainly too valuable to waste.

On practice outings don't rush around; walk the bank for a while and see what's going on. It may be that things have changed since you started your investigations back home and a little time spent watching may save hours of trial and error.

Find a peg and set up just as on match day, starting to fish the way you think is going to be a winning method. If you begin catching, fine, but don't get carried away. You are not out to see how many fish you can catch, you are here to learn. Try increasing the hook size or perhaps feeding closer in to see if fish can be caught at close range. Either change could prove to be faster on match day. Try switching baits: doubling up from a single to two maggots, for example, or perhaps changing to caster in the hope of finding bigger fish. The alternatives are endless but you must be prepared to leave methods which work and try something else in the hope it will catch even more. If the change fails you have achieved something. At least you know it probably won't work in the match.

Be brave with practice, even to the extent of trying to kill a swim off by overfeeding. If you succeed, you know not to go too heavy with match day feeding. On a water where cereal groundbait is considered a failure give it a try at some stage – just to check. After all, match fishing is about keeping one jump ahead of the rest, and getting in on the first days of a new trend can be very valuable.

Former world champion Dave Thomas of Leeds proved very successfully how something different can work when a few years ago he took the tough River Trent open circuit by storm. In those days the caster was considered unbeatable but Dave had other ideas and went along armed with a lot of bronze maggots. The result was that he cleaned up until others cottoned on to his method and quickly followed suit. Even so he had learned enough during the time lapse to ensure that he still collected his fair share of prizes.

If you are going to fish with friends it may pay to practise together. Here again it is about trusting each other and holding nothing back. In some ways you are helping the opposition, but they too are helping you and it is better to be beaten by someone you know than by a stranger.

Some small groups of three or even four anglers often fish together in this fashion and, on match day, even in matches where there are no team prizes, agree some share of any prize money. A good system is to agree to pay a percentage of any winnings, say ten per cent, to each member of the group.

Such arrangements mean ideas are openly shared and if anyone from your group comes up then everyone gets a share. It's a good way of covering expenses and coping with a run of bad draws.

One visit to a water is better than nothing, if only to give you an idea of what it looks like. You will get a feel of the pace of any flow and possibly spot a few potential problems or good-looking areas.

Besides catching some fish you will be looking for tackle modifications that might be called for. Maybe a certain colour of float tip shows up better than others. Open water may mean some black ones are needed, while on many swims thick overhanging trees produce a dark surface where a yellow or orange tip is going to be right.

● *Work your way through the various methods while involved in practice but at the same time keep an eye on what's going on around you*

If other visits follow, try to fish different pegs, and if part of a group, work out some plan of attack so that as many permutations as possible are tried during the time available.

Maybe a few very poor areas will show up if enough visits are made. If such areas are discovered it may pay to try to work out the best plan for them. Then, if you should be unfortunate enough to draw one, at least you can fish with a chance of getting a section prize.

Throughout practice and the eventual match don't get too blinkered. A method that worked in practice, or failed for that matter, might have the opposite effect when the bank is lined with other anglers.

Match conditions can do odd things to a water. A pleasure catch of 20lb can easily be reduced to 10lb when match conditions are in force. For example, baits such as hempseed and tares may be effective on pleasure and practice days, but get a lot of maggots going in either side of you and you may have a total failure. This is a typical example where three or four anglers fishing together could simulate match conditions.

Another strange thing about some waters is that they fish brilliantly all week and then go off at weekends. Often there is no obvious reason for this state of affairs and the only explanation is that fish get to know the seven-day cycle when anglers are out in force. There could of course be other factors. A river that has warm water pumped in from a factory all week may go off at weekends if the factory is not working and the water stops pumping. The slight temperature drop is all that's needed to take the edge off sport.

Continually re-think your plans as each new lesson is learned, and even on the day go prepared to scrap the whole thing if something unexpected turns up. Fishing is an unpredictable game and nothing is certain.

A big danger to watch out for is a patchy venue. They are never very good for the mind and, in my opinion, fishing time is too precious to waste. Despite what some people claim, fishing is about catching fish. Winning is pleasant but winning with a decent catch is even more enjoyable.

While most match anglers would agree that practice is important, a little knowledge can be dangerous. Unless you have spent a lot of time at the water don't become too fixed in your ideas. More than a few very good anglers have come badly unstuck because a water has changed on the day for no obvious reason

Spud bashing

The importance of good planning came home to me many years ago after practising for a national championship on the Norfolk Broads.

My Peterborough DAA team-mates had all suffered from the problem of getting groundbait heavy enough to cope with the powerful flow of the tidal rivers on which the match was to be fished. We knew some of us would need to get a fair amount of bait down in order to hold the bream which would decide the match (in those days the team prize was decided on total weight rather than points).

After searching around we came up with a cheap, easily obtainable and very effective material: potato.

My father, as team manager, volunteered to prepare enough of the stuff for the entire team. He peeled and boiled large quantities so that we all ended up with around 3lb of boiled, mashed potato to mix with a normal heavy crumb groundbait.

The plan worked well: we finished second, beaten by only ounces. Since then I have discovered that the powdered variety can be mixed up and used to good effect too. It's the sort of groundbait that's only needed once in a while but on its day it is the sort of thing that can make all the difference, as we found out in that national.

after fishing to a pattern for a long period.

Venues that are to be used for a big event such as a national seem prone to this. Maybe it is a case of their being fished hard for a long period and suddenly switching off because of the pressure they have endured. Watch out too if the match is to be on a water that normally carries heavy boat traffic and is then closed for the duration of a match. The organisers who arrange these things mean well but what happens is that water clarity improves and the fish, not being used to seeing so well, get scared.

Weed-cutting operations are yet another danger. Many times cracking waters have been ruined by having all the marginal weed hacked off a day or two before a match. Just some examples of change upsetting the best-laid plans.

Finally, go to the waters where there are plenty of winning opportunities. A match with a couple of unbeatable hot pegs is not a fishing match so much as a raffle with the prize being a peg on the fish. You can't practise drawing a peg.

4
Preparation of tackle and bait

Having obtained a ticket for a match and built up some idea of how you intend to approach it, the next stage is to begin preparing some tackle.

You will know by now what is likely to be caught and on what, so the logical first step is to call on your tackle dealer to order bait.

Some shops may not require orders for small amounts but it always pays to order if possible; that way, if there is a problem, such as casters refusing to turn on time, you will be on the priority list for what is available. Sooner or later every tackle dealer has a bait shortage. Maybe he gets let down by the breeder, a shipment goes missing or a fridge breaks down. Any of these can be a disaster both for him and for you.

Bait ordered, now tackle needs sorting through. Start with the rods, checking every ring for cracks or breakages. Clean the joints with some warm water and wipe the whole rod over with a damp cloth. A little spray polish wiped over it will help keep line from sticking should it rain.

The cork handle will need a clean too. Scrub it with a small brush and some soapy water, taking care to remove all traces of soap afterwards. A light rub over with fine glasspaper once in a while will give cork a nice fresh feel – but go easy or you'll need a new handle by the end of a long season.

While you are dealing with rods, clear out the holdall and go over everything it contained. Check pole joints. They should be clean and free-fitting. If they don't come apart easily they need urgent attention. Lap them in gently by running the joints together with a circular motion after applying a few spots of Brasso. This is a good trick with new poles that have not bedded in. If the sticking is severe a little work with

some very fine wet-and-dry paper may be needed – but again go very carefully, you can't put back what you've taken off.

Run a check also on any internal elastic that may be fitted. Has it perished, become dirty or slack? If it is getting old, change it before it lets you down. If it's dirty a wipe with washing-up liquid will remove the grime, after which a treatment with one of the special lubricants now available will be beneficial. Follow the instructions on the bottle.

A word of warning on these lubricants. While they do a good job they also tend to attract dust and dirt, which in turn can weaken the elastic. If possible clean it down after use with a soft wet cloth and a little soap.

● *A Stonfo connector is a good method of finishing off pole elastic, but make regular checks to ensure the actual elastic is sound and showing no signs of perishing*

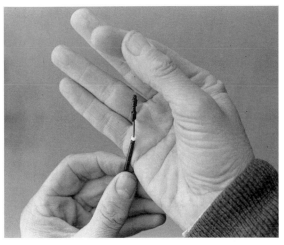

Bank stick and landing-net pole threads may need unbunging of mud. If they are new, check that they actually fit. I once went to a match with a brand new – and very expensive – carbon landing-net pole: only problem was that the screw thread was the wrong size!

Next the tackle bag. Out come landing net and keepnet for the mesh to be examined. If there is any tear, even a single mesh, sew it up with nylon thread. A tiny eel might otherwise work its way out and valuable ounces be lost.

Now the seat box contents – check everything. Nylon line wears out so change it often; but if it is required to sink, be sure to treat it with your favourite mixture of soap and fuller's earth, a special degreaser, or in an emergency just plain mud. I never like taking a brand new line to a match but prefer instead to load it prior to the last practice session so that it gets 'run in'.

Reels benefit from cleaning, especially the spool rims which can get encrusted with dried-on groundbait. This hard material will reduce casting distance. Check

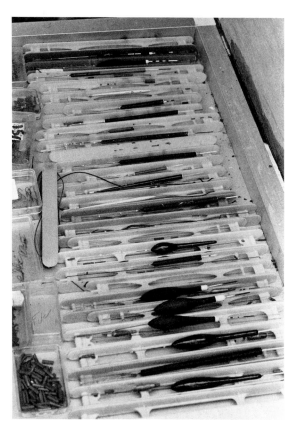

the bale-arm roller to ensure it is working smoothly, and if you are a clutch user check that the setting is correct. Should the bale-arm return spring be weak get it replaced now, before it breaks completely.

At the end of each season it is worthwhile returning reels to their manufacturer for overhaul and service. Most of the better-known companies provide this excellent service for a very modest charge.

Floats may need a touch-up with tip paint, and while you are in the float box work through all the other items that may either need replacing or repairing. Float adaptors, silicone rubber, shots, plummets, disgorgers. Run the rule over the lot and make a list of anything that needs replacing when you go to the shop for your bait.

Catapult elastic perishes and is sure to break just when you need it most. Special replacement kits are available, containing elastic and cable ties. It's worth keeping a couple handy at all times.

Hooks have a habit of getting used without being noticed. Take plenty to every match, making sure each packet is clearly marked with full details of its contents.

A clean towel, waterproof clothing, boots and everything you are going to need, should be prepared with the same care so that you arrive on the bank with every single item in the best possible condition. The whole object is to start with the least chance of anything going wrong. It's just like getting a racing car ready for a Grand Prix. Leave nothing to chance.

If during the checking stage you are unsure what you have to do, sit down and make a list and then work through it, ticking off each task as it is completed. If you have kept a diary or made notes during practice, read through them as a refresher. This will often remind you of a little item you intended to include but may otherwise overlook.

Maggots

Without doubt the thing that is going to take time to prepare is bait. Skimp on this and the rest of the work will be pointless – you might as well go back to pleasure fishing right now.

• *A good collection of pole rigs – but are all those hooks sharp and free from rust? It's worth running a check too on the winders to see that all are fully rigged and sound*

Jammed sections

Most annoying of all problems at the end of a match is that of jammed pole or rod sections.

In the case of a rod the help of the angler at the next peg can usually be relied upon to get them apart. But if they are really tightly jammed, or it's an expensive pole, don't risk applying undue pressure.

Never apply heat. For a start it doesn't work, and what's more it will only soften the resins holding the fibres together and cause serious damage.

To free the sections, get two people to hold the extreme ends of the section and pull gently but without exerting too much pressure. They should be keeping the sections under pressure but nothing more. Now, using the side of your hand – or even just a couple of fingers – tap the pole directly over the stuck joint. Use a fast but not hard action and after a matter of a few seconds the sections will fall apart.

The whole secret is in holding the ends of the sections and keeping the tapping fairly brisk.

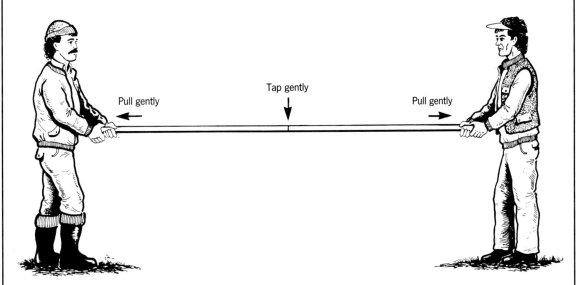

Pull gently   Tap gently   Pull gently

● *Jammed sections can be freed very easily and safely by using this method. It is essential to hold the joints at their extreme ends and then tap with the side of the hand over the jammed ferrules. There is no need for force; apply a slight pull at either end and the joints will part easily.*

Maggots supplied by dealers are usually of an acceptable standard but they can be improved upon. Usual timetable is to collect them either on Friday or early on the Saturday prior to a Sunday match.

Start by giving them a good riddle to remove whatever medium they may be in. Dealers use sawdust, maize, bran, groundbait, all manner of things.

Once the maggots are free from sawdust etc tip them onto a large riddle, through which they can pass, into a wide container. Just tip them on, spread them out with your hand and leave them. Maggots don't like light and will quickly find their way through, leaving behind any dead or dying specimens, which are then discarded.

At this stage, if the bait is really dirty, tip it into the foot of an old pair of nylon tights and wash it under a cold tap. It's surprising what will come from it. However, this operation needs doing quickly and carefully otherwise the kitchen is going to get some unwelcome visitors.

A large bowl with some dry sawdust inside will be needed, into which the cleaned maggots can be emptied. If you are washing bronze maggots that have been coloured with chrysoidine, wear rubber gloves and keep the stuff off your skin. Not only is it difficult to remove, it is also a dangerous, carcinogenic substance. Chrysoidine also leaves the sink looking the worse for wear.

A point here on shop-bought coloured maggots that you suspect have been dyed with one of these aniline substances: usually there is far too much dye on them and a good plan is to leave them overnight in a good supply of clean sawdust. This will soak up much of the residue and at least give you a reasonable chance of staying clean and safe.

If you resort to the washing process be sure to dry them off thoroughly, otherwise they will float when introduced to your swim. Once you are happy with the cleanliness they can be placed in a fresh batch of sawdust. Sawdust is best for bait which is to be stored for more than twenty-four hours, but use only clean wood dust with no hint of any substances such as preserver or turpentine. A visit to a DIY shop that cuts wood to order will usually get you all you need for a season at a cost of a few pence.

• *An old fridge can save a fortune on bait bills, but take care how you position the various types of bait to ensure best possible shelf life.*

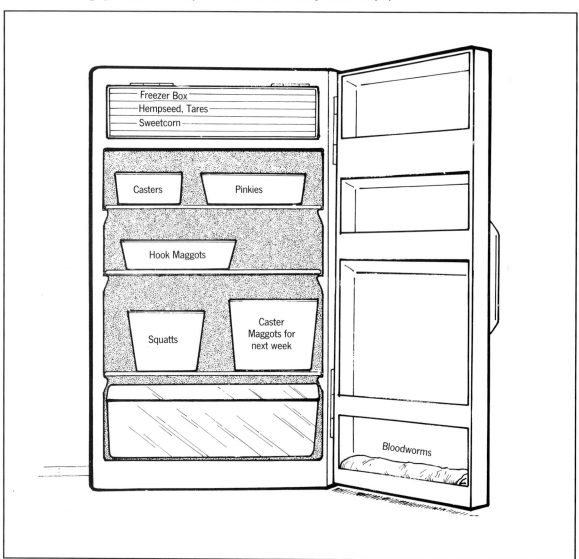

Sawdust, or any medium that is to be used with bait, will benefit from a riddle first to free it of any large pieces which may otherwise spoil the final preparation of the maggots.

While sawdust is good for storing bait it is preferable to replace it with something more edible just prior to setting off for the water. Fine maize powder, bran or groundbait all work well. Add just enough to give the bait a good dusting. You don't want to have to search through a top layer of dust every time you need a maggot.

An old fridge comes in handy when considerable amounts of bait need to be prepared. If you can obtain one that can be kept in the garage or the shed and used only for bait it will save you a lot of time, trouble and cash. It's also going to be essential if you produce your own casters.

When fridging maggots they will need to be in broad containers which are large enough to be used without the lids on. Watch out with pinkies, they must be completely dry otherwise they climb out of anything – even with the lids on.

Hook maggots and pinkies can stand a lot of fridging, but with squatts go easy. They need to be cool, but overdo it and they will stretch and, if left too long, may die. Should you find your squatts suffering in this manner take them from the fridge and spread them on a shallow container until they revive. Before returning them to the fridge turn it up a few degrees, and place them as near to the bottom as possible.

I always try to arrange my bait so that pinkies are nearest the top, then hook maggots and lastly squatts at the bottom.

Squatts come supplied in a dark sand which needs to be kept slightly damp. This sand can be introduced with the squatts when fishing but some anglers prefer to riddle it off and use slightly damp groundbait instead. I use the sand and have never found it has a detrimental effect on my fishing. If you decide to do the same it's worth riddling it to check for lumps and small stones. Just riddle it complete with squatts and then leave them to work through the riddle into the sand contained in a large bowl below.

Colouring maggots is easy with bronze chrysoidine – although obtaining the powder is no longer so simple. Your tackle dealer may sell you some if you ask nicely.

Use gloves throughout the operation, sprinkling a very small amount on the maggots, which are best coloured neat and in a slightly damp condition. Leave them for half an hour and check the shade you require. If it's deep enough, stop the process by adding dry sawdust or dry groundbait, maize or bran. Leave them now to work off any surplus dye and then change the medium in which they have been cleaning. Ideally change it as often as is practical to ensure that little is left to rub off onto your fingers.

Colouring bait is dangerous with such substances as chrysoidine and if at all possible it is best avoided. There are some completely safe alternatives available through tackle shops. Some take longer to work but there are several colours to choose from, and although the results may look different to those obtained with the old dyes they still catch a lot of fish. I have been using them for some time now and have enjoyed both success and peace of mind, knowing that I am not chancing my health by using a dangerous substance.

With all these alternative dyes be sure to follow the instructions very carefully otherwise you may kill expensive bait, or at best end up with badly coloured specimens. A good thing too about these new dyes is that they wash off your hands easily so you don't have to turn up for work looking as though you've caught something very nasty. On the morning of the match, time will be needed to run all bait through a riddle just once more and to renew whatever medium you have chosen to keep it in overnight.

If you are taking maggots to a match overnight or on long trips during the summer a cool box is essential. For short journeys just give them as much air as possible. Use large containers, and if the weather is hot, drop an ice-box cold pack in with them. If you stop for coffee on the way, park the car out of the sun, and if possible leave the windows down a little to keep some air circulating.

An idea which seems to be used less often these days is the pillow-case method. This works effectively for both maggots and pinkies. Get a cotton pillow-case double-stitched around the seams and add your bait, which should have just a little sawdust added. Tie the pillow-case up tightly and lay it on a cool floor. Packed this way the bait stays cool overnight and will get plenty of air through the cotton. It's a good method for coach travel where space is limited. The floor is usually cool, and if you can find a draught, so much the better; alternatively, hang the case up by the tie string. The whole idea is to provide as much surface area as possible through which heat can escape and air circulate.

Maggot breeding

While commercial maggots will be good enough for most of your match fishing, there is sure to come a time when something special will be needed for the hook.

Breeding your own hook maggots is easy enough and can be done with very little fuss or smell. A corner of the garden or even a shed is an ideal site at which to set up the operation. We are not looking to produce gallons of bait but just a handful or so of super-soft, pure white maggots, far superior to anything supplied by the professional breeder.

The gozzer, a very soft and white species of maggot, is the one that is best attempted and certainly the most prized of all maggots.

Gozzers, unlike other maggots, are only obtainable if the meat on which eggs are to be laid is kept in the dark. The species of fly responsible for the gozzer finds its way in through a small hole left open at the top of a suitable container.

To begin production you will need a fairly large container such as a biscuit tin or a bucket. If you use a plastic bucket, get one which is dark-coloured and through which little or no light can pass.

Now you need some sawdust, a few sheets of newspaper and some suitable meat. Chicken is good and so are sheep's hearts. If you know someone who shoots ask them for a pigeon or two.

In the case of pigeons or any other furred or feathered creature there is no need to pluck or skin it. Pigeons will be 'blown' – that is have flies lay their eggs – in the beak if it is wedged open with a small piece of matchstick. I usually pull off a few breast feathers and make a cut in a meaty part of the breast. Hearts or other meat can also be given a few cuts with a sharp knife to expose more surface area.

Liver was always claimed to be good meat for breeding but in my opinion nothing can beat a blood-free chicken breast, a pigeon or a heart when it comes to obtaining a good, very white gozzer.

In warm weather an adult maggot will usually take eight to ten days to emerge but this time varies a lot according to temperature.

Blows can be obtained more quickly by giving the meat a few minutes in a warm oven – just long enough to warm it, nothing more.

Place the meat in the biscuit tin or bucket positioned in a sheltered corner of the garden, ideally under bushes or some other overhead shelter. Next cover the top with a piece of wood, leaving only a very small opening through which the fly can enter. A brick on the wood will prevent cats and other animals from upsetting the container.

After an hour or so, take a check. If the meat has been 'blown' it will have small white eggs on it. These are cylindrical in shape and about two millimetres in length. On two hearts or a pigeon, enough eggs to cover an area something less than that of your fingernail is about right. Get too many blows and there will not be sufficient meat available for the young maggots to grow to full size.

Once the blows are to your liking take the meat and roll it inside two or three layers of newspaper. Cover the bottom of your container with two inches of clean sawdust, cover the top completely with the wood and leave nature to take its course.

Care must be taken to cover the meat completely, otherwise more flies will be attracted and too many eggs will result.

After a week the maggots will be well on the way to becoming full-sized adults, and when fully grown they will begin to leave the parcel and bury themselves in the sawdust. If all has been done correctly the meat will have been almost completely eaten, leaving behind only a little black fibre and fat, which can be buried for easy disposal.

The maggots can be left to work in the sawdust but because they are so soft it is better to transfer them to some very slightly damp bran. This is softer than sawdust and will not toughen their delicate skins.

To improve the whiteness even more, add a pinch of sugar to the bran and leave them to clean off overnight. Next morning you will have fat, soft white maggots that are ideal for bream fishing. The softness seems to produce bites when ordinary maggots fail.

Casters

As with maggots, the standard of commercially prepared casters is generally good but they cannot compare with those turned at home. Preparation takes a lot of time and trouble but the end result is usually worthwhile, if only to give you a little extra confidence.

For caster production you are going to need a good supply of big white maggots about ten days prior to the

● *A national championship is the highlight of many anglers' seasons. This one took up 12 miles of the Stainforth and Keadby Canal*

match. Riddle them and sort out any skins and rubbish in the same manner as when preparing maggots.

Good cleaning in these early stages will result in a nicely formed caster later on.

A gallon of maggots can be reckoned to produce about six pints of casters and to make the operation worthwhile you should consider turning at least two pints, for which maybe three pints of maggots will be the usual starting quantity. Clubbing together with friends can be an advantage here and certainly a small match group of, say, four anglers can gain much by taking it in turns to do the whole batch.

Store the caster maggots in a large container, the bigger the better. A gallon needs a container of at least twice that capacity and not too deep. Use the fridge to hold them back from turning as long as possible. This also has the advantage of getting a quick turn once they begin forming into casters. The sawdust should be clean and damp. Dry sawdust will cause the casters to be small and quickly dried out. A trick here is to re-use the same sawdust for several batches of casters. The sawdust seems to retain moisture, resulting in bigger casters from the batches that follow.

By Wednesday evening it is time to remove the maggots from the fridge. When they warm up a little and begin wriggling, run them through the riddle to take out any which may have died.

Store the maggots in a cool place. Too warm and the casters will be banana-shaped and of poor quality. Rushing this stage is not a good idea. Next morning check their condition, and if there are signs that turning has begun, run them through the riddle once more. There may only be a handful of casters at this stage and if that is so, give the birds a treat. If there are enough to keep, pop them in a plastic bag, seal it and store them in the fridge.

Now the work really starts and the more frequently you run off casters the more you will get that are of the best quality. As you run each batch off try to pick out old skins and dead maggots. The fewer that get into the bag the better.

Bag anything which has begun to turn and don't be afraid of opening the same bag several times, as this will let in just enough air to prevent suffocation.

In an ideal situation, where a large batch comes off on the evening prior to the match, they can go straight into a bait box filled to the very top. Cover with a couple of sheets of damp newspaper, followed by a layer of plastic bag and then the lid.

If you now have bait varying from almost white to deep red they can be used like that. The difference in colour is because they are at various stages in their development. The darkest will sink the most slowly and the light ones the fastest. This variation makes it harder for fish to notice the one with a hook inside sinking slightly unnaturally.

If you want casters all of the same colour, give them a wash under a cold tap and take them to the match wrapped inside a damp towel. This general exposure gets them all a nice even red.

Sometimes casters will be softish in texture and difficult to hook. This can be overcome by damping them and using the towel treatment, or keeping them for a while in a bait box which has not been sealed with plastic. Don't let the casters turn too far, otherwise the whole batch will float and be useless.

At times you may end up with more than you want. Don't waste them but instead crunch them up into a thick creamy pulp and add it to your groundbait. Using them this way you will have a superb additive which pulls fish from a long way off. It's a very effective trick with bream and chub in particular.

Commercial casters can be improved by tipping them onto a sheet of newspaper and hand sorting to remove any skins and maggots that may have got through during the earlier stages. Wash the sorted bait and either re-bag or, better still, fill up a bait box and seal the lid as described.

Bloodworms and jokers

These two baits can be deadly for the match angler and some would claim very expensive too, so much so that a few matches ban them on the grounds that they deter people from entering.

Collecting your own can be frustrating unless you have a good source. If you have, guard it jealously; but even with a good supply scraping takes time and no small amount of discomfort, often involving standing up to your chest in cold water.

Bloodworm is scraped from ponds that contain a level of natural pollution such as would accumulate from a herd of cattle. If you can find a friendly farmer who will allow you to scrape his pond you are well on the way towards obtaining some excellent bait.

A pair of chest waders is an essential part of the kit and there will be times when you have to get in really deep to find worms in sufficient quantity. It's cold and potentially dangerous work. Never go scraping alone and always take safety precautions. Tie a rope around

your waist and get a friend to stay on the bank at the other end. Mud on the bottom of these ponds can be very deep. A few buoyancy aids such as a car tyre inner-tube or some plastic containers strung around the waist are also a good idea.

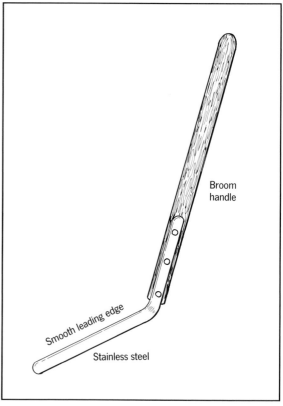

Broom handle

Smooth leading edge

Stainless steel

● *A scraper is an essential part of the bloodworm and joker collector's tools. Keep the blade smooth and well-polished to ensure the worms are not damaged during collection.*

Both bloodworm and joker can be collected all year round but during the warmer months of June and July they can sometimes be scarce due to the speed at which they hatch into gnats and midges.

Tools for the job are a suitable scraper and a double riddle which has a wooden frame and will float. The scraper is best made from stainless steel about two millimetres thick and thirty to forty millimetres wide. This is firmly attached to a broom handle.

The most important thing about the scraper blade is the leading edge. This must be perfectly smooth, otherwise the worms will get damaged and die. Check

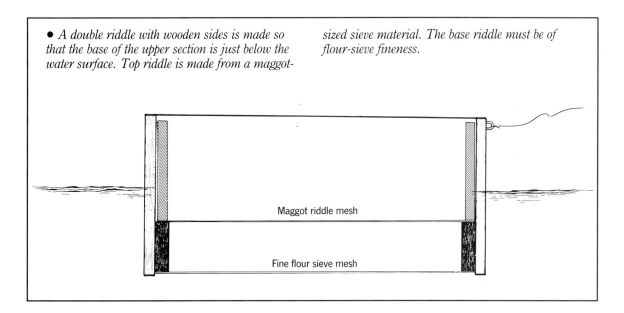

● *A double riddle with wooden sides is made so that the base of the upper section is just below the water surface. Top riddle is made from a maggot-sized sieve material. The base riddle must be of flour-sieve fineness.*

Maggot riddle mesh

Fine flour sieve mesh

it before every scraping session, and, if there is damage, file and emery it smooth.

Once in the water, the idea is to sweep the blade through the bottom mud so that the worms are swept up and fold over the blade's leading edge. Those collected are carefully slid off the blade with the fingers into the riddle, which is tied to your waist with a long piece of cord and allowed to float along behind. The upper section of the riddle has a mesh similar to the one used for maggots, while the lower portion has a very fine mesh, more like a flour sieve. This combination allows the worms to work through the upper mesh, leaving behind all the other rubbish that is scraped up with them.

Jokers are collected in the same manner but from running and more polluted water. Outfalls from old sewage plants are ideal. Work in the same fashion as you did for bloodworm.

Once the worms have been gathered give them a thorough washing in the riddle and take them home in newspaper packets. Keep these parcels flat and spread the worms out well, protecting them as much as possible from heat.

Long-term storage is possible but the worms, both bloodworm and jokers, need a lot of attention. Best way to keep them, for anything up to three weeks, is in shallow trays of cold water.

Riddle all the rubbish from the worms before dropping them into a couple of inches of water – rain water is better than tap water for this purpose and it must be changed at least once every day.

Some anglers use a fish-tank air pump to keep the water circulating and this certainly helps, especially in warm weather; but provided you never miss a water change it isn't totally necessary.

While the water is being changed tip the worms onto the riddle and be sure to pick out any dead ones. These will have turned white and are easily spotted. Leave them in and they quickly de-oxygenate the water and kill off the whole batch.

For short-term storage, or for transporting them to the water, Fison's Lawn Peat is a good medium. Lay out a sheet of newspaper, spread it with riddled peat which is just slightly damp and then add the bait, ensuring that any tight balls of the bright red bloodworms are gently broken up and spread evenly. Now fold the ends of the newspaper inwards to form a neat parcel which is not too tight.

Store in the fridge but take care not to lower the temperature below 2°C, otherwise they die very quickly.

Jokers can be treated in the same manner, but these are even more delicate than bloodworm so be careful.

If your jokers are already in peat that contains a lot of debris it can be changed by tipping the whole lot onto a riddle and submerging it just beneath the surface in a bowl of water. The jokers will slowly find their way through and into the water below. Just strain

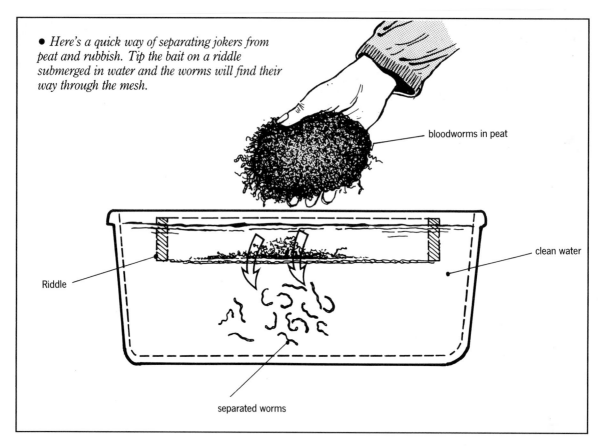

- *Here's a quick way of separating jokers from peat and rubbish. Tip the bait on a riddle submerged in water and the worms will find their way through the mesh.*

bloodworms in peat

clean water

Riddle

separated worms

them off and make up a parcel with some new peat.

The biggest bloodworms are kept aside for the hook and, once taken from the peat, need looking after carefully. Continental match-anglers keep theirs in small wooden boxes with flip-up lids. Inside they are lined with damp foam on which the worms are laid.

The rule with both bloodworm and joker is to protect them from extremes. Hot sun or extreme cold will kill them very quickly. Don't let them dry out either. A plant spray-gun is ideal for giving them a quick shower, but above all, keep them covered.

Punched bread

This is without doubt the cheapest of all match baits. A loaf will provide more than enough for a full day's fishing, both in terms of bait and groundbait.

Start with a fresh, medium-sliced white loaf. For the hookbait a few slices will need to be given some special treatment to give them just the right texture. This is

done by boiling a kettle and subjecting each slice to about twenty seconds in the steam. This puts a little extra moisture into the bread and makes it easier to punch.

Take it to the waterside in a plastic bag, and while it's in use keep it protected from sun and wind so that it doesn't dry out. To make it even easier to punch, lay it on a suitable flat surface, such as a piece of plywood, and press your knuckles into it to compress some of the crumb slightly.

The remaining part of the loaf can be used to produce a perfect punch groundbait. Start by cutting off all the crusts and then pop the white bread into a liquidiser for a few seconds, just long enough for it to be broken down into a fluffy, almost dry groundbait. Done correctly it will just pinch into small balls, which

- *Punched bread can be a superb starting bait. Use a firm board as a base for the punch and be sure to prevent the bread from drying out*

when introduced to the swim will hang for a while close to the surface and then slowly break up, sending minute pieces of crumb falling through the swim.

It's a filling groundbait and very little is needed. Bites will often come in the first few minutes of a match. If they don't, then abandon the method for something more productive.

Punched bread is a starting method. It doesn't work once other baits have been introduced to the swim but never be afraid to try it as an opener, especially in winter when the going is likely to be tough. It works for roach of all sizes, chub, and of course skimmer bream, right down to gudgeon.

Because of its filling nature half a loaf is more than sufficient for most venues. But to save time and mess make up enough for several sessions at once, packing suitable amounts into plastic bags and then freezing them down.

Hemp and tares

These two seeds are great pleasure-fishing baits but for match use must be used with care. Often they work well until subjected to match conditions when they can be unpredictable.

Hempseed is a superb feed, however, and should always be taken along – unless the rules say otherwise – to any water where chub, barbel or roach are expected.

Preparation is easy, just wash the seed under a cold tap using a small sieve, soak in cold water overnight and then bring to the boil, simmering until a tiny white shoot emerges from the split in each grain.

Hemp to be used as hook bait should be cooked slightly less than that needed for feeding. With hook samples the grain should just be beginning to open. Over-cooked it is difficult to keep on a hook.

During cooking, scum will form on the surface. Skim this away if possible. When the hemp is ready for use, do not allow it to dry out. Save time by preparing several batches at once and then bag and freeze in suitable amounts, each of which will see you through a match.

A few tares may be worth taking along if big roach are on the cards. Prepare this larger seed by washing and soaking overnight in water containing a teaspoonful of sodium bicarbonate. This treatment will help soften the grain and give it a dark appearance when cooked.

Some anglers use a casserole method taking about forty minutes in a preheated oven set at gas mark 2. My own preference is to simmer it in a saucepan and keep checking every few minutes until the grain is just soft enough to get a hook through the outer skin. But do watch it, a few minutes too long and you end up with tare jam.

The tares, properly cooked, will still be hard but this texture seems to result in fewer missed bites than when using soft tares. Small tares seem to bring better results than very large grains. As with hempseed, tares can be frozen until required.

Worms

Not much preparation is needed with worms but they do look better if allowed to run through some fresh moss. They will eject any soil that may be in their systems and the moss will polish their skins to give an attractive appearance.

A good supply of worms should always be on tap, so a little time spent preparing a good compost heap is worthwhile. Commercial tubs of worms are usually fine, but they can be expensive, and quality fluctuates.

If a proper heap is not practical, a large plastic sack full of suitable decaying matter can often produce enough worms to see you through a whole season. Make a point of placing left-over worms back in the sack or heap and disturbing only enough material to obtain the number of worms required.

Transporting worms is no problem, a little damp peat will do; but if going overseas remember that some customs regulations prohibit soil imports of any kind. If that is the case, use layers of wet newspaper or some old wet sacking cut into strips. Plenty of room and some air space are the only other requirements. As with all live bait, keep them cool.

Luncheon meat

Tinned meat is a terrific bait for chub, barbel and carp. To prepare, open a tin, cut the contents into cubes and leave in the fridge overnight in an open container. Meat straight from the tin will work but this fridging treatment and exposure to the air will cause a slight skin to form on the cubes, making hooking easier.

Take care with some of the cheaper brands. These

often contain a lot of fat and will float if introduced loose to a swim, while in extreme cases the hooked piece may rise up off the bottom in the same fashion as a carp angler fishes a 'pop up' boilie bait. This may or may not be an advantage, depending on conditions and the water being fished.

Really fatty meat can be improved by cutting it into cubes and giving it a quick fry in a non-stick pan. Do this just enough to melt the fat.

Groundbaits

A book could be written about groundbaits but so much of it is down to beliefs and personal preferences that few rules are hard and fast.

For a match angler it will pay to buy in bulk. Pure bread crumb can be purchased in 20 or 25 kilo sacks. But watch for variations in quality. Buy only the best, which is pure bread, dried and ground.

Ignore any bags containing rusk or other cereals which can result in mixing being difficult. With pure bread results will be more consistent. Check the size of grain (or grist, as it is correctly known) before purchase. Too fine and it may clog when mixed, too coarse and it will overfeed and tend to break up in the air.

● *Continental groundbaits and additives come in all sorts of flavours and colours. The biggest problem is working out their main characteristics*

Meat and veg

Luncheon meat can be a very good bait for chub, carp and barbel, but it is not an easy bait to fish at long range or when the weather is very warm.

If conditions get too warm on the bankside the cubes will soften and tend to fly off the hook during casting. To overcome this problem thread the cube on the hook, push the bend of the hook right through, turn it through 90 degrees and then insert a short piece of grass between the bend and the surface of the meat. This acts as a support and spreads the pressure of casting over a wider area of the bait, thus helping to stop the hook cutting through.

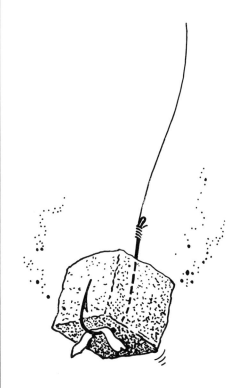

● *A short piece of grass pushed between the bait and hook bend is a simple way of preventing luncheon meat flying off during casting.*

If you find a good source it may pay to buy a whole season's supply at one go, but it does need keeping dry and away from the attention of mice.

Colour can be a guide to how it will mix. Pure white crumb mixes up heavily, while brown crumb tends to produce a much lighter mix. This is because the brown crumb has been baked longer and as a result more fat is removed.

Overall, brown will be the most useful but keep some white handy for blending a mix that might be needed for deep water or long-distance feeding.

For most fishing a fairly fine grist will do nicely. Even the best crumb will benefit from a riddling at home. The odd piece of wrapper or some hard crumb may be removed in this manner. And you can control the fineness of the finished article to suit the water being tackled.

Much has been written about continental groundbaits. Without doubt most of them work, but you will need to know which is which. Some mix up really heavily and are designed for a specific use, while others may contain things like cork dust for fishing close to, or on, the surface.

Maybe at some time in the past the continentals were well ahead of us in the groundbait stakes. Today it is not so clear-cut, and while many foreign makes do well here, some British products are just as effective and often work out cheaper.

Many public-bar arguments among anglers are over the effectiveness, or otherwise, of fancy groundbait ingredients. There was a time when I believed the addition of some of these nice-smelling concoctions improved my chances. Now I'm not so sure. What is certain is that the groundbait needs to be pure and fresh and of a suitable texture. Continental mixes certainly enable a certain consistency to be achieved – even if it is a costly exercise sorting out the many different types. Looking back over my own match fishing career I believe there has been nothing to beat a pure breadcrumb base with perhaps an additive of some description to give me a certain colour that is noted for its effectiveness on a particular water.

The real secret of good groundbaiting is not what you put into your swim but the manner in which you do it.

As to groundbait colour, that certainly is worth considering. Yellow penetrates thickly-coloured water. Red seems to do well right through the season and especially if the water is clear or cold. Bronze is a good

● *A study in concentration, Kevin Ashurst masters the long pole*

alternative to try on waters where red or natural is used extensively. My own ideal is to use a colour which matches the bait, red with red maggots or casters, bronze with bronze maggots and so on.

Pure white groundbait is something I hate. It seems to scare fish off once it has settled on the bottom, possibly because they feel conspicuous when swimming over a light patch. The only time it can really be justified is when fished in conjunction with bread punch.

Mixing any type of groundbait needs care. Done wrongly even the best of groundbaits are ruined. Start by running the dry crumb through a suitable riddle into a large tray.

Decide how much you are going to need and place all but a small amount in a wide, shallow bowl. Start adding water a little at a time, working it around quickly with both hands to ensure even distribution. If you use a square bowl pay special attention to the corners, ensuring there are no dry areas that could go unnoticed.

Continue the process until the mix can be formed into a ball that just stays together in your hand. Add a little more water and you will have a well-prepared groundbait that can be thrown a fair distance without breaking up.

Any additives that you want to use should be included prior to adding the water except in the case of liquid additives, where the best way to get an even distribution is to add them to the water being used for mixing.

Having got the right texture, run the whole lot through a riddle once more. A mesh suitable for caster production will do for most cereals. The idea is to work the groundbait vigorously, using your fingers to force it through the mesh. This will break up lumps and single out any particles which have clogged together.

Pack the results of your mix into a plastic container bag or a custom-made groundbait container and take it to the water ready for use. Just prior to the off a little extra water may be needed. For this purpose a pump-action plant-sprayer is worth taking along.

The small amount of crumb kept back prior to mixing was just in case too much water was added; it would then have been used to dry off to the required texture. If it has not been used take it along as spare dry, maybe adding some more as a reserve.

Obviously pre-mixing like this should only be done a few hours before the match. Done any earlier it may go sour.

On this point I again differ from many of the top continentals, who insist that groundbait should be mixed overnight in order to ensure good distribution of water right through each particle. One Dutch angler of international standing, with whom I discussed this, claimed that freshly mixed groundbait feels rough to a feeding fish because minute pieces of crumb are still sharp. I'm not convinced on the theory but if you want to take that idea further it can do no harm.

Although binders are not strictly groundbaits in the true sense of the word, match anglers are using them more now than ever before. They are usually in the form of a clay-type soil, of which the best-known is probably *argile*, a French word for clay. Such binders are available from good tackle shops, but with a little effort you will be able to find something suitable that can be used and collected free.

Molehills can be a good source of soil. All it needs is a careful riddling. Sandy soils will make a heavy groundbait but one which will quickly break up. Clays bind well and are good for fast water or for when a bottom feed is needed to use in conjunction with bloodworms.

Peat is another soil-type material that can be handy to have with you. Buy it from garden centres but be sure to get only pure peat which is free from fertilisers and other garden treatments such as lawn food or weed killer. Carefully riddled, it can be used almost neat with just a small amount of white groundbait added to make it bind enough to get down to where it's needed. Peat was one of the secrets of the successful Peterborough team a few years go when the local River Nene fished well for skimmer bream. We were able to pile large amounts of the stuff in without putting fish off the feed. It got our squatts down through the bleak and formed an attractive cloud at the same time. It's cheap too!

Additives

Plenty of additives are sold for angling purposes. But don't be fooled by simple food colourings and flavours. While they may do no harm they have no great attractive powers either and can be expensive, the same stuff often being sold in the supermarket at much lower prices than in tackle shops.

Real additives have a use and may contain less common ingredients.

Here are a few continental favourites which I have found useful to some degree over the years:

Peanuts: when ground they are sticky and can be used to bind a groundbait.

Pigeon droppings: sold in packets and considered by the French to be a good attractor. It comes in powdered form and makes a milky cloud when water is added.

Ground hempseed: a brilliant additive for roach and chub. Tends to make the mix very dark and slightly sticky too.

Hemp water: the water in which hemp has been boiled contains a lot of oils and flavouring from the grains. When it has cooled, use it to mix groundbait.

Molasses: a sticky, dark brown substance which is best obtained as an animal food from farm suppliers.

Add a good proportion of this to some cereal and you have a very dark, sweet groundbait that seems to work well with bream and skimmers.

Freeze-dried worms: these are usually powdered bloodworm or tubifex worms. They are expensive but a little goes a long way and the results seem to justify the cost. Very good on small fish waters.

Flour: a very powerful binder. It doesn't add much weight but it will form balls like concrete if too much is used.

Milk: produces a dense white cloud that hangs high in the water. A pint added while mixing will work well.

Baby-milk powder: old packets which have passed their sell-by date are fine for producing a cloud effect when added to fine crumb. It can be pre-mixed or used dry.

Blended sweetcorn: put a couple of cans through a food blender and then add the rich yellow liquid to some cereal. A superb mixture for use when fishing corn for carp or tench.

Steaking a claim

Match fishing has developed at a tremendous rate in recent seasons, in terms of both tackle and technique. Unfortunately some waters have not undergone the same improvements, at least not in terms of rewards for effort.

Maybe we are bordering on becoming too efficient. Fish get caught too often and as a result are becoming more educated. They associate a bait that does not behave perfectly naturally with danger and ignore it. There is also the possibility of a fish remembering what happened the last time it tried to eat, say, a bronze maggot. After a few mistakes the fish must eventually learn that it is not a good thing to eat.

If this theory holds true, then the match angler who turns to different baits, or invents new methods, gets a head start; a bit like the carp angler who dreams up a new flavour of boilie to catch a particularly difficult fish.

Take the River Trent for example. Years ago it was a maggot river. Then came the caster invasion and the maggot failed to win. Caster was 'the' bait, at least until the bubble burst and the bronze maggot once more swept all before it.

Such trends happen on all hard-fished waters and the Trent has recently seen a new bait appear regularly in newspaper accounts of match wins.

This time it is not caster or maggots, but steak. Fresh,

uncooked steak dominated matches towards the middle and end of the 1990-91 season. Weights taken on this gourmet bait were staggering. And not only chub, but bream and roach seem to love it.

Unlike similar baits such as sausage and luncheon meat, steak is fished in all sorts of ways, but the most successful seems to be with float tackle. Matches have been won on the waggler and stick with remarkable frequency. Of course those in the know are not broadcasting their success, quite naturally hoping to enjoy a few seasons of winning before the bubble bursts once more.

Favourite method, it appears, is to use ordinary raw stewing steak, baiting with tiny pieces on smallish hooks in much the same manner as more conventional baits are fished.

Once submerged the juices of this fragment of beef must permeate through the water and act as some sort of attractor. But the real secret is in the groundbait: minced beef, chopped into tiny pieces and introduced in small balls which are bound together by the addition of a little fine, dry groundbait.

It's too early to say how long the idea will continue to win but it's certainly worth thinking about on any water that holds the sort of fish that might fall for it.

5

Floats and shotting

Float fishing is the match angler's true art. Skills of both stick-float and waggler fishing, along with a few variations, will need to be mastered before any consistent results can be expected.

On whichever match circuit you intend to concentrate, there is sure to be one method that is more effective than the others. On the slow, wind-swept waters of the Fens the waggler rules. On rivers like the Trent and Severn the stick float takes many prizes. But on all waters there will be days when both methods need to be used in order to get the best possible result.

Because this is a match fishing book it is assumed that the basics have already been mastered. What this chapter is intended to do is provide a run-down on the floats and materials that are best for competition purposes.

Straight peacock waggler

The waggler comes in a variety of forms but the simplest is the straight peacock. As a material, peacock is the ultimate. Other substitutes such as sarkandas reed come nowhere near to the remarkable qualities of the true quill.

In its straight form the peacock can tackle many different situations. The thinnest end of the complete quill will provide a float ideal for delicate presentation on stillwaters or those with very little flow.

Moving up the quill as it comes from a bird, its diameter increases and with it come floats of medium sensitivity down to very thick ones that can handle big baits and cope with the forces of strong currents.

Home-made peacock floats are the best, not because the commercial manufacturer doesn't know his job but because he must produce floats that will withstand the rough treatment handed out by less-experienced anglers and which look attractive on the tackle-shop shelf. This he does by using thick paint and varnish, which while adding durability also reduce the shotting capacity and increase the float's weight.

A match angler's floats should be made to do a job. What they look like is immaterial. Thin, matt-finish paint and a tip colour of the right shade and length are all that's needed to suit the task in hand.

Make up sets of wagglers to take shot loads of between, say, 2BB and 3SSG and in various thicknesses, and it would be possible to meet most of the demands of many waters on the British match circuit.

Loading can be added to the base but this does tend to cause a float to 'bury' deeply on entry to the water, and because of this I usually prefer to add the weight as locking shots.

The bulk of shot needed to set the float correctly is usually going to be used as locking shot. At least three-quarters of the total is about right.

The other rule that is generally applied concerns the position of any remaining shot which goes down the line. Any shot positioned above the mid-depth mark is going to make casting difficult, and will eventually cause the hook to flip back over a shot during casting, and tangle.

Correct balance of the shot is more important than the actual amount used. Wrongly shotted, a 3SSG waggler will be out-cast every time by one of half its weight.

On this subject it is vital to recognise that match fishing does not always demand ultra-fine lines and

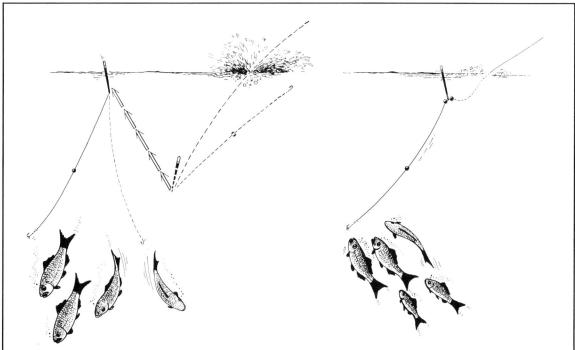

● *Loading added to a float's stem will aid casting but tends to cause burying as it enters the water. This can be a fish-scaring problem on shallow swims and also takes up time for the float to rise back to the surface and begin fishing correctly (left). The float (right) is loaded with locking shot and settles much quicker, and is fishing immediately the cast is completed.*

very light shotting. If conditions demand a big float then use one. There are no medals for battling on with tackle that does not suit the swim or conditions of the day.

Balancing begins with the allocation of the locking shot. Work on the three-quarters minimum as a starting guide but be prepared to use more if a situation demands it. Often a 2SSG float may be needed with nothing more than a couple of number 8 shot down the line.

After the locking shots a waggler can be rigged in a number of ways but the two that will be used most are with small shots strung out from mid-depth to the hook or with a bunch of shot and then a tell-tale near the hook, perhaps with a couple of other shot as a mini-bulk between the two.

Keep it simple and time will be saved. Shot patterns, like the float used, are to do a job, not to look pretty.

For example, there is no point in using a tiny size 12 or 13 shot as a tell-tale, if the peacock is a thick-tipped

one of, say, five millimetres diameter. Any movement of such a shot will just not register as a bite. The only occasion when a tiny shot may be called for is when it is to be used as a brake to slow down a thick float being trotted through moving water. Checking the float will cause it to drag under, but a small shot can be pulled along without affecting the buoyancy.

Insert waggler

The insert waggler is nothing more than a variation on the normal straight waggler, although it can also come complete with a body at the base.

Its functions are considerably more limited than the straight version, but at the right time it can be a superb float and is one that no match angler can do without.

The tip insert, of thinner material than the main stem, gives the float its sensitivity. For catching on the drop or for tackling shy-biting fish it is far superior to any other float, except a bristle-tipped pole float.

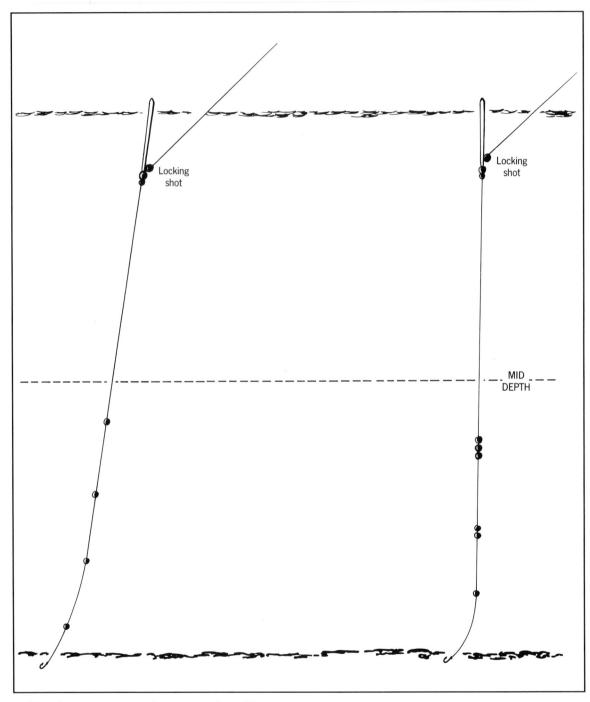

Locking
shot

Locking
shot

MID
DEPTH

● *Two simple waggler shotting patterns that will
cope with most situations. Keep all the shot below
mid-water to avoid tangling.*

60

● *The insert waggler is the ideal weapon when fish are coming on the drop. Don't try to use it when there's a strong flow or conditions are bad*

Yet it is this fine tip that also limits its uses. Try to fish an insert on a fast water and the problems begin instantly. The fine tip will just not be able to ride the flow and any attempts to check its progress, even slightly, will result in its being pulled under immediately.

On still or very slow-moving waters it comes into its own. Use it there and the full benefits can be enjoyed. Use it on the wrong venues and it's a loser.

These limitations are geared directly to tip thickness. The thinner the insert the more limited the float's scope. Kit out your box with a good set but use them only when conditions are right.

Bodied waggler

At times a straight peacock cannot be used, simply because so much weight is needed that the resulting float would need to be too long or too thick for practical purposes. Here is where the bodied version of a waggler takes over. Best used on still or slow-moving waters, the bodied waggler is a peacock to which a balsa, polystyrene or cork body is attached.

This is a superb float for casting distances beyond those attainable with a straight float. They also allow a big bulk of shot to be used down the line, to produce a stable bait such as is required when bream are the target.

Stem material is peacock as this provides a light 'tail' for the float during flight. Although sarkandas may look a little better it will certainly not cast so well.

Actual body shape will affect the way a float performs. One with its bulk at the top end will be stable in the water but does not have the same casting qualities as one with bulk at the bottom end, while an evenly tapered style will have something of both characteristics. Which you decide upon will make little difference in the long run but it is worthwhile understanding the principles, in case a problem which could be solved by a change should arise during an event.

The addition of a body makes the float that little bit more cumbersome and also creates extra resistance when striking. But the body does have one thing in its favour, in that it provides something more solid to pull

Floats and shotting

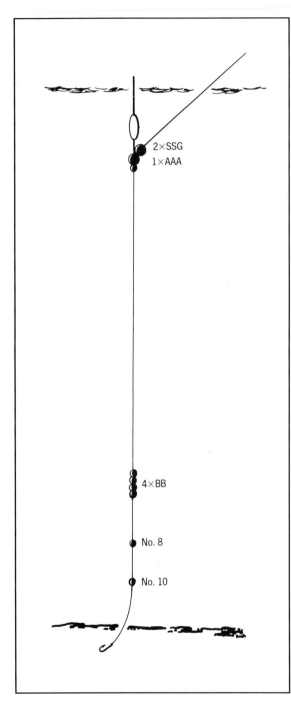

• *A body added to the normal straight peacock waggler will provide extra shot-carrying capacity. For best casting results use at least two-thirds of the total as locking shot.*

back to when conditions are bad and line has to be sunk quickly and deeply to avoid a bow forming. The body tends to keep the float on station when the line is being sunk.

Stick floats

The stick float is a big part of the match angler's armoury. On running water it is 'the' float and on rivers like the Trent it wins hundreds of matches every year.

It's not the easiest float to make and thankfully there are some good commercial ones available. Balsa for the top third is almost standard. But of more importance is the stem material. This needs to be heavy: cane, lignum, fibre-glass, dense plastic or wire.

The idea is that the balsa is buoyant enough to keep the float from being pulled under by the flow, while the dense stem acts as a sort of weight, preventing the stick from riding out of the water when held back.

As with all shop-bought floats, there are good and bad ones. Be sure the stem is of some suitable material. A stick float with a light wood stem is next to useless except in very limited circumstances.

England team manager Dick Clegg's company, Britannia Floats, has modified the more usual tapered stem by making a stem with a thicker section towards its base. This extra wood puts weight right at the bottom of the float and thus gives it terrific qualities for holding back hard.

Wire-stemmed versions are better for running through at the speed of the flow, in particular on swims that are turbulent and beyond the capabilities of a conventional pattern.

Biggest mistake with stick-float fishing is to try to use a float that's too small for the job. If it is too light it will be difficult to cast and almost impossible to control properly. A float of say four number 4 capacity might be too light where a five number 4 is perfect. Go too far and use a six number 6 and you may be overdoing things. It's all very much a case of knowing when it feels right. If things are not going well: change.

To fish a stick float effectively takes considerable concentration. Line has to be fed off the reel at just the right speed. And as the float progresses down the swim it will become increasingly difficult to remain in complete control and in touch. If the swim is particularly pacey it may pay to stand up. This seems to focus the mind on the task in hand.

Choice of reel can also play a big part. Some anglers stick with a conventional fixed spool but others find a closed-face model permits a quicker strike and less chance of knocking a fish off.

For really superb control there is nothing to beat a centre pin. But that is a skill on its own and one that few of today's anglers have mastered, simply because they grew up with a fixed spool and have had little opportunity or need to try anything else.

While stick-float fishing is generally a method for close-in work, a centre pin does restrict overall casting distance. In the hands of an expert a 'pin' can be fast and effective, but for anyone still in the process of perfecting their match skills the centre pin should come a long way down the priority list.

In stick-float fishing the thickness of line used is important. A small stick float will be hopeless if fished in conjunction with a line that is too thick. For most of this type of fishing a line of 1¾lb to 2lb is sufficient, the exceptions being big, powerful rivers that demand heavy floats and offer a possibility of large fish such as chub.

Beware of complicated shotting patterns. Two or three variations will take care of most situations. A straight string of individual small shots, say 8s, 6s or at most 4s strung down the line about ten inches apart is a conventional approach.

On waters strange to you it pays to shot a stick with a lot of small shots set in groups of two or three. By having so many shots on the rig it gives more scope to move them around until the best pattern is arrived at. Rarely will a match be started and finished on the same stick-float shotting pattern. Constantly varying the set-up can keep the angler in touch with fish as they move around in the water or become suspicious after seeing their numbers depleted as the match progresses.

Bulking shots into several groups, reducing in size nearest the hook, will get a bait down quickly but without much loss of delicacy. Even a bulk of shot well down, with perhaps a couple of tell-tales, is not unusual. However, no matter which pattern is chosen there should always be a shot right at the base of the float stem to act as a marker and to give extra stability. This one is usually the biggest, say a 4.

Tip colour on stick-floats is often black and I've found this to be one of the most widely used over the course of a season. Because stick-floating is a near-bank occupation, the float often travels over areas of water exposed to the sky and therefore with a light

● *A nice set of stick floats combining a balsa upper section and a dense stem – ideal for holding back against a flow*

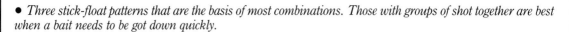

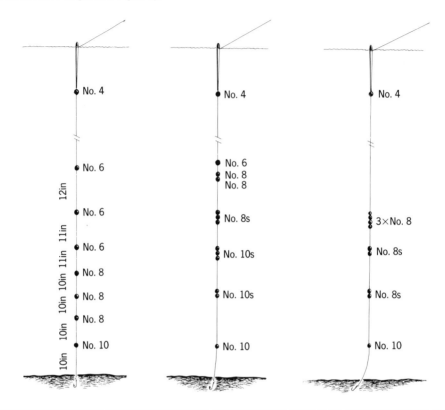

● *Three stick-float patterns that are the basis of most combinations. Those with groups of shot together are best when a bait needs to be got down quickly.*

surface colour. This makes a perfect contrast to the black tip. Bright orange is the other colour that will be needed and is fine on swims where there is a dark surface caused by overhanging bushes or a high bank.

For a stick-float collection to be fully comprehensive it will require floats ranging in capacity from about three number 4s to 7BB and in both conventional and wire-stemmed patterns.

The wire-stemmed patterns are best for turbulent swims. The thin nature of the wire reduces the surface area of the stem and so offers less for the current to act upon.

It is advisable to have some shouldered patterns in the collection too. The shoulder formed in the upper end of the balsa is a help when holding a stick float back. Current pushes against the shoulder, creating a downward force that works against the float, preventing it from riding up out of the water.

Balsa

The balsa follows on from the wire-stem stick in that it is a float for fast, turbulent waters. Shaped very much like a stick float, but lacking a heavy stem in favour of more balsa and ending in just a short stump of stem.

Usually fished without checking its progress down the swim, it can ride out water that is turning over and swirling far too heavily for other patterns. If the pattern has a shoulder at the top the balsa can be checked.

Unless matches take you regularly to rivers like the Severn, it's unlikely that the balsa will come out of the box more than a few times in a season. But a small selection of sizes is worth keeping to hand, especially in winter when floods could change a match plan overnight.

Stronger sticks

If you decide to make your own stick floats it's worth spending a little extra time to ensure they are as strong as possible.

Because of the thin section of a stick float, great care is needed when attaching the upper balsa section to the heavy stem. In the case of a wire-stemmed model there is no problem, but with cane or lignum some form of spigot is required in order that the two materials can be joined successfully.

Before starting to shape either balsa or stem, spend time cutting a short spigot on one end of the cane.

Start by making a shallow cut round the cane about half an inch from the end. Then carefully cut down from the end, back towards this line, until a spigot is formed, finishing off with a good glasspapering to get it as round as possible.

Once you are happy with the spigot, shape the stem to the required taper.

A short and centrally drilled hole in the balsa takes the spigot, which is glued in place with a spot of Araldite. Once the glue has set the balsa can be shaped to blend in with the stem.

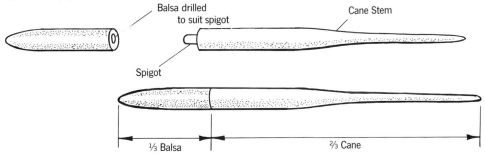

- *A spigot formed on the end of the cane stem used for a stick float is the best way to ensure maximum strength.*

The Avon

A float neglected by a large percentage of match anglers even though it has much to offer.

Made from a large balsa or pith body set on a crow quill, it is a float for fishing deep waters at medium range. As such it beats both stick float and waggler by combining a few characteristics of each.

It is a float which carries a lot of load – 14BB is not uncommon. It casts well, gets a bait down fast and is perfect where overhead room or back space are limited because of a high bank or overhanging trees.

Probably what puts off so many anglers is the bulky, rather clumsy look of the big body and the traditional large bulk of shot set down the line.

Oddly enough, bites are usually very positive, and my advice is to give the pattern a try. It really can be a winner under many situations. Even when a downstream wind makes stick-float fishing almost impossible the big Avon often copes well enough to make it a winning method.

Two or three of these floats ready rigged and stored on pole-float winders take up very little room, and will justify the space allocated time and time again.

A typical Avon peg may be one of twelve feet or so deep, on a river with a flow ranging from almost nothing to quite pacey. The wind may be blowing upstream and so making it difficult, on slow waters, to get other float patterns to run downstream at the right speed. Bleak or small fish such as dace feeding near the surface might also be in the picture, spoiling baits intended for better fish feeding near the bottom. The big bulk shot gets a bait down through even the thickest bleak shoal.

Canal patterns

Canals call for a range of smaller floats that match the nature of these fisheries. The good old Canal Grey balsa waggler is still one of the best commercial ranges around. These floats are slim in design, cast well and take a good spread of loads that are sufficient for most waters in the canal network. They also come in handy for close-in fishing on small rivers.

Nothing fancy about them, just a tapered balsa stem which bulges out to a slight body at the base.

For fishing very close to the far bank, or up against the hulls of boats, the Canal Dart is a good choice. A thin tip of little more than bristle thickness makes it sensitive. But the nature of the float comes from its loaded stem. This load accounts for almost the entire carrying capacity except for perhaps a couple of size 8 or 10 shots.

The dart is designed to be cast tight to the bank and left there, without even sinking the line as would be the case with a waggler. What happens is that the cast is made and the float flies through the air, pulling the lightly-shotted tackle behind it.

On reaching its destination the float settles quickly and the bait falls in an arc so that it falls in towards the bank. One to remember if a bait needs dropping within a matter of inches of a feature. Only drawback is that, because the line hasn't been sunk, any wind will quickly begin to form a bow and fishing time before the tackle gets pulled off line will be limited.

Drinking straws and all sorts of other floats will eventually find their way into a tackle box. That's fine, but the more you collect the harder it becomes to make the right choice.

● *(Right) A good draw on a productive canal. Note how this angler has positioned his spare kit well away from towpath traffic*

● *(Below) The loaded canal dart float is perfect for getting a bait to fall right up against the far bank, but fished correctly it will only present a bait well for limited periods.*

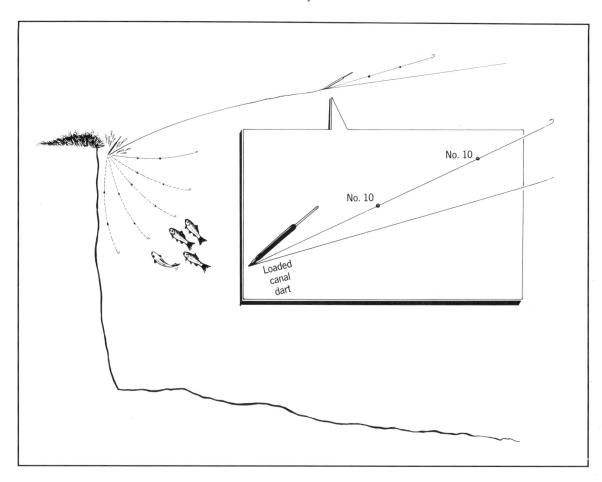

No. 10

No. 10

Loaded canal dart

Missed bites

In match fishing, missed bites cost money, making all the difference between success and failure. But of course even the best miss them occasionally, so don't get all worked up if you suddenly find the connection rate falling.

Solution to missed bites is usually to be found in the shotting, so turn to that first to see what can be done to improve things. Begin by shortening the distance from hook to bottom shot. If that doesn't work, check that the shot is actually large enough to have some effect on the float. A minute number 12 is no good if the tip of the float is a great chunk of peacock.

First indication that something is wrong is when a bait comes back nipped but no bite has registered. Usually in such cases shotting is to blame but it may also be worthwhile checking that the rig is not set too far overdepth.

In a situation where no bites are forthcoming, begin by reversing the whole procedure, lengthening the distance from shot to hook. Once all is well the rig should be such that bites are not only frequent but easy to see and hit.

Going the distance

Never worry about using heavy floats if conditions demand them.

It is far better to use a float that allows you to get the required distance into your cast and then, having reached the target, be able to control what's happening to your bait.

But simply increasing float size will not automatically increase casting range.

Too much shot down the line in relation to what is being used to lock the float in place will dramatically reduce the distance it is possible to cast.

Aim to use at least two-thirds of the total load as locking shot. If you are catching regularly and simply want to make casting easier, add the extra load to the float rather than interfere with the actual pattern.

6
The pole

Pole fishing is an ever-growing part of the British match fishing scene, so much so that it is no longer possible to compete on equal terms without one.

Like all methods it has to be used sensibly. A good pole costs several hundred pounds, but it must not become the automatic choice simply because the expense seems pointless if it is left inside its case.

Selecting a pole needs care. Price is the first stumbling block so begin by deciding how much you can afford. There are a lot of long, cheap poles around but many of them are really second class in terms of performance.

A minimum length of 10 metres will be needed and even better are ones of 11 or 12. But this increase in length must not be at the expense of rigidity.

Watch out in particular for poles which have their length increased by extensions. For while some of the more expensive ones are fine, there are others that become sloppy and unmanageable once the extension is added. A far better option is to find a pole designed specifically to fish at its full length.

What is needed is a pole that is stiff, of small diameter and light enough to be handled right through a match without fatigue setting in. Spend time finding one in your price range which offers the best of all these features.

Apart from the less-popular telescopic style, two types of pole exist. The variation is in the manner in which joints fit together, known either as 'put in' or 'put over'. The 'put over' method is by far the better of the two. With this system of assembly the lower section fits inside the one above it. This makes assembly while fishing much easier because the end of the male section is of a considerably smaller diameter than the mouth of the female and is therefore easy to locate quickly. In the case of the 'put in' type two parallel ferrules have to be lined up accurately. There is also a greater risk of the sections jamming with this method.

In terms of useful life the 'put over' fittings will last far longer than the others because the taper effect compensates for wear on the joints, which with the 'put in' type can result in loose joints.

Ideally there should also be spare top, second and if possible third sections into which different strength elastic can be fitted.

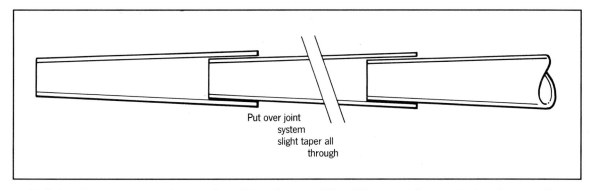

Put over joint
system
slight taper all
through

● *(Left) A cold, clear day: not the sort of conditions that make fishing easy. Those spectators standing in full view of the fish are not helping either*

● *(Above) Put-over joints are the best for poles. They are easier to connect and are less prone to jamming.*

A fine flick-tip top also comes in handy and is well worth the extra outlay.

If a flick-tip top set is available it will save having to lay out more money to purchase a whip for speed work. If you can't get these sections then a whip of six or seven metres must be considered as a part of the pole armoury.

Rigging up the main pole sections will mean possibly cutting off a short piece from the top section so that a PTFE bush and internal elastic can be fitted.

Take care when doing the cutting. Use a fine-toothed junior hacksaw and ease it through gently. Keep cutting back, a little at a time, until your PTFE bush can just be pushed home. These bushes come in both internal and external types. The external ones usually mean less pole has to be cut off, but overall the internal ones look neatest. If you do fit an external type, be sure to get one that protrudes from the pole end far enough to prevent the elastic from rubbing over the end of the pole and becoming damaged. Once the tip is cut to the required length, give the sawn edges a wipe around with fine emery paper to remove any sharp fibres that might otherwise damage the elastic.

Some form of bung to which the elastic can be anchored must be fitted inside the bottom end of the second joint. Best types are of tapered nylon which can be cut to fit any size of pole. Cut back the bung until it fits inside the pole, far enough up to clear the next section if the joints are 'put over' types.

Bungs need a short length of strong nylon attaching to them so that they can be pulled out when the elastic needs replacing.

Having got bung and bush to the correct fit, elastic can be threaded inside the two sections by using a diamond-eye threader. This is a length of special wire with a diamond-shaped eye at one end through which the elastic is passed. The opposite end of the wire is threaded down the pole from the bushed end and the elastic pulled through.

A Stonfo connector is now tied to the elastic. This is a special nylon fastening that has a tiny hook and sleeve at one end to which the tackle is attached. Remember to thread the shroud over the elastic

• *This world championship angler has pinned his faith in the pole. Although it is a method now widely used in British match fishing it is not the complete answer, and should be used only as a part of the overall approach*

before passing the elastic through the fixing eye. Knot the elastic securely and then push the shroud back over the knot.

A personal liking of mine is to get the loose end of the knotted elastic just protruding out of the back of the shroud.

Finally the other end of the elastic needs to be tied to the bung, ensuring that there is just enough tension to make the elastic slide back inside the pole after being extended. Getting this tension right is very important. Too much and there is a danger of bumping fish off on the strike. Too little and you end up with

elastic hanging out of the end of the bush after a few fish have been caught.

If tension is proving difficult it is worth adding a special tensioning device to the elastic. These are small pieces of plastic rod with open eyes at each end. The elastic is passed through one eye and then spiralled along and anchored through the eye at the other end.

Elastic comes in a whole range of sizes and breaking-strains, but for general use number 4 is a good starting strength. Match the elastic to the size of fish you expect to catch and the tackle being used. If it

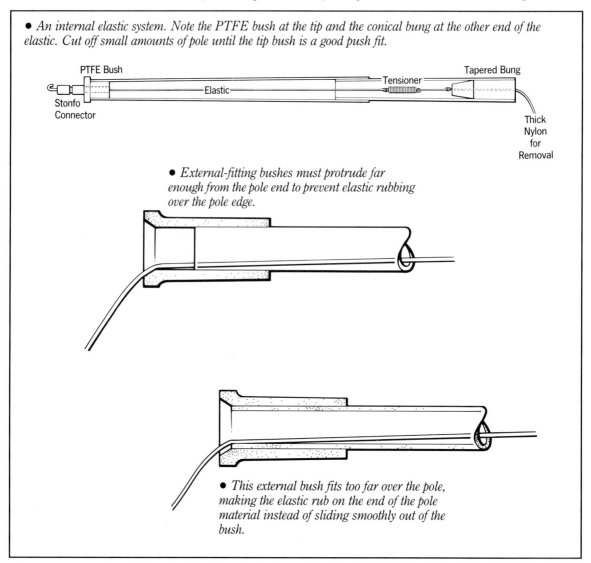

● An internal elastic system. Note the PTFE bush at the tip and the conical bung at the other end of the elastic. Cut off small amounts of pole until the tip bush is a good push fit.

PTFE Bush

Elastic

Tensioner

Tapered Bung

Stonfo Connector

Thick Nylon for Removal

● External-fitting bushes must protrude far enough from the pole end to prevent elastic rubbing over the pole edge.

● This external bush fits too far over the pole, making the elastic rub on the end of the pole material instead of sliding smoothly out of the bush.

- *Tie on a stonfo connector using this simple knot. The elastic can protrude just through the end of the stonfo sleeve.*

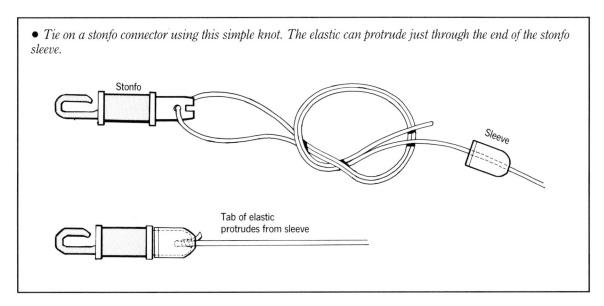

is set up correctly it should extend just a few inches as a small fish is struck and played, but with bigger fish will come out as much as several metres to provide a sound shock absorber.

Different makes vary a lot in strength but the number 4 just mentioned as a good general size is usually rated as being suitable for hook lengths of 1.1lb and hooks of around size 20.

For more delicate fishing, say for small canal fish, with size 24 hooks and 8oz bottoms, a drop to a size 2 elastic would be about right. If you are going to a lake where carp might be the main target then a powerful size of 7 or 8 may be needed to set hooks of up to 12 or 14. The whole thing is a matter of balance. Get it too fine and you either don't set the hook fully or spend ages playing each fish. Too powerful and fish are bumped off or the tackle is broken.

Elastics are sold in a variety of colours, usually white, black or orange. There is no difference in the performance – although some brands may prove to be better than others. But choose a colour you can see easily. Being able to see how much is outside the pole makes it easier to assess the amount of pressure you are applying to a running fish.

While setting up these pole tops it is also worth making up a couple of spare lengths of elastic. Attach a Stonfo to a suitable length of elastic and store it on a pole-rig winder so that it can be quickly threaded through the joint and attached to the bung should you be unfortunate enough to get a break during a match.

If a break occurs, it is better to spend a few moments rethreading an elastic of the correct length than try to struggle on with other spare elasticated sections which have been set up for a type of peg completely different to the one you are fishing.

Once everything is to your liking, run a few spots of pole-elastic lubricant down the tip bush and pull the elastic to get an even distribution.

Elastic eventually either wears out or perishes and if left too long is going to break. Check regularly and renew it often. Elastic is cheap, lost fish are costly.

The reason for having the third section as a spare is so that reasonable lengths of rig can be attached and the three joints set up as a complete unit, easily interchangeable with the main pole without having loose line hanging around.

All pole joints need to fit well and come apart smoothly, but there is a great danger that even the best sections can get jammed together if they are rammed home too enthusiastically during the heat of match action.

To prevent this happening, work out which joints will be broken down as a fish is landed or the hook is rebaited, and then fit them together correctly. Next wrap a couple of turns of electrician's adhesive plastic tape around the male joint at the point where the female ends. This then acts as a stop and should prevent trouble. A bonus if you go for a bright colour is that it makes the section easy to identify, so there is no danger of breaking down the wrong joint.

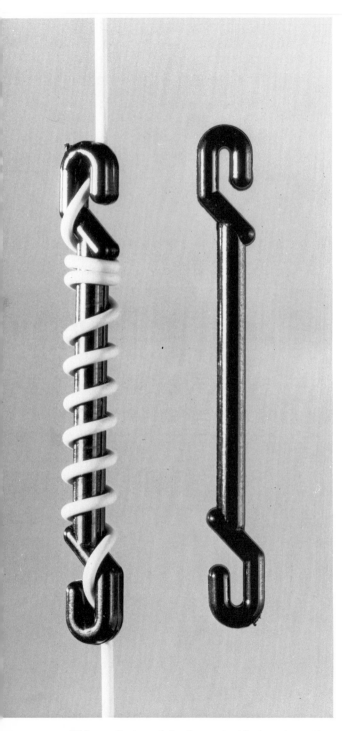

• *This small piece of plastic goes inside the pole and is used as a means of increasing the elastic's tension*

Whips

The whip is a superb method for catching fish fast at short range. As a tool for catching bleak it cannot be beaten. A whip of 6 metres with a full-length line that can be fished to hand means that a swim 1½ metres deep can be fished at almost 10 metres range without any need to break down sections. It also allows much smaller floats to be used than would be possible on running tackle.

The soft flick tip does all the work when a fish is hooked and it is surprising how even powerful species like carp and tench can be beaten on fine tackle.

There is not much difference between whip-fishing techniques and those of long pole work with elastic. The main variation is in having to learn to handle long line rigs so that fishing to hand becomes a fast and efficient operation.

Once fully mastered it is a most enjoyable way to fish, and can completely outstrip any efforts opponents may make to compete at similar range with rod and reel.

Attaching rigs is simple, and if the correct method is employed they can be removed in seconds too.

Several different ways of attaching a rig have been devised but the one I favour most involves using two small pieces of silicone rubber tube (see diagram in Chapter 11).

A piece around ten millimetres long needs to be a good fit right on the extreme end of the tip so that when in position it overhangs the end slightly. This overhang is important as it prevents tangles. A second, larger-diameter piece about five millimetres long goes along the tip about 150 millimetres from the end.

The tackle rig has the end piece of silicone slid on and is best kept there permanently. The line of the rig has a conventional loop tied at its end. Line is passed through the loop to form a second loop, which is then slipped over the tip and located behind the second piece of silicone. Now twist the nylon of the rig around the tip in a spiral, and finally push the tip silicone tube into place. The spiral stops any bowing effect between pole and line and the whole set-up is perfectly safe.

To remove a rig it is a case of slipping off the end tubing, untwisting the spiral and opening up the double loop. The second silicone tube stays on the pole.

Three choices of whip type are available: telescopic throughout, take-apart or a combination of both. My own favourite has five metres of telescopic and then two more take-apart sections to make up the total length to seven metres. These two removable pieces are handy when a big fish needs to be netted or the float requires adjusting.

Pole floats

Floats for pole fishing are a subject in themselves, but understanding the basic shapes and their uses is all that is needed to get started on the match scene.

Many of the strange patterns that appear on tackle-shop shelves are best left there. They have been designed for very specific jobs, often for continental waters where weather and flow conditions are considerably different to those found on our waters.

Five or six patterns in a range of sizes can see you through a varied season and, as with all my fishing, I have adopted the principle of keeping them simple.

Straight balsa

This pattern is fitted with a bristle tip and is perfect for still or slow waters where tackle does not need to be

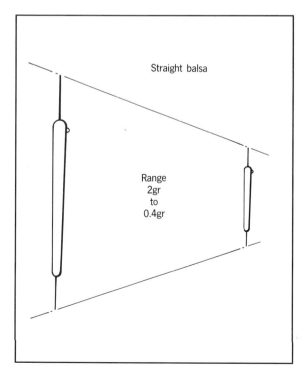

Straight balsa

Range
2gr
to
0.4gr

held back excessively. It can be fished either with an olivette for bottom-feeding fish or with a string of shot or styl weights to present a slowly-falling bait. Overall a versatile float that can vary in size from a small one taking three or four number 8 shot to a big model carrying a large olivette.

A bonus with this float is that because it is so slim in profile it permits a clean strike and creates little disturbance in a shallow swim.

Stillwater balsa bristle

If conditions are choppy but the water is still, a tapered body with its bulk near the bottom will give extra stability. This one also has a tip bristle and is generally fished with a bulk of shot or an olivette down the line to keep the bait steady.

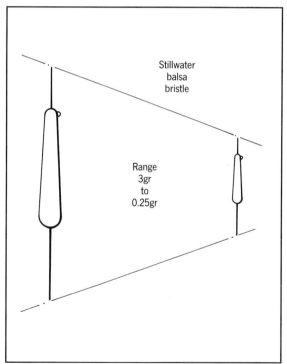

Stillwater
balsa
bristle

Range
3gr
to
0.25gr

Flat-topped balsa

For shallow water a balsa-bodied float with a flat top is a good choice. Usually very small – up to perhaps three number 4s at most – this one comes into its own with small fish and is great for catching fish quickly in

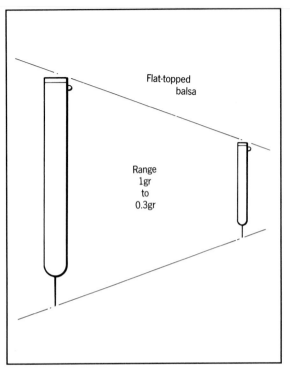

Flat-topped balsa

Range 1gr to 0.3gr

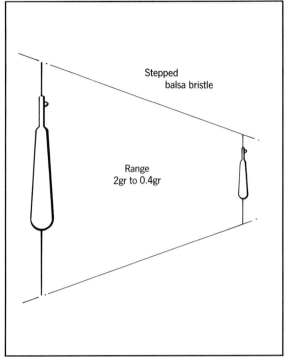

Stepped balsa bristle

Range 2gr to 0.4gr

only inches of water. A point to remember, though, is that the flat top has to be shotted right down flush with the surface.

A variation on these balsa patterns can be made from tiny pieces of peacock quill into which a short length of wire is pushed to form a stem. A side eye made from a small eyed hook is glued to the quill and a nylon bristle cut from a broom is fixed into the top. These are excellent little floats that carry a good load for their size and can be very versatile.

Stepped-bodied bristle

A specialised float for bloodworm or squatt fishing on canals and stillwater, this one has a bulbous body with an upper part that slims down to form a balsa stem ending in a bristle.

By rigging with an olivette and a couple of drop shot it can be set so the bait is just on the bottom. Then, by a minute upward movement of the pole, the float is made to ride up a fraction in the water. This causes a little flutter of the bloodworm, followed often by a bite. It takes a gentle touch and some practice to perfect its use but it is a good choice when fishing is hard.

Balsa specials

For fishing right across canals, or close up against overhanging trees on small waters, I keep some very small all-balsa specials. These are fished like a waggler but with only a couple of tiny shots down the line. Rest of the load is used as locking shot.

This is a short line rig used with elastic and is pushed out with the pole kept low so that it can be fed right beneath the branches.

River balsa

River work will need a wire-stemmed, balsa-bodied bristle. The stem needs to be long and the body almost spherical in shape. This one holds back well without riding out and is a terrific float for most river venues where a pole is needed.

The longer the wire stem, the more stable the float becomes, but the extra wire does of course reduce the amount of load the float can carry.

The bulbous nature of the body sets up a considerable resistance and in the case of the larger sizes this must be taken into account when striking;

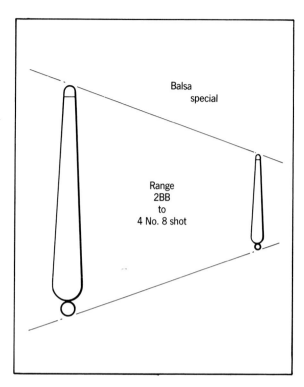

Balsa
special

Range
2BB
to
4 No. 8 shot

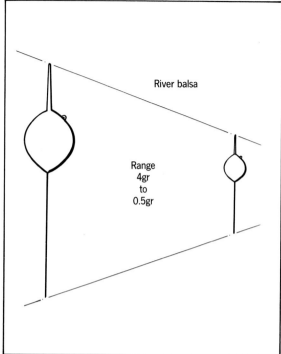

River balsa

Range
4gr
to
0.5gr

otherwise a lot of fish may be lost because the hook has not been fully driven home.

Pole wagglers

Small wagglers can be useful to beat a bad skimming wind that insists on blowing line around, and yet they are all too often overlooked in pole-fishing situations.

Nothing fancy is needed and the ideal solution is often a simple balsa pattern, perhaps with a slight body at the base for extra stability.

Set-up is similar to those for rod and line, but scaled down to suit the shorter range being fished. Keep line short, but if the wind is strong enough to make holding the pole steady a problem, it may be necessary to increase float-to-tip line length by an extra metre or so to prevent the pole's movement affecting the float.

Large patterns

Biggest of the lot are the monsters that only come out of the box a few times a year. These have fat balsa bodies and can support a big olivette. Body shape is such that the top is either flat or almost round in shape

so that it creates a face against which the current pushes downwards when held back. These are the floats for flood conditions or for fishing the prolific, powerful and deep rivers of Ireland where big catches are always on the cards.

A point about loading of pole floats is worth making here. Some floats will be marked with their approximate load in grammes. That is straightforward enough and can be used as a guide to get the loading started. Others might come marked with, say '4×12'. That coding refers to the number of styls it will carry.

In the case of a 4×12 it is four size 12 styls, each of which weighs 0.064g, so four times that totals a little over 0.25g. Watch out for some English-made floats which may be marked with a similar system but using normal shot sizes instead of styls. The 4×12 marking of a float for styls will compare roughly with a 5×10 one intended for shots. It's all a bit rough in any case so use them only as a guide.

Even when a Dosapiombo is used it is not always possible to get the more delicate bristle-tipped floats loaded exactly right. A good dodge with one that appears to be just a shade overloaded is to leave the load complete but, before starting to fish, give the

Bristles

The tip bristle of a pole float is what decides the level of its sensitivity. The thinner the bristle the more sensitive it will be.

Whether it is made from cane, plastic, quill or wire makes no difference. It is the diameter that decides the sensitivity through the laws of displacement. That is to say, a cane tip of a given diameter will require exactly the same force to pull it under as one of identical diameter but made from a light quill.

Watch out for wire bristles, however, as they do seem to be affected easily by any turbulence on the water surface, such as the after-effects of a passing boat.

bristle a dip in a jar of Vaseline or similar grease. The little extra buoyancy provided by the grease is often enough to keep the float above the surface.

Other items

Armed with those few patterns you will be well-equipped for most waters. Only addition may be some floats with cane stems rather than wire. These wood stems are excellent for use with styl weights or anywhere where bites may come on the drop. The drawback is they do not hold back so well in a flow as their wire-stemmed equivalents.

There was a time when my box contained hundreds of pole floats, many of which were on winders complete with entire rigs. While some are still carried that way, I have reduced the collection considerably without really missing any of them. Now it is a case of checking over what is likely to be needed and ensuring that these are included in my match kit in a variety of sizes.

A good idea is to keep several different boxes of made-up rigs of similar types so that if, for example, the venue is a canal, only the appropriate box needs to be taken to the match.

Prior to a match, time should be spent rigging up new sets of tackle. Easiest way to do this tedious job

● *The Dosapiombo pole-float shotting device makes balancing delicate floats much easier, but watch out for air getting trapped under the platform*

is with one of the special shotting aids such as the Dosapiombo or the one made by Preston Innovations.

Both types involve pushing the base of the float into the hole or clamp at the centre of the cup that is to take the shot, and then gently lowering the whole thing into a water-filled container. Take care here to shake off any air bubbles that may be trapped beneath the cup, otherwise a false setting will result.

Shot, olivettes or styls are now added to the holder until the correct load is achieved. They are then tipped off, dried and set up as required on the rig.

A completed rig goes on a winder that is marked with details of hook size, shot load, line and hook length, strength or diameter.

Whenever an evening is spent setting up rigs I like to have the pole to hand too. That way, by assembling the required number of sections I can fix a spool of line to the Stonfo and then run the line along the pole until I reach the joint where I will want to break down. By

cutting the line there the resulting rig ends up at the right length rather than half-way along the section.

I use my teeth a lot for biting off pieces of line, but if olivettes are to be threaded on never use your teeth in this fashion. If you do, the end of the line gets flattened and makes threading difficult. A far better idea is to cut the nylon with a very sharp razor blade.

A word here about hook lengths. For general rod and reel work mine are about two feet long, but for pole work that is reduced to six inches. This is so that olivettes etc, which are often fished very close to the hook, can be positioned on the line rather than the hook length. In order to make identification easy I mark packets containing these short lengths 'pole'.

Another difference with pole hook lengths is that I

● *Biting nylon with your teeth crushes the line and makes it difficult to thread into fine-bored olivettes. Use a sharp blade and cut the nylon at an angle.*

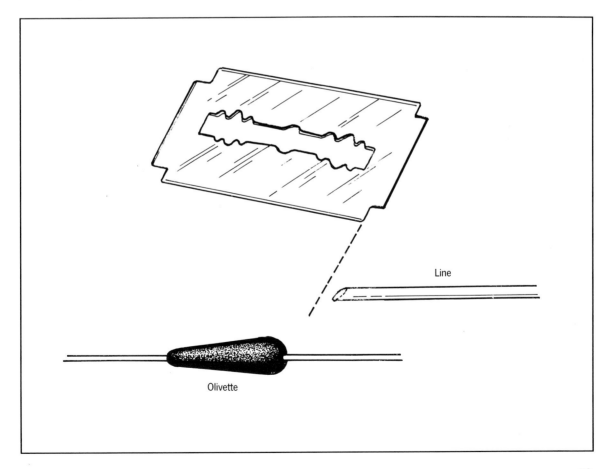

Line

Olivette

leave them without loops, preferring instead to use a four-turn Water Knot to attach them rather than a loop-to-loop or loop-to-Half Blood Knot method. It's a small point and if you go for the loop method you will have lost little or nothing.

Hooks for use when fishing short-line pole rigs should be barbed. My personal preference is for a micro-barb pattern. While barbless hooks are very much in fashion with many match anglers they do not work well when the pole is being broken down, as with a short-line set-up. As a joint is unshipped there is a danger that a slight slackening of the line can occur. In the case of a barbless hook this usually results in the fish coming off.

It is the current fashion to use all sorts of fancy hook patterns, often originating from obscure continental sources. While they may well be good hooks, I fail to see why they are considered by some anglers to be so essential for pole fishing. The patterns I use for my general match fishing have been tried and tested over many seasons. They work well and catch just as many fish as any others. Again it is all a matter of confidence and I certainly don't believe in change for change's sake.

All anglers go through periods when they seem to lose a lot of fish. Nine times out of ten the hook is blamed and the search begins for something new. That may be fine if you have shares in the tackle trade, but it probably isn't going to solve the problem. Before doing anything drastic try looking at technique. We all slip into bad habits occasionally, or maybe the fault will be traced to something like wrong tension or wrong strength in an elastic.

Turning back to hook patterns for pole fishing for a moment: I have little time for barbless patterns unless perhaps to use with a long line being fished to hand. In that situation they are fine if you have confidence in them. They save time and are better for the fish. And unlike the short-line rigs there will be no slackening of line, because joints are not being taken off. It is a case of strike and lift, swinging the fish to hand in one motion.

That then is the basics of my pole fishing which began twenty-five years ago with a 7 metre telescopic glass-fibre pole that took me all my time to lift. Looking back it was a hopeless tool, and I must have lost a few matches as a result of trying to make it work where it was totally wrong.

Those early years taught me a lot, though, and I began to progress through the pole-fishing maze to a point where my approach became over-technical and my fishing again began to suffer. This second time around it was a case of chucking out a load of unnecessary floats and complicated oddments so that I could see more clearly what the method was all about.

Pole fishing is an essential part of match fishing, but, just like legering, the feeder, waggler or stick float it is not, and never will be, the complete answer to every problem.

Simply best

One of the most successful canal anglers of recent years is Browning Starlets member Dave Berrow. Watch him fish and you cannot help but see that everything he does is as near perfect as possible. His feeding and general presentation cannot be faulted.

In the 1990-91 season he finished runner-up in the Silstar British Pole Championship and went on to end the season as winner of the tough Kamasan Matchman of the Year series. But he has no secrets and puts down his success to one thing . . . simplicity.

There are no rows of poles set up behind him. No fancy shotting patterns and very little bait, even though he works on a bait farm. He rightly points out that far too many anglers confuse themselves by setting up massive arrays of tackle and then spending most of the match trying to find the one which works.

A far better approach is to set up two or three rigs that you know will work and then stick with them.

Dave is also a great believer in resting a swim frequently during the course of a match. Often three or four fish will be caught quickly from one section of the peg and then he switches lines, maybe from the far shelf to the inside, catches three or four more and then goes back to the far swim.

By constantly alternating between several areas he can keep fish coming throughout a match which in any event, and on canals in particular, is an essential ingredient for consistently good results.

● *Former world champion Ian Heaps lands a nice pole-caught fish. Often there are times when fish seem to come off regularly, but don't just blame the hook: take a look at technique too*

7

Legering

Many major events are won on the leger, possibly because it is a very positive method that can account for big weights on venues holding large fish, bream in particular.

Unfortunately it is a method often used only as a last resort when all else has failed. Adopting such thinking is completely wrong. Legering can and does win, often in the most spectacular fashion. Check back over major match results and it is easy to see that mastery and confidence in the 'bomb' is going to play an important part in making the grade as a match angler.

First let us consider the advantages it may have over float or pole. For a start it can be fished at extreme range, often when conditions would make float fishing impossible at similar distances.

Once in the water it presents a bait that is not going to be pulled off line or made to move unnaturally by wind or surface skim. It can get a bait down quickly, too, so that small surface-feeding fish cannot intercept it.

In winter when fish movement is minimal it puts a bait down hard on the bottom where semi-dormant fish will be lying. They may be tempted to take a bait that calls for no effort on their part while ignoring one that moves and needs chasing.

Those are just a few benefits but don't get the idea that legering is easy. It can of course be done by casting out and sitting with the rod in a rest. That is not the match angler's way. To make the method win, the rod must be made to work hard and search out as many bite-producing situations as possible.

To achieve this means working just as hard as with a float. The bait may need to be twitched constantly across the bottom. Feeding will have to be thought about too. Adjustments to the end rig may be called for, just as shot might be moved to give a float-fished bait a different form of presentation.

Match fishing seems to have come down in favour of the quivertip against the swingtip. Reason for this is

that a swingtip can be difficult to use accurately and is more prone to tangling than a quivertip.

In truth both types of indication have their uses, and at times a swingtip can out-fish any other method. One situation where the swingtip scores is with bream that seem shy of giving a good indication on a quiver. With a quivertip, a fish taking a bait will feel increased resistance the further the tip is pulled round. To appreciate this fully, consider the tip as a complete rod. Pull on the tip slightly and there is resistance. Pull harder and the next section of the rod comes into play, thus increasing the resistance. As a quivertip is pulled round by a bite the same thing occurs but in miniature.

In the swingtip's case once a fish moves it there is hardly any increase in the amount of force needed to keep it moving upwards. Result is a more leisurely bite because the fish is not being scared off by the unnatural pull caused by a quivertip. It's a small thing but it does often make all the difference.

A quivertip is likely to be the most widely used indicator and on running water it really comes into its own. It is easier to set up to show a bite, and overall becomes more effective.

The good match angler goes prepared to use whichever is the right indicator on the day.

As to actual legers, the Arlesey bomb is the one that offers most. It casts well, is not tangle-prone and, if cast correctly, enters the water with the minimum of disturbance. In sizes from ⅛oz to 1½oz it should deal with most pegs. Large shot can also be used on a link to tackle more delicate situations. It's worth remembering too that a string of shot of equal weight to a leger will hold bottom better.

Terminal rigs are always kept as simple as possible. For straight legering, swivels can be discarded

---

● *A summer bream comes to the net after falling for the still bait offered by a quivertip rig*

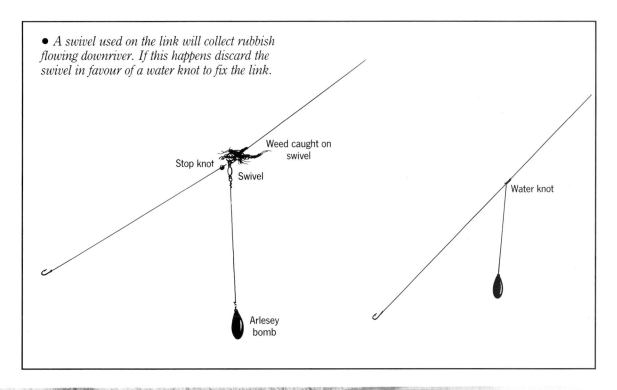

● *A swivel used on the link will collect rubbish flowing downriver. If this happens discard the swivel in favour of a water knot to fix the link.*

Weed caught on swivel

Stop knot

Swivel

Water knot

Arlesey bomb

altogether. Links can be tied straight to the main line so there is nothing more than a knot to get in the way of rubbish rolling along the bottom or to tangle in flight.

Length of tail and hook length will vary a lot from water to water and between summer and winter. In summer longer tails generally encourage bites to come 'on the drop'. But as the colder months reduce water temperature so the tail is shortened so that less-positive bites can be detected.

On a bream water a starting rig in summer might have a tail of perhaps five or six feet and a link length of up to ten or twelve inches. In winter both these sets of figures could be halved.

There are all sorts of knots that can be employed to attach link to line. A loop as used on a hook length is one way, but because the line comes out of the knot at a steep angle I suspect it considerably reduces the line's strength. My preference is to cut off a suitable length of line for the link and then tie it back to the line at the required position by using a four-turn Water Knot. This method has served me well enough and I have no reason to attempt anything else that can only complicate the issue.

Only drawback of course with tying on a link is that it means cutting the line to alter length of tail. This can be overcome by using a swivel running along the line and stopped by a small shot. It works, but against the method is the fact that the swivel often tangles, picks

---

● *Shots pinched on a nylon link make perfect weights for delicate leger work.*

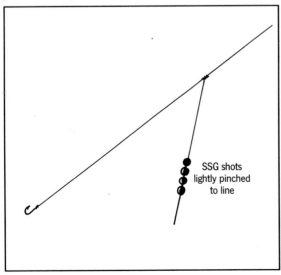

SSG shots
lightly pinched
to line

up rubbish and is the one piece of tackle that can offer a resistance to a biting fish.

If shot are to be used instead of a leger then it is just a case of pinching them onto the link close together. This idea can be handy in snaggy swims with rocky bottoms that may trap a leger and result in a fish being lost.

In such a situation pinch the shots on very lightly so that in the event of them getting snagged they will slide off the link when pressure is applied.

Setting up your pitch on a river for a legering attack is best done by positioning the seat box so that you face at an angle, looking downstream at about 30 degrees from the bank.

The rod now needs to be set on rests so that the tip is just touching, or only slightly above, the water. It is vital here that the rod is correctly supported. One rest needs to be very close to the tip – no more than a foot away. This may mean a second rest is needed about half-way along the rod. Done correctly the rod will show no sign of sagging.

A good tool for holding a tip steady is a special leger rest. This is a three-inch-long V-shaped plastic rest that lets the tip sit snugly. The other rest can be a standard wide one but take care to set everything right. Once you are happy with the settings, the rod butt should be resting on the edge of your seat box so that the reel is in easy reach and your hand can rest either on, or directly above, the rod handle.

Only time this arrangement changes is if the flow is very strong or there is a lot of debris being washed downstream by floods. If either is the case it may mean setting the rod up high, beach-caster style, so that the minimum amount of line is in contact with the water.

In the case of a swingtip it is best if you view it from an angle, so again set the rod some 30 degrees out from the bank. It is then possible to watch for movements of the tip as it swings outwards or drops back. The rod itself can be used as an improvised sight to give something to mark the tip against.

Target boards are popular, and not only do they make indication easier, they also provide some shelter for the tip if conditions are rough. If one is set up be sure to place it clear of the rod, remembering that line may come away from the tip at an angle. On no account must there be any chance of either rod or line hitting the board on the strike.

A good plan on clear swims where weed is no

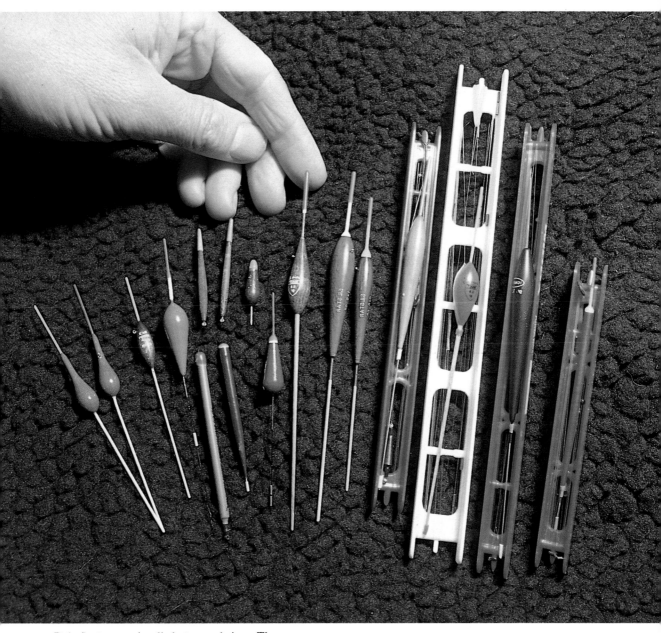

● *Pole floats come in all shapes and sizes. These are
some of the more practical ones suited to British waters*

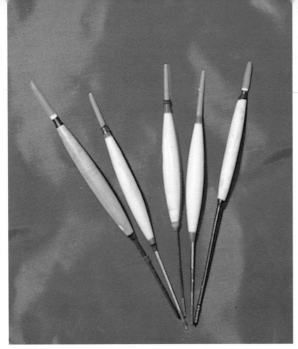

● (Above) The crowquill and pith or balsa-bodied Avon float is a winner on deep waters where bleak are a pest. This range takes up to 14BB shots

● (Above) A good selection of non-toxic shots and a tub of legal-sized lead styls are an essential part of the match angler's kit.

● (Right) If you take the kitchen sink with you there's no reason why the fire can't go too! This enterprising angler stays warm during a winter event and as a result fishes more efficiently

● Handling a long pole is easy if you get everything balanced and well-supported, and this angler is using his knee as a rest. The left hand acts as a steadier, while the right pushes downwards

● *A vee section rest is perfect for holding a tip steady in rough conditions. use a second rest to prevent the rod sagging in the middle.*

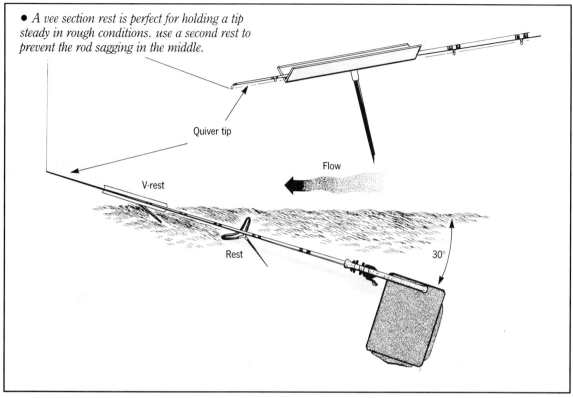

Quiver tip

Flow

V-rest

Rest

30°

● *If the flow is very powerful a beachcaster style set up is called for. This keeps the rod tip high to hold as much line as possible clear of the water.*

Quiver tip

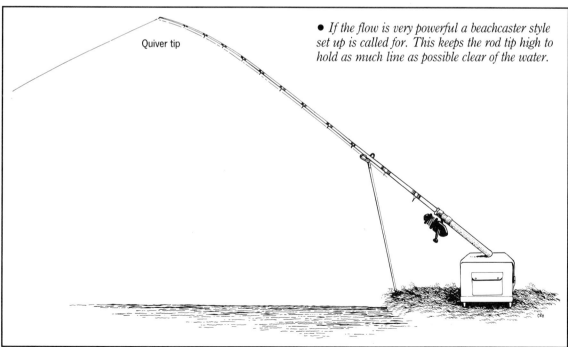

• *Legering is not just a case of 'chuck it and chance it'. But Syd Meads of Wisbech, Cambs is a master of the art and makes the whole operation look very casual*

problem and wind has not pushed up waves, is to set the swingtip up so that when set at a slight angle to the vertical – the normal setting that will show both pulls or dropback bites – it just touches the water surface. Like this the slightest bite is very easy to spot.

There are two schools of thought on how a bomb should be cast. Some anglers claim the cast should be made and the bomb allowed to sink to the bottom before the reel pick-up is engaged and slack taken out. Supporters of this method claim that it is then possible to tell exactly where the bomb ends up, and that the other method in which the pick-up is closed as soon as the leger hits the water, causes the tackle to fall through the water in an arc, back towards the angler.

The arc theory is, of course, true but a little mathematics will quickly show that the distance the bomb actually swings towards you is very small, except in the very deepest pegs and then only if fishing is at short range.

In favour of the closed pick-up drop is the fact that the tackle is under control all the time, and any bite that might occur as the bait falls will register. When the bomb hits bottom it will show as a slight drop back on the tip. Now wind up slowly and carefully, watching the tip all the time, until it is set correctly. By taking care with this operation it is often possible to detect bites that come as the hook is still falling.

After all has settled and the tip has been set, raise the rod and pull the bomb along the bottom a few inches, again winding up the slack. By doing this the hook length and tail will be straightened out fully and bites will be more positive.

Here is where the work starts. For while at odd times a big weight can be built simply by casting, tightening up and then waiting for a bite, there are far more days when every bite has to be earned.

Having cast to the baited area and followed all the right procedures for the first few moments, the bait may need to be worked across the bed. This 'twitching' action often spurs a fish into grabbing a bait that might otherwise be ignored. Oddly enough, bream are notorious for wanting this little bit of extra incentive.

● *By closing the reel pick-up a leger will fall in a slight arc back towards the angler. This fall-back is only slight except in very deep water. But by closing the pick-up in this manner bites that come on the drop can be easily spotted.*

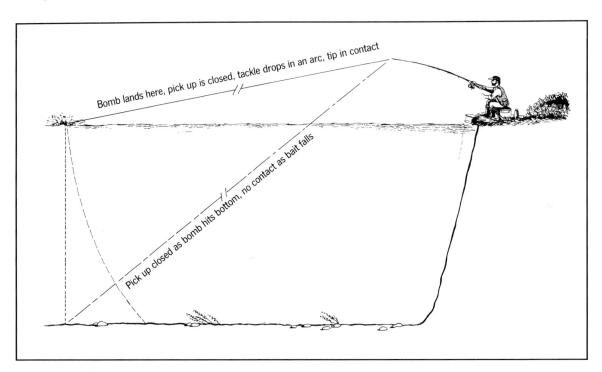

Bomb lands here, pick up is closed, tackle drops in an arc, tip in contact

Pick up closed as bomb hits bottom, no contact as bait falls

To begin a twitch, the rod can be lifted just clear of the rest and moved a few inches backwards from the river. It requires a gentle and slow sweep so the bomb drags rather than bounces across the bottom. As soon as the rod is replaced in the rest, the reel is used to pick up the few inches of slack the movement has created. But watch out all the time for the bite that can come at any time during the operation.

With a swingtip it is possible to use the same technique, or, instead, the reel can be used to wind up until the bomb is moved. This causes the tip to rise and it will stay out almost straight until the bomb has been allowed to settle again and the line re-set. What usually happens here is that as the tip is being re-set it will suddenly pull upwards, or the fish will move the bomb towards the rod, causing a drop-back bite.

Legering in this manner takes concentration equal to anything required with a float, but the rewards are good.

Feeding the swim needs to be done well in order to keep it on the boil. The idea is to make it work just like a float peg. It is easy to forget to feed properly when legering, and often it is easy to fall into the trap of feeding a ball of groundbait or some loose feed and then adding nothing for some time. This may be the right plan in some situations, but if all is well and you have fish feeding, something more regular is going to be needed. Try to work out a pattern so that something is falling through the water on a regular basis. Little and often is always a better bet than a big ball of cereal or a pouch full of casters every half-hour.

Swimfeeders

The feeder seems to have taken over on many match rivers. So much so in some cases that attempts to win on anything else are almost certainly doomed.

There are those who argue that this has taken away the skill in winning. That may be true to a degree but, as with legering, feeder work is still not just a straightforward chuck-it-and-chance-it method. Watch a good feeder angler in action and you will see a classic time-and-motion exercise.

In the case of small feeders or stillwater fishing the basic set-up is little different to that used for quivertipping. The indicator will be a quivertip simply because throwing feeders with a swingtip is difficult

and usually results in a lot of crack-offs. Accuracy is also difficult to control when a swingtip is involved and it is no good throwing feeders full of bait to every corner of the swim.

Small feeders can be dealt with using a normal quivertip, but if the size increases too much then a rod with more backbone and a steeply-tapered quivertip is needed. A good rig for these small feeders is to tie the feeder to a short link similar to, but shorter than, the one used for straight legering. About five or six inches is fine.

Block-end feeders for use with maggots vary a lot in design but those where line comes out centrally from the end cap are the best. They cast well and come back through the water cleanly on the retrieve.

One real favourite of mine has interchangeable end-caps into which different weights have been cast. They can be used with a plain plastic cap and no weight or with a choice of medium or heavy ends. Additional weight is provided via a metal rod running down a tube cast into the feeder body. This rod can also be removed if required.

Larger block-end feeders also need this central line attachment if possible and any purchased with other arrangements are usually doctored very quickly.

If long-range fishing with a big feeder is needed, a good plan is to replace the nylon with a loop of Power Gum. This stretchy silicone-like monofilament can be looped through the cap and tied to the opposite end. A bead with an eye large enough to take both Power Gum and line easily can be threaded on. Alternatively, use one of the special leger beads available. These have a central eye like a normal bead and another small eye through which line can be passed.

A swivel may be used in place of beads but they can tangle easily. If you insist on using them try slipping a piece of silicone float tubing over the link. This will at least reduce the chance of problems.

These Power Gum feeders, or for that matter any big feeder, can be fished on a type of bolt rig similar to those used for carp fishing.

The feeder is then threaded onto the line and a loop between three and six inches long is formed. A much smaller loop is tied at the bottom of this main loop and to this the hook is attached in the usual manner. When a bite occurs the fish pulls the loop through the bead and hits the full weight of the feeder, at the same time setting the hook exactly as with a true bolt rig.

Power Gum is used with these large feeders to take

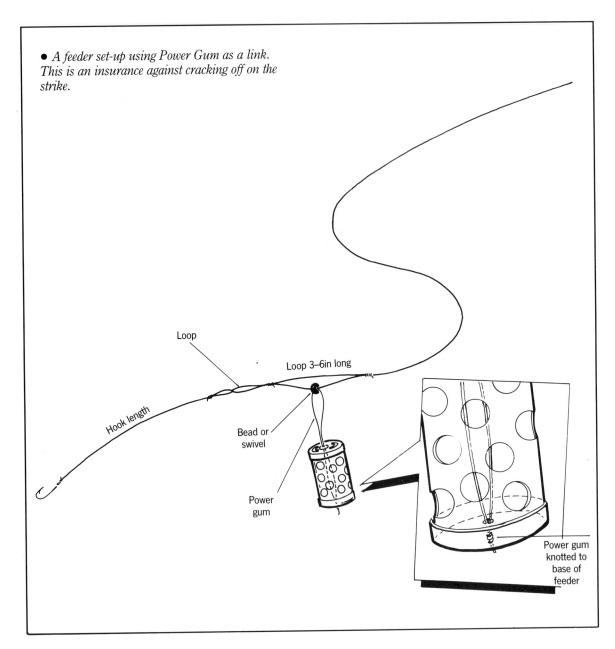

● *A feeder set-up using Power Gum as a link. This is an insurance against cracking off on the strike.*

Loop

Loop 3–6in long

Hook length

Bead or swivel

Power gum

Power gum knotted to base of feeder

some of the shock out of the strike hitting the full weight of the feeder.

All rigs can be adapted to house an open-ended feeder for use with groundbait. Variations on these basic set-ups appear regularly on the match scene. They all work, and each inventor will claim that his particular way is superior to the rest. In the end most anglers finish up using those they find the best, but the simple ones are eventually proved to be the longest-lasting.

One thing that has emerged, as feeders have grown larger and the demand for the ability to throw them further than the angler at the next peg has increased, is the shock leader. Here we have taken an idea from the beach angler who may need to cast a 5oz lead close to 200 yards with a line of 15lb or so. To overcome the

shock of the first surge of power, a length of much thicker line is tied to the main line. In the case of sea angling this may be 65lb or more. For match fishing 10lb is about the maximum needed for even the biggest 'jam jar' feeder. Often an 8lb leader is enough, allowing feeders of considerable proportions to be cast on lines of 5lb or so.

A shock leader of about twice the length of the rod

● *Feeders come in all sorts of shapes and sizes. This simple open-ended pattern is a popular choice in match circles. Be sure to carry a full range of sizes*

is tied to the main line. Tie a full Blood Knot to make the join, and take care to get the knot neatly formed and of a size which passes easily through the rod rings.

Extra weight

Additional weight to cope with powerful flows is added to feeders by clipping some form of lead strip to the feeder body.

Small amounts can be added in the form of trim leads, pieces of lead cast with thinner arms at each end. These are pushed into the feeder-body holes and then folded down inside. Several trims can be added until the correct load is achieved.

For heavier weights, tackle shops provide either larger versions of the trims, or ski leads. Ski leads are sledge-like weights that sit outside the feeder body.

Trim leads are attached by fold-through arms. A few spots of Araldite make the job more able to stand up to rough treatment.

Araldite or Super Glue can also be used to fix other pieces of lead strip to the body wherever required. Made up like this, a larger feeder for fishing the strong flows of the weirs on rivers such as the Trent may weigh upwards of three ounces.

● *Big feeder work demands a reel with sturdy gearing and a good handle that provides plenty of leverage. This type of 'T' bar grip is a good choice*

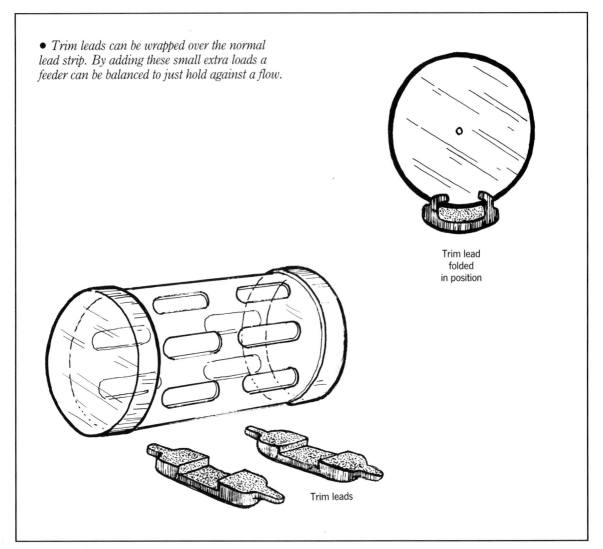

● *Trim leads can be wrapped over the normal lead strip. By adding these small extra loads a feeder can be balanced to just hold against a flow.*

Trim lead
folded
in position

Trim leads

It takes a good reel and a powerful rod to cope. A line of at least 6lb is also going to be needed, whether or not a shock leader is employed.

This heavy feeder fishing is usually aimed at chub or barbel and is extremely hard work. It calls for large amounts of bait and a lot of concentration. The feeder is loaded, cast and, within a matter of maybe a minute, retrieved, loaded and cast again. Bites on the good pegs come as soon as the feeder hits bottom.

Such is the competition among the shoals of fish that they will even attack the feeder to get at its contents. To overcome this the normal round holes of the feeder are elongated into each other to permit the bait to be washed out almost instantly.

As an experiment I once painted a batch of these feeders matt black to help reduce the visual attraction of a feeder full of bait. It worked and also set me wondering whether fish, on more difficult pegs, get used to seeing the usual transparent green or clear feeders and associate them with danger. My tests didn't prove anything conclusively but it is certainly something worth taking further.

Move right to the opposite end of the feeder scale, and mini-feeders will be discovered. These thimble-sized pieces of tackle are capable of holding maybe a dozen maggots or a tiny amount of groundbait. They really come into their own when fishing is very hard and especially in winter. Their biggest asset is being able to deposit that small amount of feed right next to your hookbait. Even canals will respond to this delicate approach so be sure to keep a few mini-feeders handy for those difficult days.

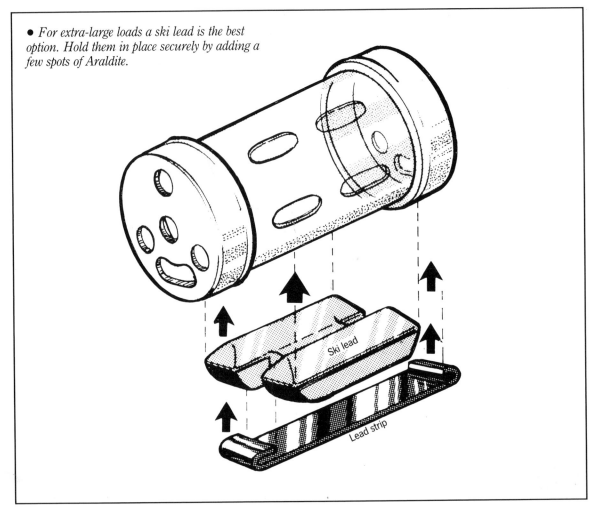

● *For extra-large loads a ski lead is the best option. Hold them in place securely by adding a few spots of Araldite.*

Ski lead

Lead strip

Part II

A Match-fishing Season

Part I has dealt with the theory of match fishing and what is required to begin an event with the best possible chance of success. Now it is time to put the theory into practice with a full season of club and small open matches, on a variety of waters that will call for a wide range of skills. Each match is a case history that can be used to plan future competitions.

8

A skimmer bream sprint

First event of the new season, which opened yesterday, is to be an evening sweepstake with a local club. The match is expected to attract thirty anglers and the venue is a slow-moving river that usually fishes well during the opening weeks.

It has been a mild winter, and spring came early. Over the past weeks waters in the area have been showing signs that they will be in good condition when the season begins on 16 June. Walking the bank the previous weekend has provided some insight into how the river is looking. Small fish have been spotted on the surface but the worrying thing is that the roach do not yet appear to have finished spawning completely.

Rainfall has been average for the time of year, and after a flush-through two weeks ago the river has settled down to normal June level. As usual, the green algae that gives the river a nice tinge later on has not yet fully bloomed, leaving the water with a slight brown colour.

With the season opening only a day ago there has been no chance to fish the venue, but an hour spent walking the match length last night showed that skimmer bream and bleak had been the main fish taken by pleasure anglers. Two anglers sitting at what would be the bottom end of the match pegs had each caught a bream of 2lb but reported tiny eels as a nuisance.

Armed with that scant information a match plan needs to be formulated, bearing in mind the duration of the event is only three hours.

It seems the roach are not worth considering for a few weeks yet and there has been no sign of the chub population so far. The bleak, eels, skimmers or, if good pegs are drawn, the bigger bream could figure in the result.

Although this is only a sweepstake, there is a points competition based on each angler's best four results from the six-match series. Prizes for this should be good and will cover the top three. Normal sweepstake money for each match pays the top four and one section prize in every ten pegs.

Because of the short fishing time there will be little room for error. The last half-hour or so might also suffer from poor light conditions if the weather stays dull.

Bait has been collected and duly prepared. There has been no need for a big outlay: 1½ pints of squatts, half a pint each of white and bronze hook maggots and half a pint of pinkies. Groundbait is 5lb of fine dark-brown crumb. To save a little time and to get a nice even texture it was mixed before leaving for work on the morning of the match.

It's been a rush to get home, collect tackle and bait and get to the river by draw time, but the effort was better than having to leave bait in the car all day. Just time now to stop in the car park long enough to check with some pleasure anglers that the situation had changed little since last evening, except that the two bream pegs had been fished all day and a big weight of bream had been caught and returned only an hour ago.

The prospect of drawing one of those pegs is now something not relished. If they have been hammered all day and had fish put back they are unlikely to figure. But it's worth keeping an eye on the area for the

---

• *Hefty bream like this can upset the form book during the opening weeks of the season. Keep an eye on the venue during the run up to a match and you may be able to pinpoint their location*

following evening matches, by which time they may have settled into a new location.

Target weight to make the prizes is 6lb, and a 10lb winning weight is possible even without the bream pegs. It's a gamble now between settling for a placing with bleak, or going all out for a win. Well, it's a new season, the bleak technique really needs working on during practice, so it has to be the skimmers.

The actual match length begins about 400 yards below a set of lock gates and for the first ten pegs has a little more flow over maybe five feet of water and a gravel bottom. These are good early-season pegs because a lot of fish stay on the gravel to clean up after spawning and to enjoy the high oxygen content of the water after it has tumbled over the locks. Twelve pegs below them are deeper, varying from eight to ten feet, and then finally, at the lower end of the stretch, the remaining swims widen and deepen to an average of eleven feet.

The bream have been in that last eight pegs, just three and four from the very end of the match. Past form suggests that the early swims will hold a lot of smaller fish but there is always a chance of a skimmer bream weight here. The mid-match pegs may also be good and a few slightly bigger skimmers can be expected.

Once the widest section is reached, anything can happen. Those bream are there and it is a good area for a chub or two or even a mixed roach, chub and skimmer weight.

Pools have been paid and the draw has resulted in peg 10, right at the end of those gravels. There is little to choose between any of the pegs in terms of cover or weed growth.

Once at the peg, a few moments are spent weighing up the swim. It is noted that there is a slight downstream skim but nothing too serious. Flow is pushing gently through and suggests a good match is in prospect. Wind is nothing but a gentle breeze and there is no ripple. Bleak, or some small fish, are topping.

No point in setting up too much tackle because of the limited time both between draw and start and actual match duration. A 13 foot match rod with a 2½lb line, a straight 2SSG waggler and a 22 hook to 1lb bottom is the starting float-rig.

That skim might be a problem if the wind gets up, and from previous experience it is known that the skimmers often want a stable bait. That means a pole

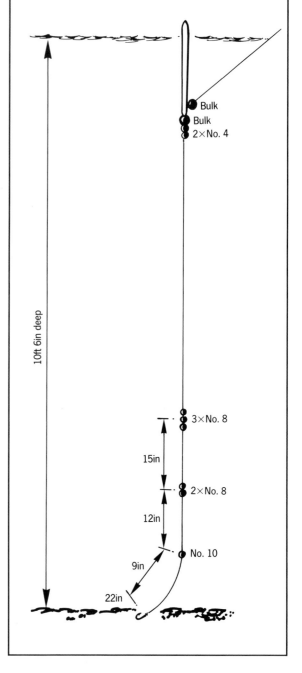

● *Plenty of bulk beneath a long peacock float will enable line to be buried effectively. The low-down bulk is intended to get the bait past small fish feeding high in the water.*

Bulk
Bulk
2×No. 4

10ft 6in deep

3×No. 8

15in

2×No. 8

12in

No. 10

9in

22in

A skimmer bream sprint

- *1g balsa bodied and wire-stemmed pole-float is used to provide a stable bait for the skimmer bream.*

1gr balsa bodied
bristle tip

Wire stem

No. 10

Olivetti

No. 10

No. 12

– 11 metres – and an olivette rig beneath a 1g balsa-bodied float. Again a 22 hook to 1lb but a 20 is also set out ready just in case the bigger skimmers show. In these short events you have to hustle the fish out quickly.

Rules allow plumbing before the start, so after setting everything out in place, the remaining time is spent working around with the pole and a plummet. This has shown a slight drop-off from nine down to ten feet deep between the ten and eleven metre marks.

With the waggler down the middle the depth has been found to drop again by another six inches. The waggler is set to trip bottom, with a number 10 shot as a tell-tale nine inches up and then two 8s together a foot above it. Fifteen inches above these is the main bulk of a number 4 and two more 8s. Rest of the load is used as locking shot, but with two of them as number 4s which might be brought down to the bulk if bleak are troublesome.

Ten minutes left to the start. Groundbait has been damped a little more to give it a consistency that will allow fairly firm balls to be made up. The landing net is positioned within reach, but with the frame hanging over the bank at the point where any fish that may drop off while being swung in will fall.

Catapults, towel, disgorger, hooks, shot; every-thing is laid out in the way that has been worked out as the best. The pole rig is clipped onto a rubber holding-ring on the fourth section and the remaining pole is in two parts laid parallel with the water, well clear of the cyclists and walkers who use the bankside path.

Seconds to go. The rod is ready on the rest and the hook can now be baited for a quick start. White maggot is usually a good bait on this water during the first weeks of the season. Once the roach and chub begin feeding later in the year, then bronze seem a better option.

Off we go, the first cast of a new season. A line right on the middle of the river has been decided upon, but no feed goes in yet and the cast is dropped well short just for the moment. While this first cast is running through, keep an eye on the anglers each side. The one upstream has gone for a line well beyond three-quarters of the way over and the other appears to be fishing a whip close in, possibly for bleak.

What this situation has presented us with is a clear line where we wanted to fish, right down the middle. Effectively, that means all the fish in that section of the river can be worked into the catching area without the

A skimmer bream sprint

• *A neat layout of the peg can save valuable time in any match but in these evening events every second counts. Note how the landing net is placed to catch any fish which might come off as they are swung in.*

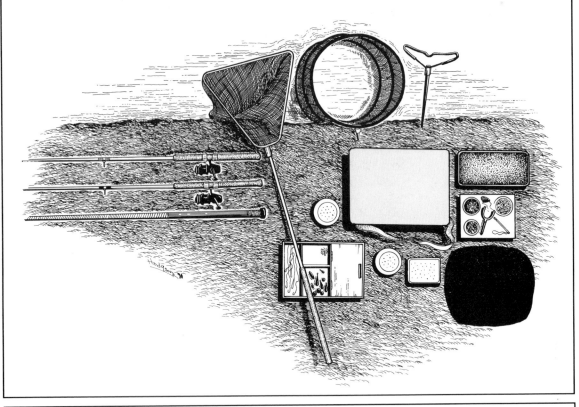

• *The plan of attack. The angler upstream has chosen a far bank line, and one downstream is fishing close in, leaving the middle line clear and perfect for waggler and long pole.*

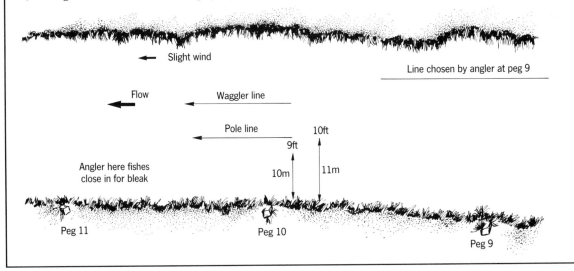

← Slight wind

Line chosen by angler at peg 9

Flow

Waggler line

Pole line

10ft

9ft

Angler here fishes
close in for bleak

10m

11m

Peg 11

Peg 10

Peg 9

● *A nice fish nears the landing net. Keep calm and don't rush it*

distraction of other feed going in on the same line from a peg away. Had either neighbour gone for the same line it might have meant choosing a different attack; possibly, because of the poor light, one closer in. Because our first cast has not gone directly to the line to be fished, we have not shown our hand should either of the anglers nearby have been waiting to see what we would do.

A run through produced nothing but it has shown that the tackle is set right, just bumping bottom. Now it is safe to feed, just a single small ball slightly downstream of the sitting position. In goes the ball and a cast just beyond it. The pick-up is closed and the line given a flick to sink it. Two runs through and nothing! Meanwhile the angler upstream has landed a tiny chub and the one below has caught a bleak.

Concentrate now. The third run down brings a bite, a small skimmer of little more than an ounce. But it's a start and a little more feed goes in on the same line.

Each ball of groundbait has a sprinkling of squatts in it, and it is moulded hard enough to get it through those surface fish before breaking up.

A bite missed: the end of the white hook maggot has been bitten off. Possibly by a bleak that took it on the drop. If that happens again one of those number 4s around the float might need pulling down to give a faster fall to the bait.

That's better, a good skimmer of 3oz. Such fish can win these evening matches if they keep coming. Now it's feed, cast beyond it, wind back to sink line and concentrate. For the next half-hour all goes well and the weight is building nicely, with skimmers to 6oz coming to the white maggot. It takes only a couple of dozen of these to top the 7lb mark.

Now the fish are coming it is important to keep going; feed, bait up, cast, sink line, run through, strike, wind back and check the bait.

While the middle, which is just beyond pole range, has been the main area of feed, the odd ball has been dropped short just in case a change is needed later on.

A few spectators have begun walking the bank now, and when two pause just behind you, bites stop suddenly. They move away and as if by magic the fish return. A friend arrives to watch you fish but is spotted in time to get him to sit down behind and slightly above

• *Ray Mumford demonstrates how the contents of a feeder can be quickly pinched into place by using thumb and forefinger*

you where he can do no harm. From his account it seems that the early pegs are not doing so well as was expected, but a few anglers are picking up small dace and a few bleak. The bleak don't appear to be coming with any regularity, maybe because they have not yet fully spawned. The decision to leave them alone for at least another week was a good one.

The skimmer attack has been going well but bites have gradually slowed. Six inches on the depth and the tackle is sent through again, but this time holding it back as much as is possible with a straight waggler. A bite straight away, and a better fish too, probably the best part of half a pound.

A slack time followed that skimmer, and despite a couple more adjustments and alternating bait colours the peg seems to be drying up. Time for a change to the pole.

The rig has been set so that the last six inches of hook length are on the bottom when the rig is held back. For a start the white maggot is again the bait and straight away there's a fish, but only a gudgeon. A little feed soon brings a response and the skimmers are taking the static bait with more confidence, but still a lot of bites are being missed.

Those pinkies, which were brought along in case bleak were to be fished for, may be the answer. The smaller skimmers sometimes hang onto the end of a big maggot and don't take it all in. A start with two pinkies, one hooked in the normal fashion and the other through the head, go on. Hook is still a 22 micro-barb to 1lb bottom. Change is immediate, with bites becoming easier to hit.

For the next hour the pole continues to bring enough fish to justify its continued use, but they seem to be smaller than those that were being caught down the middle with the waggler.

These evening matches always attract a lot of spectating anglers who use them as indicators as to how the river will fish at the weekend. From their passing conversations it appears there's going to be a clear winner from the bottom end peg. The angler there had caught nothing after an hour and, in desperation, had switched to fishing worm and caster on the leger. Result has been four bream to 4lb, putting him well out of reach of anyone else. Backing weights are reckoned to be in the 5lb bracket, with the second-best looking safe with 6½lb. There's twenty minutes left and we are just short of that figure but the skimmers seem to have had enough. Now it's time for

• *A single maggot should be hooked so that the hook point faces outwards from the bait. Try to pass the point through the rough skin that protrudes from the blunt end so as not to damage the maggot. If the point faces inwards it is not only shielded by the maggot but also allows it to flick back on itself and become double-hooked.*

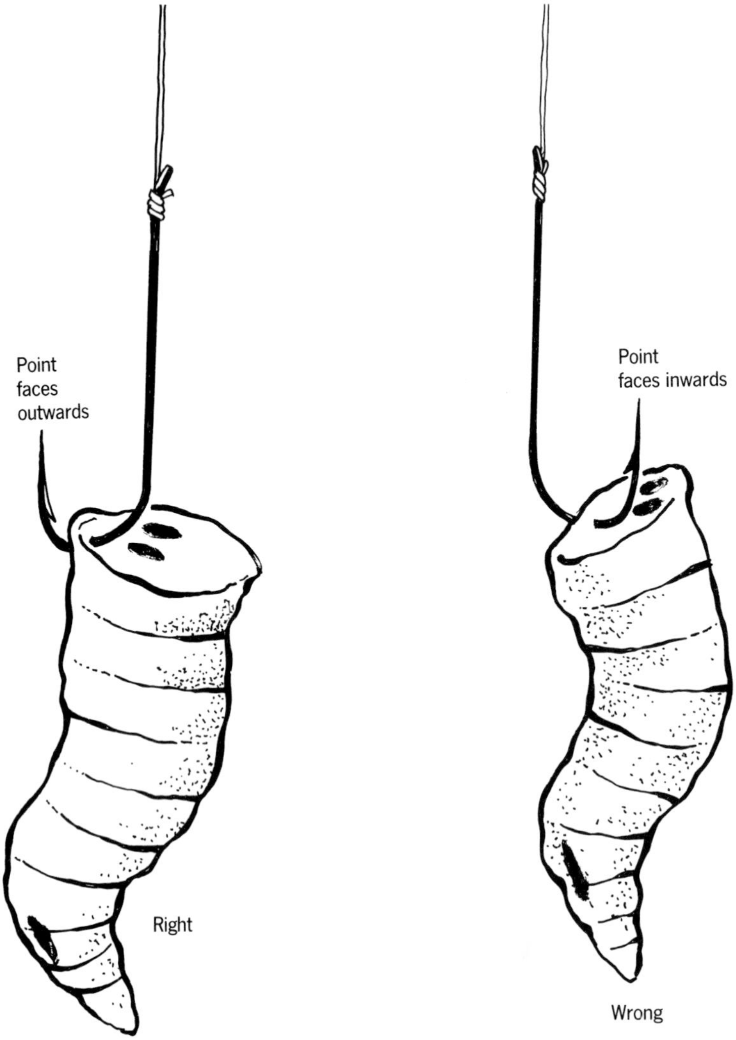

Point faces outwards

Point faces inwards

Right

Wrong

a bit of a gamble. The pole goes up the bank and the waggler comes back into play, but this time with pinkies rather than the big maggot we had used earlier.

As dusk has fallen so the few bleak previously present have disappeared. Two runs through without a bite so the shotting is opened up, leaving the tell-tale in place but with the two 8s split a foot apart and the rest slid up under the float.

A catapult launches a dozen hook maggots into the swim, just a yard beyond where the mid-line has been fished for most of the match.

After this feed the waggler goes in again, but the bait has been switched to a bronze maggot. Response

● *Two pinkies are a good bait when a larger hook maggot is either refused or bites are being missed. Note one maggot is hooked at the head end. This prevents the bait spinning and causing kinks to form in the hook length.*

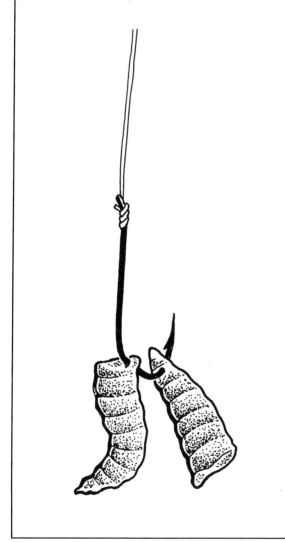

is immediate – a small chub of 3oz, followed by two more of the same size within three casts. Not long to go now so there's little point in changing no matter what happens. For the final ten minutes the loose feed can keep going in. The tackle has been left to search out what it can and a couple of dace, plus a stray roach which feels rough and has obviously still not fully recovered from spawning, have added another few ounces.

That's it. The whistle goes and the match is over. Not a bad start despite those bream upsetting the plan. If our result gets a place in the top three that's a reasonable placing from which to begin the series.

Those late chub suggest that they might be worth fishing for before too long. Maybe a week or two and they could be winners. That roach shows the species is well behind, so hemp and tares needn't be worried about for a while.

Biggest danger comes from the bream shoal. It's noted for hanging around all summer but to go for them in these short matches is a death-or-glory job. The eels didn't show, even on that pole rig that gave them plenty of time to have a go.

Bleak were caught, and a few warm days will bring them right into the picture. Fishing for them from the off could make 3lb an hour possible and that is going to win most three-hour events here.

The approach we took was simple, almost certain to work well enough to get a decent placing, and didn't call for a lot of switching around. With only three hours' fishing you usually get the best results by picking a method and sticking with it.

Scales have started weighing from the bottom end and those bream recorded 13lb 6oz. From there upstream the average has been 3lb, with a couple of low 5lb. Our effort just hit the 7lb mark, so those last-ditch chub swung the extra place and a section win. Upstream, fish had been small and only fed in spasms, maybe because many of the pegs had been fished during the day by pleasure anglers.

With the experience of this match to go on, the majority next week will come to fish for skimmers or maybe have a go for those bream if drawn on a high number. Because more will be fishing the method that has worked for us today, it may be worth thinking about a different approach to keep one step ahead.

During the next week it will mean a few evening sessions here to work out a plan. An evening at the bleak to sharpen up on the speed work; and a session fishing a slowly-falling bronze maggot right across for some chub is worth a try. A possible plan for the next match would be a pole for the 10 metre line fishing maggot over groundbait and squatts, and a waggler set to fish on the drop along the far ledge with bronze maggot and loose maggot feed for the chub.

The match could be broken down to a first hour on

the ledge and then, if it dries up, straight to the pole line which will have been fed and should have stopped anglers either side from taking your fish.

Groundbait worked well enough tonight, but those spells when things went slack suggest the skimmers were getting over-fed. With that in mind perhaps the feed should be riddled peat with just a little white groundbait added to bind it. All this can be worked out during the week.

● *The small waggler approach is a good method for sorting out early season roach and skimmer bream, but don't fish too light and ruin presentation when conditions are not so good*

9
Four ways in Fenland

The Fens of Cambridgeshire are criss-crossed by hundreds of miles of man-made waters, many built by Dutch engineers to drain the low-lying farmland. These waters are prolific, if somewhat temperamental in nature.

Matches can be won here with huge bream weights but it is very much a case of drawing a flyer. Sit two pegs away and unless the fish decide to move you can forget them. So planning a match must be done with these fish considered as nothing more than a bonus if a dream draw comes your way. But it also means going prepared, bait-wise, to fish for them.

Throughout the summer, club matches are usually won either with a bream weight or with some small roach and skimmer bream that have been boosted by eels and a tench or two. These tench are big, often 3lb or more, but as with the bream, fishing for them is a bit hit-or-miss. For consistent results something more positive is needed.

A typical Fen water is lacking in flow and can be anywhere from 25 to 30 yards wide. The banks are steep, with cut-outs at each peg. Depth varies a lot but could be six to ten feet, with a ledge on either side. Some pegs have a lot of weed too. Lilies are the usual cover, and if you have a dense patch they probably hold a tench.

Target fish, apart from the big bream and tench, are roach, skimmer bream, eels, small perch and a few rudd and bleak.

The eels are big by match standards, often topping 1½lb and averaging perhaps 8oz. The roach can be of good quality and a few weights are made every summer on hemp. Skimmers vary from small to maybe 10oz and the perch about the same, although generally no more than 4oz.

Past records show that most club matches start well, but the fish have a habit of going off once feed starts going in and a few have been caught. The good thing is that the roach, eels and skimmers are at every peg.

Today's match has attracted fifty anglers so the payout will be decent, and with a team match here in a few weeks' time it will be a good chance to put a few ideas to the test.

The bream might show, but the match length is not one noted for them so early in the year. As a solid plan the smaller fish are to be the target, but the problem of the swim dying needs to be overcome.

This sort of water is a worker's dream. Sitting with a bait doing nothing is the pleasure angler's way of catching a tench but with five hours to go at them there will be a lot of changing around to keep fish coming all day.

A lot of tackle is going to be needed to fish four different lines, the idea being to take fish from them all in rotation rather than fish one out completely before making a change. It is going to take thought and self-discipline to leave a line that is producing and start fishing elsewhere.

A target weight of 10lb to 12lb should be enough to win a breamless match, and even if the big fish do show it will still be enough to finish well up the frame.

The peg drawn is typical. The bank is like a miniature ski slope but at the bottom there is a nice flat area which can, with the help of adjustable legs on the seat box, be made into a comfortable pitch. Because

the plan demands a lot of changing around, including long pole work, it is vital to be safely and comfortably seated. The water has a nice colour, probably caused by a couple of days of wind stirring things up. There is a little near-bank weed and a nice lily patch along the far bank.

Most anglers will go for the groundbait and squatt approach, but rather than follow sheep-like, the loose-feed-and-eel plan is the secret.

Bait requirements, even with so many lines to fish, are not large. Groundbait and squatts would seem an obvious combination but in fact are being taken along only in case the bream show. Should the eels decide not to feed, then a little cereal and a few squatts may come in handy for the small fish too.

A pint of casters, a pint and a half of assorted hook maggots and a pint of hemp should be enough. Anything else, worms, extra casters and maybe a slice of bread, are being taken only for the tench or bream draws.

Conditions are not ideal. There is a wind coming from behind the pegs but because of the high banks it is swirling slightly and tending to funnel in and push down the waterway.

Tackle is to be a 13 foot waggler rod to fish a 3AAA straight peacock waggler with a thin insert tip and a 24 micro-barb hook to 1lb bottom. Shotting is with a number 10 as a tell-tale, then an 8 a foot away and another 8 fifteen inches from that. The rest are used as locking shot with a couple of 8s that can be pulled down if required later on.

An 11 foot leger rod with a bit of power but fitted with a fine quivertip takes a straight link leger rig and a 22 hook to 1½lb. The other rigs will be changed to the same hook if the eels show well.

Next come two poles, a four-metre rig and another of ten metres to fish at nine.

For the long pole, a 0.35g or 0.4g wire-stem float with a balsa body is ideal. For the shorter rig a similar float, but possibly of the smaller size, will do nicely. Both poles have elastic through the top section and, while a number 3 will be fine for the usual fish, those eels will demand a size 4 to get them moving quickly off the bottom.

• *A superb tench – but pinning your hopes on catching one is not a good tactic*

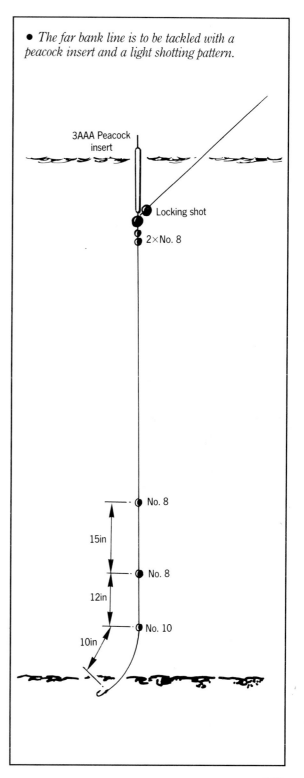

• *The far bank line is to be tackled with a peacock insert and a light shotting pattern.*

3AAA Peacock insert

Locking shot

2×No. 8

No. 8

15in

No. 8

12in

No. 10

10in

Four ways in Fenland

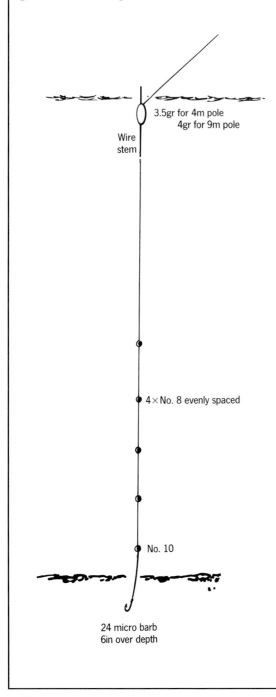

• *The same rig is assembled on each of two poles. The only difference is that a slightly heavier float goes on the 9m set-up.*

3.5gr for 4m pole
4gr for 9m pole

Wire stem

4 × No. 8 evenly spaced

No. 10

24 micro barb
6in over depth

Shotting the pole floats is to be done by stringing out number 8s. These can be moved around according to how the fish respond. A point here is that, but for the wind, a cane-stem float would have allowed styls to be used for fishing on the drop to collect more roach and maybe a rudd or two. But the wire ones I've chosen will give more stability and the shots will get the bait down quicker.

A start with the plummet finds the near shelf. A line just beyond it and to one side is where the short pole

114

will be used. The idea of fishing well to the side is so that hooked fish can be played away from the catching area.

Next the nine metres mark is plumbed up and the long pole set to fish six inches overdepth. Once this is done the waggler is set at the same depth, which in this case is about 9½ feet.

Normally the inside line would be the first one fished and then we would gradually start working outwards as the fish became shy. But today the eels are going to

play a big part, and because they take about forty minutes to move onto the feed we have introduced, the waggler will be used to fill in that time, taking what it can from across the far side.

The whistle sounds and feeding can begin. The long pole line and the inside both get a few hook maggots and a few grains of hemp. This hemp is only to act as an attractor and must be fed sparingly so the roach don't get obsessed with it. The far line is fed with maggots and hemp too. And once all these are covered

● *A ski slope of a bank like this demands a bit of care and considerable organisation. Take special care when breaking down the pole otherwise there's a danger of joints slipping into the water*

a few casters go in on top. Only eight or so in each area. They are for the eels, which seem to like them on these Fen waters.

It's now a case of feeding all three regularly but carefully, while fishing the waggler right across close to the lilies.

The waggler is getting over with no problem, but the wind is making control difficult and the tackle isn't in long before it needs recasting.

This opening period sees a few tiny roach come to the waggler and a perch of 3oz is a bonus. But it's obvious the conditions are going to defeat this method before long. Half an hour gone and maybe 8oz to show for it. No need to panic and in any case the area needs a rest. Time for a try with the short pole to see if those eels have moved in yet.

A maggot on the hook gets a bite straight away. They're there all right. First fish is an eel of maybe 4oz

and it gets the landing-net treatment, as will all the others that might follow. Once it is netted, the landing net is slid over the keepnet mouth and the eel unhooked and tipped straight into the keepnet. No chance of one slipping through the fingers and escaping if it's done this way.

Fifteen minutes at this and three more eels, two small roach and a gudgeon have gone in the net. Time for move two, this time to the long pole.

Same method and a try to see if the casters are working there too. A catapult is used to drop in a few maggots and a bit of hemp.

Interesting to note that the anglers on either side

• *The swim has weed cover on both banks and a slight shelf at 3½m. At least three lines will be fished during the next five hours. A break from the normal routine is that the far bank gets fished first rather than the inside.*

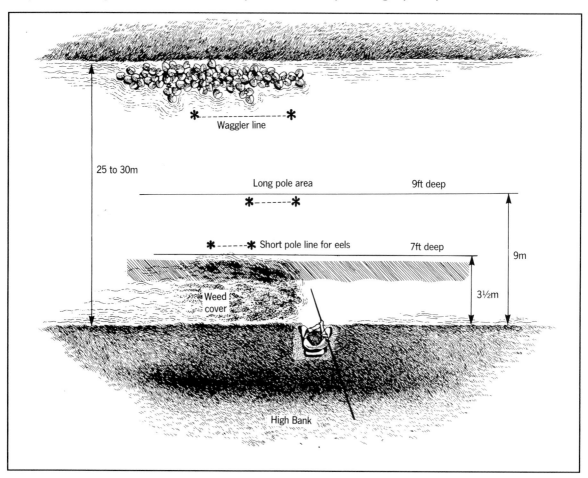

25 to 30m

Waggler line

Long pole area   9ft deep

Short pole line for eels   7ft deep

Weed cover

9m

3½m

High Bank

have been fishing the middle all this time and are probably doing just as well. But they have neglected to feed anywhere else so if their swims die they could be struggling.

My long pole line is still fresh and a bite comes first drop in. It's a skimmer bream, and that is followed by two more and then two eels and a roach.

As each fish is netted, the pole is being broken down and the disconnected sections are slipped just inside the keepnet rim so they can't slide into the water. A couple of spare sections are propped behind the groundbait bowl so that they are within easy reach should a bream or tench need playing.

The pole line has taken a hammering over the last twenty minutes and the wind seems to have died off a little. I'll use this steady period to try over with the waggler again. In between catching two more eels over there, the other lines are constantly being topped up. The weed bed is producing odd perch among the eels but the wind is getting up again.

Into the second hour now and still the leger hasn't been touched, while the other lines are all producing

• *You can't legislate for bream like these. You need to take the bait required to catch them if you draw a dream peg – but more often than not it doesn't get used*

fish. At no time will I wait for the area being fished to slow down. It's a case of catch a few and leave the rest to feed, while catching more from the other areas. But a minor setback: a lost fish has caused the elastic to bump back, wrapping the hook length of the pole into a knot. It will take a short time to fix on a new one, but, to keep fishing, the leger can go out on the far line.

The hook takes a matter of seconds to tie on but the leger is out now and fishing all the time. It gives a break, too, which can be used to feed all three lines.

The leger has a tail of five feet and after each cast the bomb is allowed to settle and wound up to, but not moved. The bottom is littered with bits of peat and dead vegetation and it is easy to get a bait buried if you start dragging it about.

The tip twitches and it's an eel, a good one, of well over 1lb. Those are the ones that win matches if you get 'em coming. Half a dozen casters on all three lines and the tip goes again, another good eel. But did you notice the tip didn't rattle round as you'd expect? Some of these eels are really shy and bite just like a roach.

This leger approach is doing fine and some roach and a couple of little skimmers have come, among a series of missed bites. Maybe the tail is a bit long. Take it down to half what it was and the problem is cured and shown to have been the result of little roach nipping the bait.

The eels have obviously gone off again, so it's back to the short pole where straight away the skimmers and some more eels are waiting. It's amazing how these different areas keep producing a few fish if you rest them every few minutes. It makes fishing hard work but it does pay off nine times out of ten. The secret is to keep them all fed just right and to rest them while they are producing bites. It is easy to get carried away and catch too many from one spot. In fact, this inside is taking a lot of stick so the waggler had better come back into play quickly.

Fishing the inside was easy, but the wind has certainly got up now and the float is pushing through much too fast. A bleak took on the drop that time, but eels or quality fish will not chase such an unnatural presentation. Out comes the waggler, and the leger with that shortened tail, this time with a caster just as a change bait.

Nothing! Back to a maggot and the tip goes straight away. Missed it. Try again. The same thing happens three times on the trot, a sure sign that the fish are getting touchy, so maybe the far side has been fished too hard or the fish have moved off because I forgot to feed it regularly while swapping around those tail lengths.

The long pole hasn't had an outing for a while and with a maggot back on the hook the eels are soon coming again. Strange how they seem to roam about on these drains. The one I have just caught coughed up some squatts that must have been put in by one of the anglers nearby. Interesting to note that neither of my neighbours is making much impression now. One has abandoned the middle line and is sitting it out with a waggler just off the near shelf. Probably that is a tench-or-bust tactic but it isn't going to put him ahead

of what's in my net. To the other side a leger is plopping well over, but the area hasn't been fed all match and short of a miracle he's unlikely to catch much now.

Another eel of well over a pound, so that 24 is coming off and the 22 to 1½lb goes on. The swim is showing no signs of going off so the extra size and hook length thickness shouldn't make any difference.

Even on the pole it is getting difficult to hold the tackle still against the wind, but there's not long left, so after catching a few more small skimmers, a nice roach of 4oz and two superb eels, it will be a try on the short pole for fifteen minutes and then finally back on the leger but dropped on the long pole line instead of the far swim for the last fifteen minutes.

The plan has worked well, maybe double figures from what has been a tricky match considering the wind and the moody nature of the water.

This resting tactic can work on all sorts of waters, and even when a move away from a line that is producing doesn't yield as much it still often pays in the long run, by letting the main catching area settle down after a bashing.

The groundbait and squatts didn't get used today, but had the eels not fed well some might have gone in on the pole lines to catch the skimmers and roach.

These waters need watching carefully and by August hemp can do a lot of damage with the bigger roach. When using this bait it is worthwhile using the three-line technique, keeping the inside one just for hemp and the other two as catching areas before the seed begins working, and as resting places just as they were today.

At the scales the hard work has shown 11lb 3oz, top on the board and looking good for the section, and almost certainly well in the frame again. The anglers on either side have weighed 3lb and 2lb 6oz. They paid the price for putting all their eggs in one basket.

This eel-and-small-fish plan doesn't always work but over a season, at least through the summer, it takes a lot of beating if the bream don't figure.

As a team plan this is certainly going to be the way to tackle the water in the next match here. It will get high points for each member and is certainly not going to eliminate anyone individually from a winning chance.

10

Big bream

Late July, and the big bream shoals are the target if top weight in the 100 peg open is to be achieved.

Venue is a wide, very slow-flowing river that was canalised many years ago from a twisting, narrow and flood-prone waterway into a featureless and barren place. This is a match angler's river that would get very low marks for scenic value.

Much of the river is about nine feet deep and there's a lot of marginal weed on the pegged bank side. Eels can be a problem – or winners, depending on the size

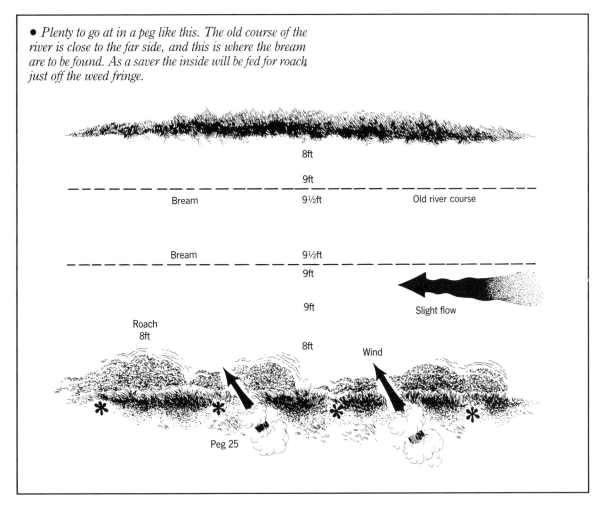

● *Plenty to go at in a peg like this. The old course of the river is close to the far side, and this is where the bream are to be found. As a saver the inside will be fed for roach just off the weed fringe.*

of match and the opposition. Today the field is strong and the bream have been showing for three weeks. No way will the wrigglers figure this time.

Results in the national angling press have shown winning weights of 45lb and 48lb in consecutive weeks and there's been a string of 20lb nets in both events. The roach are feeding on hemp but fishing for them is not the way to win outright. At best they will be the savers if the draw is unkind.

With 100 anglers stretching along the best bream section of the moment it is going to take at least 40lb and maybe even 60lb to win. Even to make the frame 25lb is a fair estimate.

Favourite area is towards the upstream end and a draw anywhere between numbers 15 and 35 is going to be needed for the best chance. It's worth remembering that these fish do move around, especially if they have been hammered a few times during the week by pleasure anglers who follow the match results for their fishing ideas.

This match is an expensive venture. The pools are 'all in' with the ticket price and bait outlay is also considerable. Although it's a bit of a lucky dip there are enough winning chances to make the gamble reasonably sound. If it was a case of two or three outstanding pegs and nothing else then I would be fishing somewhere else!

Bait for the five hours is going to be four pints of casters and the same quantity of red squatts. A few home-bred white gozzers, a good supply of small redworms, a pint of red hook maggots and a few dark casters hand-picked from the main bait supply. A few slices of fresh white bread can also go into the bag just in case it turns out to be one of those silly days when things don't go to plan.

Also as a standby, I'll take two pints of hemp to feed an inside line for roach. These are only to be fished for if the bream go off or the draw is hopeless.

Groundbait is going to be 7lb of fine, well-riddled brown crumb to which a kilo bag of Masterclass Red Bream Feed is added. This is a strong-smelling additive that gives the crumb a deep red colour and has worked well for me in recent seasons. Mixing it is easy. You get red hands in the process but it is a safe dye and washes off easily afterwards.

Because the river is very slow-moving and the water fairly shallow, the groundbait needs to be mixed so that it moulds into balls easily but will break up well before hitting the bottom. With this in mind, at least

half of it gets mixed at home before leaving on match morning. After mixing the Masterclass with the dry crumb the whole thing is gradually wetted and then riddled again. Lumps left on the riddle can be rubbed through with the fingertips, and then the whole lot is packed into a couple of plastic carrier bags.

Target fish are bream – big ones of 2lb to 4½lb – and the method most likely to succeed will be a straight paternoster leger and a swingtip or quivertip, depending on conditions. Ideally the swingtip is the weapon for these bream because they don't like to feel resistance as the quivertip pulls round. In my experience a long swingtip gives a broad arc of travel and plenty of time for the fish to get hold of the bait before the strike is made.

A float rod will be set up for the bream and a second one for the roach. The roach rod is made up even if I draw the bream flyer – just in case.

The other float rod is likely to get a waggler of some 2½SSG capacity. It will be a straight peacock with perhaps a slight insert but still thick enough to take the pull of a bow forming in the line.

For me the feeder is out of the running today. The water is fairly clear and these bream don't take kindly to lumps of plastic landing on their dinner. The river is forty yards or so wide, so getting groundbait out isn't a great problem by hand. If you aren't up to it then use a Whopper Dropper catapult.

Well, that's the plan. The only things that can ruin it are a sudden change in the settled weather, a real stroke of bad luck such as finding the swim drawn has been hammered the previous day, or a draw right out of it at the downstream end of the match.

Remembering that the match is bigger than the usual club event, it is essential to arrive that bit earlier. There are no pools to pay on match day but parking may be a problem, and if I feel lucky it will take time to get a bet with the bookie at the draw.

Arriving early the car can be parked in the direction of the river so as not to get mixed up in the post-draw panic as everyone tries to set off at the same time. These bankside roads are narrow, and in the excitement a few anglers seem to think that Grand Prix driving is all part of the fun.

It also helps to get off to the river as soon as possible after the draw, which hopefully will be one where you draw on arrival rather than having to line up at a given time.

Bet on, a few chats in the small queue at the draw

table and – bingo – peg 25 comes out of the bag. A flyer if ever there was one, just five pegs from where a match was won last weekend.

On the way to the car, the bailiff who pegs the bank is spotted in the car park. A few minutes with him confirms that some bream have been caught there during the week but he can't remember anyone fishing the peg yesterday. Yes, I'm getting the feeling that it's a good day in prospect.

A short drive along the bankside road and the pegs are in sight. Park well off the road and clear of the farmer's gate. No bonus for getting called away to move the motor half way through the match.

Over the bank and quickly off the skyline to walk close to the water. These bream are crafty creatures and may be walked away by the careless. Hopefully anglers who follow me will take the same route. If they do, we all get to catch a lot more fish.

A few minutes sitting on the box to recover from the walk is time well spent. There's over an hour to the off, so no hurry to set up the gear. On go the polarising sunglasses and it's easy to see there is a bit more colour here than where I stopped to look at the

water on the way to the draw. Could be the bream are here in good numbers.

Oh yes, one just topped at the next peg, that's a good sign. Anglers are arriving now and in no uncertain terms tell me and the anglers at the next pegs how lucky we are. Well, we all need a bit of luck now and again, don't we?

Enough of this chatter. The first thing out of the bag is the keepnet. It needs placing carefully with the minimum of disturbance, not as the angler five pegs away has just done: he launched a 10 foot net complete with weighted bottom out into his swim. The splash and resulting shock wave has probably shifted all the bream from that peg and the ones either side of it too.

My net is dropped into the margin and slowly pushed into place with the landing-net pole, taking care to gently part the floating weed and cot that festoon the first three yards of water.

Now the landing net is assembled and placed alongside the keepnet. Next, one of the bags of groundbait is emptied into the tray and given a good stir. It will need just a few spots of water adding to bring it back to its original mixed texture.

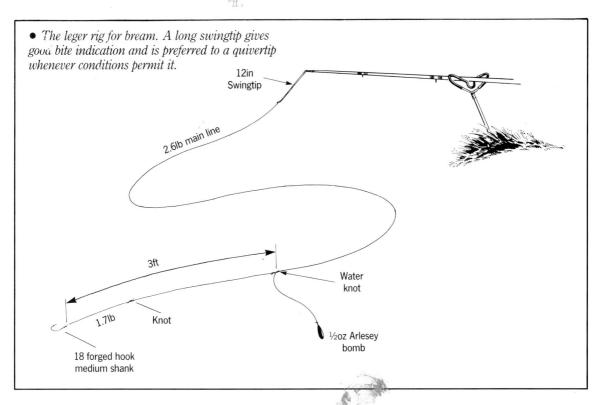

● *The leger rig for bream. A long swingtip gives good bite indication and is preferred to a quivertip whenever conditions permit it.*

12in Swingtip

2.6lb main line

3ft

1.7lb

Knot

18 forged hook medium shank

Water knot

½oz Arlesey bomb

Everything else comes out of the box and is laid in place. Only then is the holdall approached to select rods and rod rests.

Conditions are good, and with that marginal weed in front an 11 foot swingtip rod is going to be handy. With the swingtip the rod can be fished almost straight out in front so that the line is kept well clear of the cot.

There's just a ripple on the surface and what wind is blowing is from over the upstream shoulder. The sky is slightly overcast but the sun may break through later and as we'll be fishing from 11am until 4pm it might get warm by mid-match.

The actual tip is a 12 inch long nylon one with a nylon link. These are favourites on the wide and windy bream rivers of Lincolnshire and the fenlands, and even in this age of the quivertip they win a lot of matches on rivers like the Witham, Welland, Nene and the lower Ouse every season.

Line is a 2.6lb on and the starting hook a size 18 forged medium shank tied to 1.7lb. If the fish come a 16 might go on later, but the first thing to establish is that they are there and feeding.

Bomb is a half-ounce Arlesey tied to a fixed link nine inches long and about three feet from the hook. It's that simple. Nothing fancy, no swivels, stops or other ironmongery to worry about. The link has been Water Knotted in place and if the tail needs altering it is a case of breaking it off and starting again. The whole operation takes a matter of seconds, and in my opinion is better than risking leger stops and shots to stop swivels, all of which can tangle.

The rod is ready and can be placed on the rest, with the butt resting on the seat box, which has been set firm and level by adjusting the front legs. The rod rest can now be pushed downwards until the swingtip has the top ring just touching the water surface. Set this way even the slightest twitch is going to show, even though the tip is tending to move away from the line of sight. Had it not been for all that weed, the rod could have been set to one side and the tip viewed almost at right angles.

• *The swing tip is set so the end just touches the water surface.*

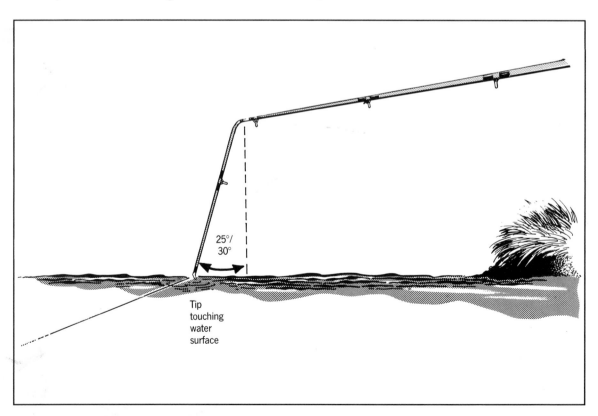

25°/ 30°

Tip touching water surface

First of the waggler rods goes up next, a 13 footer to which the waggler is set to fish a foot overdepth. I'm not going to cast it out even though the rules allow it. The disturbance might just cause a bit of panic if the fish are already touchy following the bankside noise as anglers walked to their pegs.

Shotting is mainly as bulk, with a number 10 six inches from the hook, then a number 8 a foot from that, followed by three more 8s as a bulk a foot higher. Part of the locking-shot load at the float is made up with two more 8s that can be brought down to add to the main bulk should additional weight be needed lower down.

Finally the standby rod for those roach. There's a little cot in a clump, about two rod lengths out and to the downstream side of me. That's where the hemp will go for roach.

This float is another waggler but of only 3BB capacity. Depth there is confirmed with the plummet as eight feet so that's the starting depth with a 20 hook to 1lb botton. Shot is mainly locked around the float. Down the line is a series of styl leads. These are ideal when feeding hemp as the roach will not mistake them for the seed, which can often result in false bites if small individual shot are used. If shot are preferred be sure to use them in multiples of two or more to reduce the false bite danger.

First styl is a tiny size 8 a foot away and then three more size 12s spaced at one-foot intervals above it. Rest of the load is as locking shot.

Five minutes to go and a few more bream have showed at the next peg upstream. The first box of casters is opened and placed at the back of the groundbait tray. The other two pints remain sealed until needed.

A quick stir of the groundbait, and three good handfuls of casters and a few squatts go into what is to become four tangerine-sized balls. These are made up carefully and into a uniform shape and size, then left in the tray for a while.

A spare bait box is filled with river water and placed alongside the tray. This water will be used to wet the hands and put a skin on the groundbait just prior to throwing. This prevents the balls exploding in mid-air

• *The peacock waggler rig that may be needed for bream if the leger fails. The tackle is set to fish a foot overdepth.*

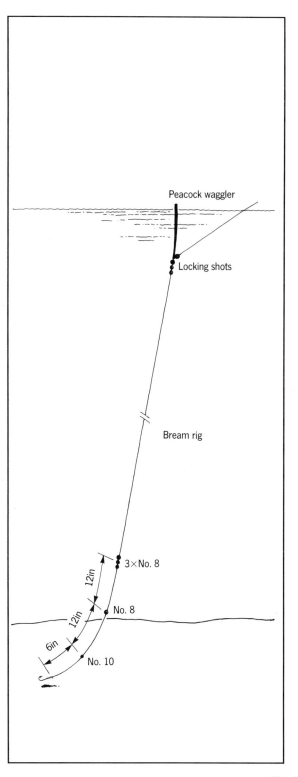

Big bream

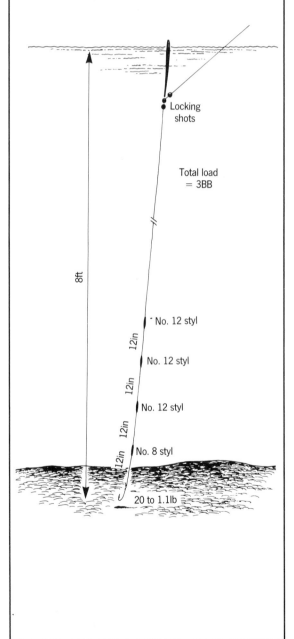

● *For the roach a rig using styl weights is used. These slim weights are ideal whenever hemp is used and there is a danger that normal shot could be mistaken for food by feeding fish.*

Locking
shots

Total load
= 3BB

8ft

12in — No. 12 styl

12in — No. 12 styl

12in — No. 12 styl

12in — No. 8 styl

20 to 1.1lb

but does not make them too hard to break once they hit the water.

Target area is going to be about three-quarters of the way across the river where I know the water is just a fraction deeper. This extra depth is only a matter of a few inches, but it is the original bed of the old river before the widening operation and for some reason seems to hold bream better than elsewhere.

The whistle goes and there's a barrage of groundbait all along the river. This is danger time. Pile too much on top of their heads and the bream go. Feed too little and they still go. The man in most danger is that angler upstream. He has the fish right in front, while I suspect my swim has only the edge of the shoal. He has put in three big balls about half-way across so I am free to feed that old channel with my four tangerines. One goes in on the near side of the channel, a second two yards further out and one a yard to each side mid-way between the two.

Those four balls have accounted for almost three-quarters of a pint of casters and a good handful of squatts. By spreading the four to form four corners of a square, with a corner facing me, I have four places to cast in rotation. These shoals are big and the whole lot can't feed in one spot. It also means that each fed area can be rested in turn as fish are caught.

The feed is in: now the first cast. Baiting the hook with a caster and a white maggot, the cast is made to the nearest of the four baited areas. The bomb hits the surface and the bale-arm is closed immediately. This results in the tip staying out at an angle and it needs watching carefully for the next few seconds as the bait falls. Should a fish take on the drop it will register as a bite.

If the bomb is cast and allowed to fall unchecked, no indication will occur and a fish might be missed.

Once the tip has been set the reel's anti-reverse lever is flicked on. I prefer to leger for bream this way so that the strike can be made one-handed. The lever is then flicked off once the fish begins to move towards me.

Reason for fishing the nearest feed first is to avoid line bites as fish move around before settling down to feed.

Nothing happened, but that's a good sign. On these bream waters it is best if fish move to your feed rather than being there at the start.

Now is the time to take it easy. There's no hurry. Five hours to catch fifteen bream or so means just

• *A typical feeding pattern where a big shoal of bream is involved. The four areas of feed are fished in turn as shown by the numbers. This system ensures hooked fish are not drawn through the feeding shoal.*

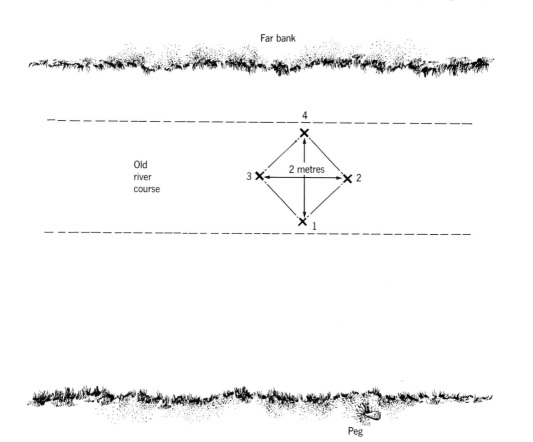

Far bank

Old
river
course

4

3 ✕ — 2 metres — ✕ 2

✕ 1

Peg

three an hour. Early match nerves can all too easily result in trying to strike at every twitch. That is a dangerous game because it can involve pricking a fish early on and having the whole shoal move off in panic.

The swingtip is set at 15 degrees from the vertical and then the waiting begins.

Fill in the time by watching carefully, while feeding in a few grains of hemp to that patch of cot. Try to keep trickling in a few grains regularly throughout the match.

The tip has been still now for twenty minutes. The angler upstream has struck four or five times but, as yet, has caught nothing either.

This is the pattern of things in these matches. He is probably getting line bites as fish move around, slightly panicked by the feed going in. He strikes again and for a second or two is into a fish, but it comes off. He's in big trouble now and feeds in two more balls straight away. That has probably killed off what chance he had left. Hopefully it will also help my prospects if the fish move my way.

The wind is favourable so it is possible to fire in some loose casters by pointing the catapult high and dropping a few at a time over the groundbait.

Suddenly, without warning, the tip twitches, lifts a fraction and then drops back before rising again, this time with some purpose. A sweeping strike and a good fish is on. The rod is kept high and to the left in the direction I had struck. A slight pause causes the fish to move off the bottom slightly, and the reel can be wound gently but firmly to steer the bream away from the shoal.

Keep winding carefully rather than adopt the text book 'pumping' action. Gentle but firm continual pressure does not allow the fish to turn back down towards the other fish. Even bream flash when they turn, and if there's a pause between 'pumps' there is a real danger that the others may see this flash and panic.

Bream are not the world's hardest fighters but keep them away from that marginal weed until they can be surfaced and turned on their side, at which stage they can be steered towards the landing net.

A fish of 3lb, not a bad start after half an hour and it has been hooked nicely in the bottom lip. A bit of a gamble now with a change to a 16 hook, but if these fish are going to come regularly the extra size is an insurance against loss. The maggot is replaced with a second caster and the cast again made to the first feed

● *The correct way to pick up a sizeable bream; but get the keepnet as close to you as possible so as to avoid any mishaps*

area. The dark casters picked from the main supply are lighter in weight and are easily flicked up off the bottom by browsing fish. The difference often works if the going gets hard.

Three minutes and out goes the tip again, even more positively than last time. Another fish of the same size is netted, followed by a third less than ten minutes later. That's nearly 10lb towards the target. Time for a cast to the right-hand side of the square, followed by a couple of smaller balls of groundbait to which more casters and squatts have been added.

The angler to the right has not caught again except for an eel and two small roach. It looks as if his race is run, and all because he got that opening attack wrong. He now resorts to a bombardment of four big balls of

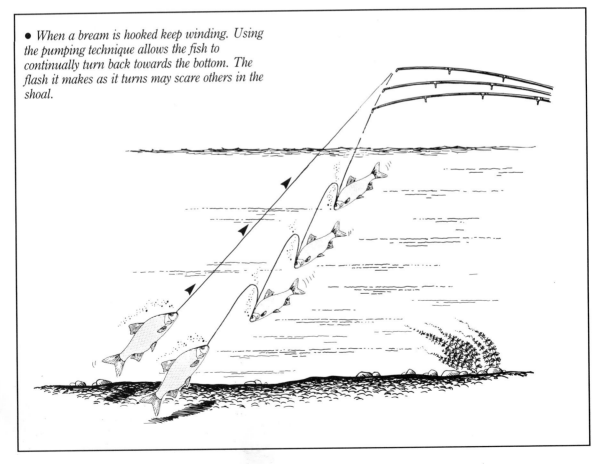

● *When a bream is hooked keep winding. Using the pumping technique allows the fish to continually turn back towards the bottom. The flash it makes as it turns may scare others in the shoal.*

Big bream

feed in the hope that he can pull some fish back from my swim. That's unlikely unless I also make a mistake or lose fish through rushing them or striking at half bites.

Downstream the angler has caught two fish but they are smaller than mine and my tip has just twitched again before rising slowly, only to produce a 1lb fish. Maybe the bottom end of the feeding area is where the smaller fish have taken up residence. Next cast goes to the upstream feed area and the size again increases, this time to a fish knocking 4lb. Safely landed and a ball of groundbait tops up the near spot.

It is now a case of alternating around the three near areas until bites slow down. Then it is safe to go to the far corner of the feeding pattern to see what it holds. Thankfully it is more bream and by mid-match there are eleven in the net, possibly worth close to 30lb.

Others have been catching downstream but the

signs are good for a result in my favour. But it's twenty minutes now without a bite, so off come the casters and on goes a small redworm tipped with a red maggot. As if by magic a fish takes it as it hits bottom, but a repeat baiting brings nothing. Maybe the shoal is drying up. Now is danger time. Two hours left is too long to sit it out, so the feed is kept up, but only as loose feed and the occasional small ball of cereal. Constantly casting around the feed area keeps a few bites coming until a sudden lull in the proceedings. Oddly, we have all stopped catching. The angler below comments on the situation but continues as before.

A rebait with two small redworms on the 16 hook,

● *A lively worm tipped with a maggot or caster is a good combination for bream. The worm can be made to wriggle even more than usual if the extreme end of its tail is pinched*

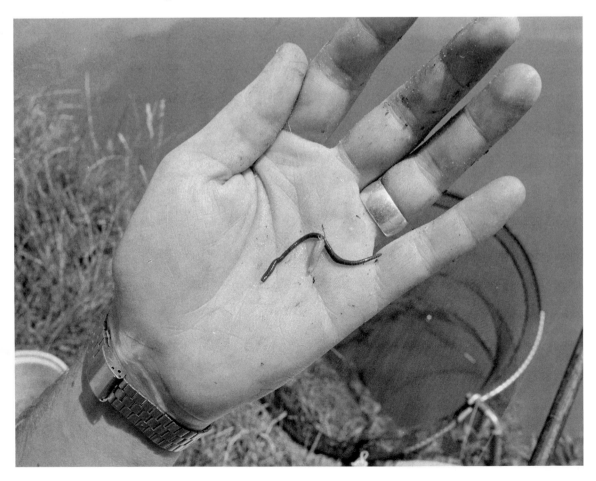

and a cast to the far corner of the feed. The tackle settles and is given a couple of minutes. Nothing. Now the reel is given a few turns and the bait is dragged a few inches across the bottom, a pause for a minute and another two turns of the handle given. Out goes the tip and a fish is on. Often this twitching technique triggers off a feeding response in fish that have ignored a static bait.

The same trick is repeated several times, but no more fish come and there's an hour left. One more try with a worm but this time the tail end is pinched with a finger nail before casting. The worm twitches attractively and soon proves too much for a browsing fish of 2lb.

Half an hour to go and it has gone really dead now. Another angler a few pegs away has had a golden last hour and could be getting close to my weight, but he too has stopped catching. It certainly looks as if they have had enough for one day.

What I need now is a bonus few pounds from somewhere. The wind has got up a little and there seems no point in float fishing over the bream area, so that leaves only the roach. Now it's make-your-mind-up time: continue with the leger and risk nothing or a lucky bream, or fish the hemp-fed area and try to work up a couple of pounds of roach. Option two is chosen and a caster is offered just off the weeds. Second cast and a bite produces a 4oz roach. More hemp and the bites continue until a tench takes the caster and goes mad, diving into the weed and getting well stuck.

Time now to show a bit of real nerve. The rod is laid on the rest and I wait. The float is visible and after a few seconds begins to move off. The fish has swum out again, its head covered in cot. It is reluctant to swim blindly and is easy to net. It's the best part of 2lb and, with six nice roach to go with it, has ended the match on a high note.

Scales show seventeen bream, the tench and 1½lb of roach for a total of 47lb. Possibly enough.

The angler upstream had 8lb at most and below me 20lb. There are a lot of others in the mid to high 20lb range but it's looking good. The day has been one of luck, in that the angler below killed his own chances but didn't affect mine as can so often happen if mistakes are made on these close pegs. I was able to get those extra fish by working at the swim, feeding with thought and working round the feed in a pattern. Ringing the bait changes also paid off. It's as if the

● *Big bream are the target and for this angler a positive approach has paid off resulting in nine good fish*

bream get wary of one type they have seen for a while but readily go for a change.

That tench was out of the blue, but it often happens that an area that has been constantly fed but left unfished for a long time produces a bonus. In this case it was better than expected.

Finally the fish go back and it takes a few moments to wade into the margins and steer them clear of the cot. They swim off almost casually as if they know it will be another week before the performance is repeated.

11

In the fast lane

Love 'em or hate 'em, bleak are match winners at times and so should not be ignored or overlooked as target fish.

Some anglers criticise those who fish for them as being unsporting, even claiming that 'bleak snatching' is not fishing. But it's usually those who have never mastered the art of catching three or four fish a minute who are quickest to condemn the method. A few small clubs ban bleak and that's fair enough, but if conditions dictate and the rules permit, then fish for them.

No match angler can claim to be an all-rounder unless he – or she – has taken the trouble to learn how to catch them, so as to be able to make the best possible use of a poor draw if faced with one.

There's a chance that the match to be fished is going to be hard work. The river is not in the best condition and only a few pegs have shown any consistent roach form. But club championship points are at stake and for that reason it must be fished.

Bleak offer the best chance of success unless one of the form pegs is drawn, but even they are unlikely to produce much more than 10lb. The weather has been warm and bright for a few days and practice has shown that once the sun gets high the roach become very hard to tempt.

Preparation must be planned carefully. Bait and tackle is to be included that will enable the roach pegs to be tackled effectively, but at the same time bleak remain the first priority. For this reason there is going to be some waste involved, but even if the draw is unkind the roach bait will not be totally neglected.

Hemp and caster have been sorting out the good roach but maggot has taken smaller specimens, along with some skimmers. The danger to a bleaking plan could be someone making seed baits work from early on in the four-hour contest.

Bleak bait comes in for the first attention. To catch several fish fast without having to rebait demands something that is tough. The fish are small and don't really want a big mouthful, so pinkies and hook maggots are called for. The hook maggots need to be a week or so old and smaller than usual. White maggots seem to be the best for bleak but a few bronze as a change bait are worth taking along.

The old maggots will be tougher-skinned than fresh ones, and in order to thicken their skins even more they have been kept in dry foundry sand – the dark-brown stuff used for squatts.

Sand works well but anything sharp and dry such as ground rice or even groundbait is ideal. If the bait looks a bit too large it is worthwhile hand-picking a few hundred of the smallest from whatever is available.

Pinkies for feed and also as a hook-bait alternative are going to be needed. Again toughen up some old ones for the hook, but use fresh for feed so that the fall rate through the water is slow. Two pints of pinkies should be plenty and chances are a pint is going to be enough. Generally, the faster the river the more bait will be needed. Squatts are fine for feeding but only if the fish can be brought in very close, otherwise they are difficult to throw the required distance.

The prospect of a good draw is going to call for some hemp, a few tares and a couple of pints of casters.

Groundbait hasn't figured in winning performances but 3lb of dry cereal is going into the bag just the same, for reasons that will become obvious later in the day.

Main attack on the bleak is going to be with a whip at five metres but hopefully reducing to four later on in the match if all goes well.

The roach are shy and, although they have been caught on seed, seem reluctant to come in close. For that reason a smallish waggler rather than a pole is going to be the method to tackle a line some ten metres out. The pole would work for a while but I suspect it will be a case of searching right down the swim, something that the waggler can do well beyond the pole range.

Draw time: the peg that comes out of the hat is not one of the favourites, but it does have a bit of flow and is ideal for a bleak attack.

First job is to get comfortable. Bleaking is best done sitting down on a stable base. A platform or box legs are vital tools for this game. As with all match fishing, everything needs to be to hand but be sure to keep the area as uncluttered as possible. Get bait stands so that they are right to hand but out of the way of fish being swung in.

A point too, is to get the peg as 'fish safe' as possible. Do this by positioning the box and then building a barrier just in front of your feet that will stop dropped fish jumping back into the water.

The barrier today is a few handfuls of the long grass that was lying around the peg, but stones or even a couple of spare towels or some bits of driftwood could be pressed into service.

So bleak it is, but, just in case they don't want to feed fast enough to make a weight, the plan needs an option clause. The seed isn't going to work at this peg but there is a chance that small fish might come to a maggot. To try to make seed work is pointless. But here is where the maggot plan can help even if the bleak do not come up to scratch.

Half of that 3lb of groundbait is mixed and into it go some pinkies and some squatts left over from the previous day. Introducing maggots and groundbait provides the chance of catching skimmers and small roach, while at the same time helping reduce the prospects of anglers on either side catching on seed. It is bordering on gamesmanship, perhaps, but match fishing is all about beating people and this is one way of doing it perfectly legally, while at the same time giving a second line of attack should the bleaking prove fruitless. The biggest danger is forgetting to feed this second line while working at the bleak.

Tackle for the bleak is a whip and a line long enough to fish to hand. Measure this off exactly so that a hooked fish swings straight into your hand. Something about a foot shorter than the pole is about right, but allow for the suppleness of the fine tip which will bend and effectively lengthen the line of swing.

This soft tip is one of the most vital parts of the whole rig. Too stiff and fish will be bumped off. Go for a fine and very soft one that puts the hook home and nothing more.

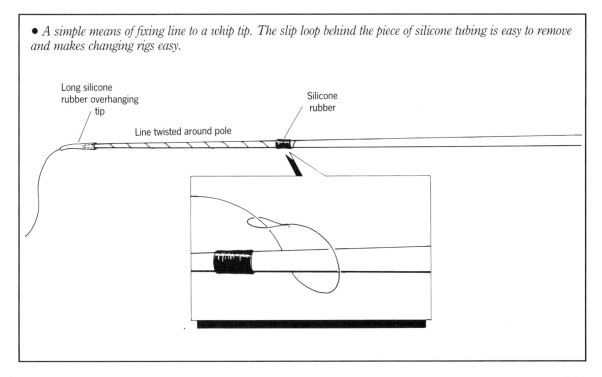

• *A simple means of fixing line to a whip tip. The slip loop behind the piece of silicone tubing is easy to remove and makes changing rigs easy.*

Long silicone rubber overhanging tip

Silicone rubber

Line twisted around pole

Attaching line to the tip is done in a number of ways, but I prefer the slip loop used behind a piece of silicone tubing and the line twisted along the tip before ending with a long piece of tubing protruding from the tip. This method allows some degree of adjustment and also rapid removal should a change be needed.

Hook pattern is a long-shanked crystal barbless. Micro-barbs are fine too for bleak fishing but if you feel confident with a barbless it will give you the edge on speedy removal.

Tying hooks for bleaking needs a different approach. For a start don't go ultra fine with the hook length. Rarely is anything finer than 1lb necessary and to go lighter can result in breakage when flicking fish into the net.

Best line for bleak is a clear one, either near-white or very pale green. The dark-brown types are not so good in my opinion because fish can see them as they come up from below towards the surface light.

Tie the spade knot in the usual fashion but leave a longer-than-normal tag of line protruding from the knot. This is going to prevent the bait being blown up the line by a hooked fish. Micro-barbs can help in the converse direction by keeping the maggot from slipping off during repeated casting and unhooking. The actual spade end of a hook should normally be as small as possible, but in the case of bleak hooks a larger one can be an advantage by again acting as a stop.

Hook size for bleak can vary a lot – anything from a 24 to an 18 or larger – depending on conditions and the mood of the fish. Always use the largest you can get away with.

At the far end of the hook length, which should be about twelve inches long, tie a loop for attaching to the main line.

Float is a 1½ inch long piece of ³⁄₁₆ inch diameter balsa. The ends have been tapered down to give it a streamlined appearance and to make attaching rubbers easier.

At each end of the float pieces of silicone rubber are used to fasten it to the line. Be sure both rubbers protrude well beyond the float so that tangles are avoided. To make casting easier and to provide extra weight, add a small shot either side of the float, pushing them right inside the rubber. By using shots of the same size at either end the float remains flat on the surface.

Final part of the rig is the knot used to attach the hook length. This can be a loop-to-loop system or a Half Blood Knot to the hook length loop. In both cases leave an inch or more of loose line protruding from the knot.

Now pull the line – not the hook length – between

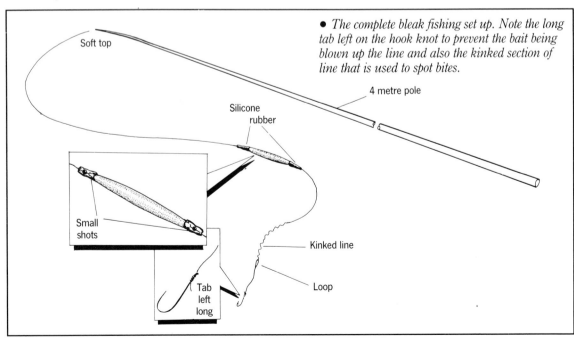

● *The complete bleak fishing set up. Note the long tab left on the hook knot to prevent the bait being blown up the line and also the kinked section of line that is used to spot bites.*

Soft top

4 metre pole

Silicone rubber

Small shots

Kinked line

Tab left long

Loop

your thumb and finger nails to make it kink into spirals. It helps too to use a thick line, of, say, 3lb strain, so that it can be easily seen on the water.

Smear some grease on these curls and also on the long tag of line left at the knot. You now have a series of floating coils and pieces of nylon which can be easily seen.

This rig has caught a lot of bleak for me and it's one in which I have a lot of confidence. Other methods exist, including substituting for the balsa float a few inches of trout-fishing floating-fly line. This line is heavy and so casts well, and if a bright colour is used it has very good visibility.

The whistle goes and for a start I put in two smallish balls of groundbait on the 10 metre mark. But time is valuable, so this must be done quickly and the real fish-catching method begun.

Polarising glasses and a peaked hat or sun visor are absolutely essential because, even though there is a float and those coils of line to show bites, the best method is actually watching the bait.

The bleak float has been set two feet from the hook for a start but this length will be shortened if fish are easy.

Cast the rig in the manner you find most efficient but try to get the tackle to land with a splash. This seems to attract bleak to the surface. My own method is a sort of underhand cast a bit like that used for a stick float. It starts off with the palm of the pole hand facing slightly downwards and flicking the pole from the side to the front while at the same time turning the hand over so that it ends palm upwards.

A pinkie is chosen as the starting bait, but before casting put in a dozen as loose feed, followed by the tackle. Now watch to see what happens. Chances are that bleak will rise from nowhere, and if you are lucky, one will take the hookbait. If you can see the bait clearly don't react too quickly. As it vanishes, just lift the pole in an even upwards movement. There is no strike, no jerking, just a smooth sweep that should lift the fish from the water and in towards your waiting hand.

If preparation has been thorough the keepnet's wide mouth is placed so the fish can be dropped straight into it. The net needs to be low enough to be clear of operations but positioned so that transfer distance from hand to net is as short as possible.

Because the hook is barbless it should be possible to shake the fish from the hook and into the net without touching it. To do this, the fish is swung in and the left hand moved behind it with the fingers facing downwards. The line comes between thumb and forefinger, and giving it a slight shake drops the fish into the net. It sounds complicated but once you've tried it a few times it is easy to follow.

Feeding now takes a lot of concentration. Ideally it is done without breaking the rhythm. But the most important thing is to feed regularly but with only very small amounts of loose pinkies. The idea is to get fish chasing about for the little that's available so that it all gets eaten and does not result in the bleak dropping either downstream or deeper in the water.

Sometimes bleak are reluctant to come right to the surface, and on those days a tiny shot may be needed to take the bait to them.

If you can't see a bleak take the bait, then watch the line, which, apart from the hook length, should be floating. As a bleak takes, line will slide across the surface and you lift to the fish. If it's missed or bites are hard to see, just keep casting. With bleak fishing it often seems that the more you cast the more you catch.

Another good tip is to count fish as they are caught. Begin by breaking the match into, say, fifteen-minute segments. Then, by making a mental note of the catch in each segment, it is possible to see if the catch rate is constant or improving. If it begins to fall, try to work out what is wrong.

Half an hour has passed and the catch rate has been thirty in the first fifteen minutes and thirty-seven in the second. That shows it took a little time to get going and work up both the bleak and the other line, which must now be topped up constantly to hold any other fish in the area and prevent them being drawn to the anglers feeding on either side.

It is important to hold any fish that may be there, otherwise your neighbours get the advantage of an untapped source of supply.

While the catch rate has been reasonable, size leaves something to be desired. The bleak caught are running at maybe forty-five to the pound whereas on this water they are usually closer to thirty-five to the pound. So off comes the pinkie and on goes a hook maggot.

The extra splash made by the bigger maggot works like magic and a better-quality bleak rushes from the depths to intercept it. Two or three hook maggots are now added every so often to the usual six to eight pinkies going in. But two or three is all that are

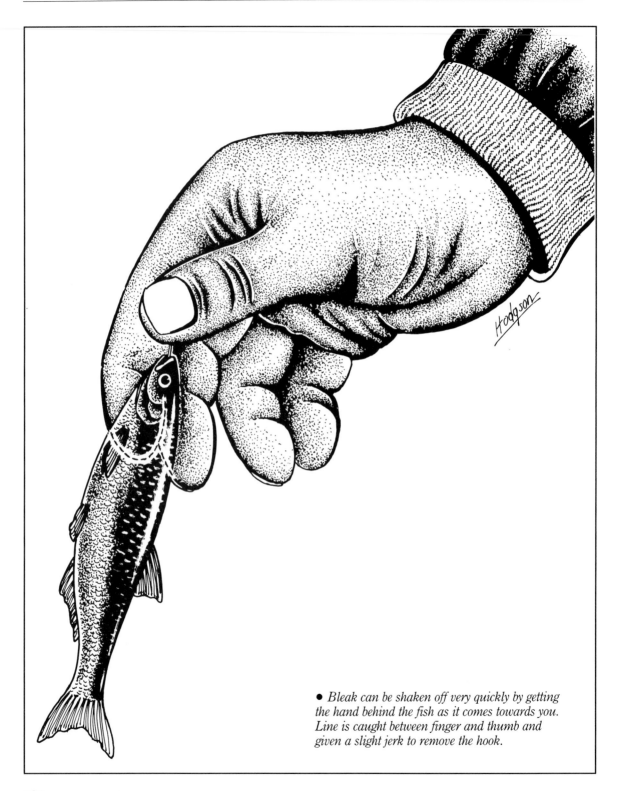

● *Bleak can be shaken off very quickly by getting the hand behind the fish as it comes towards you. Line is caught between finger and thumb and given a slight jerk to remove the hook.*

needed. It is easy to feed-off even a big shoal.

Hook the maggot at the blunt end as usual but get the hook well into the skin so that there is less risk of it being pulled off by a succession of bites.

Today it has been a loose-feed operation but there are times when some form of groundbait is needed. This feed needs to be very fine, and mixed to form a dense cloud which hangs in the water.

Very fine brown crumb to which a packet of dried pigeon droppings has been added is mixed with milk until it is either just damp enough to hold together or wet enough to form a slop.

This tactic can work well when the water is very clear and there is no cover such as weeds in which the bleak can shelter.

Feed in small amounts every few seconds. Pieces smaller than a thumbnail are about right, and eventually a dense cloud will hang constantly in the water and become shelter to a bleak shoal. The trick now is to keep that cloud there no matter what happens. Forget to feed for even the shortest period and you're dead.

I first saw this method used at the next peg to France's Jean Pierre Fougeat during a world championship in Austria. The angler at the next peg was catching bleak and was ahead of Fougeat until the Frenchman hooked and landed a bream on the long pole. This prompted a change of tactics by the other angler, an Italian named Roberto Trabucco. Out went his long pole in search of bream. Meanwhile Fougeat, seeing what was going on, quickly began feeding a light bleak groundbait. The Italian's bleak, suddenly neglected and now in clear water, soon swam to this new cover. Fougeat didn't fish for them but he kept feeding that cloud groundbait for the remaining time. He ended with another bream from the long pole line and went on to win the world individual championship. The Italian, finding no bream in front of him, returned to his bleaking only to find he had none of those either!

I have looked back on that match many times since as a salutary lesson on tactics and how to make the best of someone else's mistakes.

Another thing to watch for is bleak suddenly going off. This may be just a change in depth or something more sinister such as a pike. The change of depth can be followed but if a pike moves in there is little you can do. Just stop feeding and hope that the dispersing of the shoal also means the pike moves away. It sounds drastic, but spend the time trying for other fish away from the pike and switch back occasionally without adding any feed. If you catch it is probably safe to begin building the shoal up again.

After a shoal has taken a hammering it might just move out further or perhaps drop downstream a metre or so. Search around, but keep an eye on the catch rate and be prepared to do something about it before too much time is wasted.

When bleak are feeding confidently bites will show as easy runs that are hard to miss. But if they are unsure the rig will register short sharp knocks that tear off at high speed and are almost impossible to hit. If they become a problem try scaling down the hook and bait size. If that fails, fish deeper. Check too that the maggot is sound. One which has been nipped repeatedly can often result in lightning-fast bites and missed fish.

Bleak fishing is just like other methods. It needs thought and a flexible approach. Switch to something a little different if the required results aren't forthcoming, and above all don't be distracted. If you feel you can end up with enough fish to earn a good result, stay with it. Only when it appears hopeless and there may be a better proposition available should you abandon the idea.

So that's four hours of hard work over. The sun did come up and the roach don't appear to have made much of a showing. Anglers on either side may have caught 3lb of little roach and skimmers apiece, and although there are stories along the bank of a few better fish being caught on hemp, the 11lb of bleak which have resulted from good planning may well be enough.

12

Beating the bleak

Last match was one where bleak played an important role but now the problem has been reversed. For the match is on a deep section of river that holds a good head of roach, skimmers and some bream. 'Some bream' may be an understatement, because there have been a number of pleasure weights topping 100lb and a few over 50lb in matches.

Bream apart, the club event planned for the weekend is likely to be won with between 8lb and 15lb depending on conditions. Bleak fishing might hit the lower target weight but it is too risky going for them in this match, simply because too many anglers will be sitting on pegs full of better fish.

Bleak are a pest here. The water is deep – 13 feet on average – and a bait has to be got down to run along the bottom. Fish the waggler and nine times out of ten the maggot gets intercepted by a bleak and ruined. It's frustrating and time-wasting, and in any case it is hard to get the tackle to run through properly against a wind that seems to skim along the river. This odd characteristic is created by far-bank trees that cause a sort of turbulence as the wind hits them.

Many anglers see the trees for the first time and immediately get it all wrong, expecting to catch a lot of chub from beneath the far-bank cover. They fail miserably. There are chub here, but more often than not they are less than 1lb apiece and turn up in the main area of the pegs among the roach and skimmers.

Overall this is a superb stretch of river, but it is one where knowledge of the river's contours and those trees is vital to success.

A few seasons ago the stretch was dredged, with the dragline working from the pegged bank. Result is deep water from two rod lengths out to the middle, which is about twelve metres away. From then on it shelves upwards to the far bank and in some pegs can be four feet at most. Under your feet there's a bit of a ledge to a rod length out but it's still maybe eight feet there.

There is flow but it's minimal. Too slow and too deep for a stick float. The waggler catches but those bleak are a problem. Maybe the leger? Well, it works, but it will not usually beat a good float angler who has sorted out a method.

The answer is a bit of versatility and confidence in the crow quill and balsa Avon float. That is going to be the opening plan for the match, coupled with a fair amount of feed.

Oddly enough, many anglers go to this venue and try to loose-feed it. Result is that the bleak get a real feast and very little gets down to the bottom. Any that does make it is spread out all over the place.

It's been a low turnout of thirty anglers but that number makes it a fairly even match except that three anglers get a draw on the noted bream pegs. Fortunately the draw has put us off that area – fortunately because they are hit-or-miss fish here and the shoal gets hammered, making it unpredictable. If you draw the area you have to try for them, but don't waste too much time at it.

Anyway, the draw puts us on a swim mid-way along the stretch. No particular features. Every peg looks the same – very promising. But the bank is dangerous. Vegetation is long grass, a few nettles and docks, making the actual edge difficult to find. Tackle is left at the top of the bank and a bank stick is taken to the undergrowth to hack out a spot. Go easy on this bank work and make as little disturbance as possible. Even on these deep swims the fish can be easily upset.

A hole has been made and the tall bits of growth behind are folded down so as not to foul the tackle during casting.

The box is unloaded of its contents and positioned nice and flat by using two adjustable front legs. On this

● *Wide, deep and ideal territory for a big Avon float. The heavy string of BB shots placed well down the rig gives stability, and if bleak are a problem will get the bait down quickly before it can be intercepted*

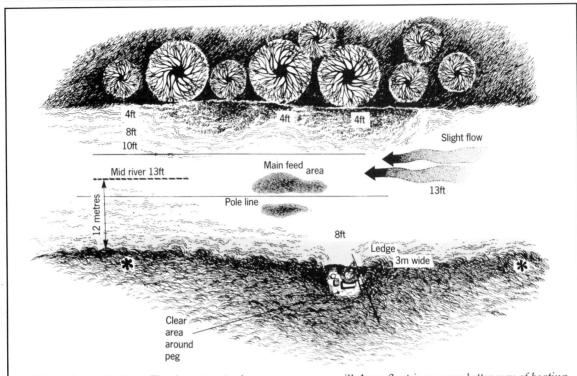

4ft 4ft 4ft

8ft

10ft

Slight flow

Mid river 13ft

Main feed area

13ft

Pole line

12 metres

8ft

Ledge
3m wide

Clear
area
around
peg

● *No need to go far here. The deepest water is no more than 12m or so out, making it ideal for the pole. But the crowquill Avon float is an even better way of beating nuisance fish such as bleak.*

water legs are better than a platform, firstly because it's a long walk and secondly because the bank terrain puts you high up above the water. A few anglers have opted to sit on the bank with their legs hanging over the edge, but they may find casting a fixed float set to fish at over thirteen feet a problem.

The box in place, next comes the landing net and then the keepnet positioned nice and low at the feet. A bait tray on the left, behind which is the groundbait bowl.

Everything is laid out to the format that's been worked out over the seasons. Now the rods can be assembled. It's going to be a three-method approach, but only one is likely to be used if all goes as planned.

First out of the bag is a 10½ foot quivertip to which a small open-ended feeder is rigged. A three-foot tail ends with a size 20 hook to 1.1lb bottom. Nothing fancy here. The feeder, a small Drennan, is tied to a six-inch fixed link.

Next a pole – 11 metres – to which a 1.5g balsa-

bodied wire-stemmed float is attached and set at around 12 feet. Shotting is an olivette two feet from the hook and a number 10 shot a foot away. Above the float there's five feet of line, which will allow for some adjustment. Hook is a 20 and the elastic is a number 5 so that any bream that show can be dealt with quickly.

Before setting up the final tackle the pole is used to plumb around and has shown 12 feet at 10 metres and remaining even to the bottom of the ledge about three metres out, from where it stays at four feet right to the bank.

● *(Inset overleaf) The author with a big weight of carp taken on a light leger rig. These are the sort of fish that ensure sell-outs on well-stocked lakes*

● *(Overleaf) You can't judge an angler's skill by the amount of tackle he uses. Top canal man Dave Berrow believes in setting up only what he needs*

● *Who says pole fishing only catches tiddlers? This fine River Nene bream fell to a well-presented caster offered on a short-line pole rig*

• *The man you have to beat to win on the canals! Dave Berrow, the 1990/91 season Kamasan Matchman of the Year, with the sort of canal catch that earned him the title*

• *It's easy to smile when you're catching. Dave Howl went on to win this* Angling Times/Ruddles League Championship *on the Twyford Farm length of the Warwickshire Avon*

Beyond the 10 metre line is where the float rod is going to be fished and this is the one with the secret weapon – the Avon float – carrying an incredible 14BB! That sounds a big load and, considering it is being fished at a range of some 12 metres, seems a bit silly. But it works, and any bleak fast enough to take a bait on this outfit is going to get a severe case of the bends as it is pulled downwards.

The beauty of these floats is that if they are shotted with the traditional big bulk of a string of BBs they will actually pick up any flow close to the river bed and run down against an upstream wind at exactly the right speed.

Variations that work include a piece of tungsten tubing held in place either with shot or with a cocktail-stick wedge. An olivette is fine too, but for this match it is going to be the ready-made-up outfit stored on a pole winder. It carries 14BB and a tell-tale number 6. A 6 sounds big but that can even be increased to a 4 without trouble. The bigger this shot, the better the bites. And, oddly, the fish don't seem put off by it.

Having fished the water a lot I knew it would be around thirteen feet deep so my rig is made up on a piece of 2.6lb line some ten feet long. Hook length is 1.1lb to a 22 hook.

By making the rig short the knot will be beneath the float and is less likely to be broken on the strike. It also means it doesn't get caught in the tip ring.

This one could be plumbed up as normal, but because of the even bottom I'll set it at a few inches short of the full length of my 13 foot rod. I prefer a 13 footer but if you can cope with a 14 foot model then it would be a good choice under these conditions.

A few runs through sort out the exact depth as 13 feet and the tackle is set to trip bottom at 12 metre range.

Next comes the bait. Groundbait is brown crumb to which a bag of red additive has been added. Around 4lb of dry has been mixed and riddled at home and carried to the water in a plastic bag. There's a further 3lb of dry held back as reserve.

A tip here to cope with the high bank is always to carry a sponge or spare piece of towel which can then be used to soak up water for mixing extra bait. Tie it to a piece of string attached to the keepnet stick and leave it hanging in the water.

For adding to the cereal there is a pint of casters, a little hemp and two and a half pints of red squatts. Hookbait is going to be red maggot with a few bronze

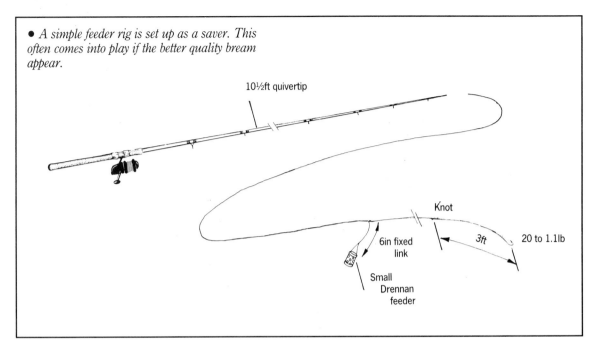

- *A simple feeder rig is set up as a saver. This often comes into play if the better quality bream appear.*

10½ft quivertip

Knot

6in fixed link

3ft

20 to 1.1lb

Small Drennan feeder

ones as a change bait, along with some small red worms.

Everything is simple and with that Avon float the fishing can be so easy it seems unreal.

Final few minutes are ticking away to the start. A handful of squatts, a few casters and some hemp all go into one corner of the cereal bowl and three good balls are prepared, each mixed fairly solidly to get them down through that deep water before breaking up.

The whistle goes and the three balls go in straight away just a metre downstream of the peg. On goes a red maggot and we're fishing. The bright orange of the Avon float shows up well against the dark tree cover and within a matter of two metres it slides away positively. No rush to strike but the bite is hit in an upwards direction to give the most direct route through to the hook. A fish is on, but despite that terrific bite the result is a tiny roach no more than three inches long.

In goes another ball of cereal and the process is repeated. Another two small roach follow on consecutive casts. The tackle is going through smoothly so an extra couple of inches are added to the depth and as if by magic the size of fish immediately doubles.

At the upstream peg a waggler is constantly being cast some three-quarters of the way across but judging by the amount of casting – and a few curses –

the bleak are doing their stuff. It wouldn't be so bad, but they are so small!

Feeding is continued every other cast but with the size of groundbait ball reduced slightly to something about egg-sized.

So far so good. The roach are getting bigger and a few close to 6oz have fallen to the red maggot. Time to slip on a caster and go for a bigger one still. A run through produces nothing but next time down a chub is hooked right at the end of the swim. It's one of those on the 1lb mark that I mentioned in the match plan. The same line has been fished for close to an hour now and it's getting harder all the time. There's maybe 2lb in the net and that chub has pushed it over 3lb. Things are on target for a four-hour 14lb or so.

Downstream the angler is feeding hemp on the inside but so far has caught only a few small roach. He might be a danger later on but the amount of bait going into my swim is likely to take the edge off seed fishing. It's a bait that seems to work best when there is no other feed going in.

In an attempt to keep up the catch rate the bait has been changed back to a red maggot, and this time the tackle is cast a yard lower down than normal and held back as it reaches the extreme end of the swim. Down goes the float and this time it's not a roach but a bream of maybe 1½lb that glides over the landing net. Now

Beating the bleak

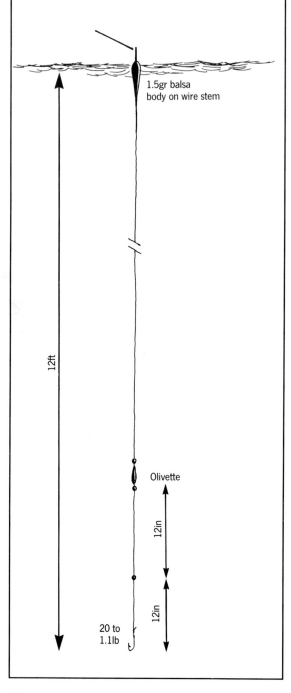

• *A hefty No 5 elastic will cope should the bream show. An olivette is used to get the bait down as quickly as possible. By having 5 to 6ft of line above the float a lot of water can be covered.*

1.5gr balsa
body on wire stem

12ft

Olivette

12in

12in

20 to
1.1lb

we're cruising. An extra three inches on the depth and the same tactic is repeated, but this time a gudgeon is the result. Either the gudgeon are moving to the fair amount of feed that is now down, or there are a few bream stirring up the bottom and drawing them in.

Give it another few minutes to see what pattern forms. If the skimmers or bream come, then fine. If not, it may be that a change is needed.

The catch rate has slowed right down so maybe going so much overdepth has not been a good idea. Off come the three inches added earlier, along with three more to try a run through clear of the bottom. A point here is that before starting to move anything around I'd made a careful note of exactly where the tackle was set, to give a true depth. This was done by winding the float right to the tip ring and noting the hook position on the butt.

Running through off the bottom has brought some more small roach and a few tiny skimmers, but I've a feeling there are better fish to catch. So up the bank goes the float rod and the block-end feeder is given a try. A bronze maggot and a caster go on the hook and the rig is dropped mid-way down the swim. I'll give this method ten minutes and then switch back to the float if it fails.

Two minutes seems like ages but eventually the tip indicates a quick knock, possibly a roach. If I had struck at it, chances are I'd have missed by miles. I do nothing and the tip goes again, this time more positively and a bream is on. Another pound goes in the net so that change has paid off. Bait is again caster and maggot, but nothing happens, so off they come in favour of a worm. Result is another bream, this time a skimmer of maybe 8oz but it all helps.

The quivertip and feeder are getting a few fish but not as many as I'd have liked, so it is now a case of fishing the match through by alternating to catch whatever I can. So far the pole hasn't been given an airing, but with an hour left on the clock it might be worth a go and if nothing else it will rest the main feed line.

The hook is a 20 and maybe that's too big considering how hard the main attack has become but it's worth a run through with a bronze maggot to see what happens. Straight away a roach – but not a big one and the bite was a poor affair. Off comes the hook and a 22 goes on in its place. The olivette is not working as well as that big string of BB shots. A bleak or two have managed to upset the rhythm but most of

144

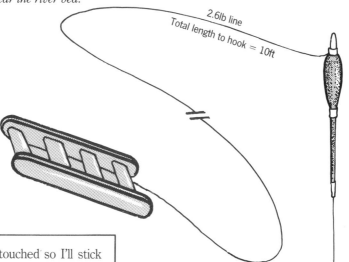

● *A crowquill Avon float rig. Three rubbers keep the line close to its contours and the whole outfit is stored on a large pole rig winder. The long string of BB shots carry the tackle along at the same pace as any flow that may be present near the river bed.*

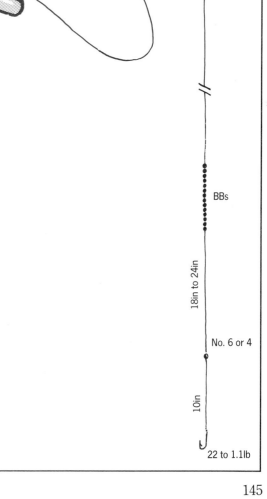

2.6lb line
Total length to hook = 10ft

BBs

18in to 24in

No. 6 or 4

10in

22 to 1.1lb

the time the rig has got down untouched so I'll stick with it for a while, running the bait along the edge of the main feed line.

The pole is being worked so that the bait moves down a few inches and is then held still again. On the check bites produce some roach and a few skimmers, but still the better-quality roach have not shown as I'd expected. Maybe it is one of those days when they aren't having it no matter how you present the bait. The river does look a little off its best and maybe would benefit from a good flush through, then the Avon and a lot of feed would really come into their own.

A few fish on the pole but now it's time to finish off on the starting method. Overall the Avon has made up the bulk of the weight, except for those bonus bream on the feeder.

Something that has shown up is how the fish respond to feed. Every time a ball has gone in there's been a run of three or four bites shortly afterwards. That suggests the feeding pattern should be continued right to the end.

There have been a few boats through in the last hour, which has also upset the form book a bit and no doubt stirred up some of the feed slightly. So the tail end of the swim is going to be fished out now and anything that shows will be taken as a bonus to nudge the total into double figures. If those big bream have

Beating the bleak

• *As an alternative to a string of* BB *shots a piece of tungsten tubing can be used. Stop it in place with shot top and bottom or a cocktail stick down the bore.*

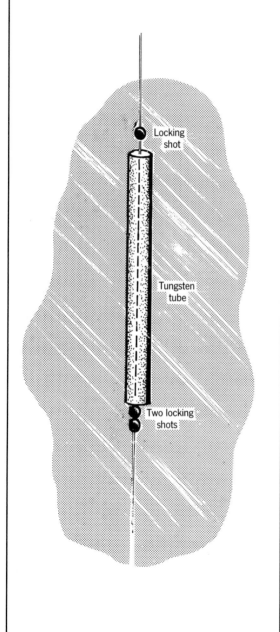

Locking shot

Tungsten tube

Two locking shots

shown at the top end of the match it will only take three of them to beat my collection of odds and ends, but it has been a case of making the best of an average swim.

The waggler, as expected, hasn't performed too well either. The angler nearby gave it up after two hours and has spent the rest of the time messing about with a leger. He started too carefully too. The loose feed he fired in with a catapult was wasted on the bleak, and all he collected on the leger was a sprinkling of roach, a few gudgeon, three eels and a perch, totalling maybe 3lb at best. The seed used at the other side never got in on the act and he finished off with a bleaking stint just to pass the time and maybe earn a few championship points.

The scales edge over the 11lb mark so maybe we haven't done so badly. But looking back on the day, maybe the opening feed should have been cut to just two balls and then the remaining feed gone in as smaller pieces but more frequently. Some hemp might also have been introduced loose with a catapult to help hold the better roach in one spot.

Because fish have come in spasms I feel that they were moving around a lot and never really settled to feed seriously. If they had stopped totally it might have been a case of overfeeding being the cause, or, more likely, one of the many pike in the section of river had moved in. If that happens then it often spells trouble in a big way and unless you are lucky enough to have it hang on to a fish long enough to be netted it might mean a complete change of tactics.

A marauding pike leaves few options, but one is to fish right away from it, casting to the end of the swim and taking whatever you can. The problem then, of course, is getting a hooked fish out without attracting the attention of the predator.

Alternatively, go for the leger and sit it out for a bream too big for the pike to worry. Either way it will be hard work to get the swim going again at full steam.

Again, on reflection, perhaps a few pleasure stints on the venue might have paid off by giving a good indication of the river's true form. I had gone to the match expecting too much.

13

Carp on the pole

The recent increase in the number of lakes stocked with small carp has brought a new dimension to match angling and the good all-rounder is now required to master the technique of catching these hard fighters in large quantities and at considerable speed.

Although winning weights on these types of waters can be as high as 60lb and even into three figures, it is not always easy. Carp learn quickly and in any case fight hard. Only those anglers with everything right, both in tackle and mental approach, will win.

Biggest danger of all is getting obsessed with this style of fishing. Yes, it's great fun to crunch out a big weight of fish maybe topping 5lb a time, but it will do little to improve your general match fishing. So fish these waters with the idea that they are a treat to be enjoyed once in a while and no more.

The match this week is on a typical privately owned fishery, a lake housing around sixty-five pegs, all of which will be taken on match day as usual.

During the early months of the season weights well over 100lb have been needed to win but the pattern usually shows a drop-off from mid-September to around 60lb and then, as the water cools, weights again drop to nearer 20lb.

At present the lake is still in good form and maybe 70lb is a fair assessment of what it will take to win. Backing weights too will be close, maybe four over 50lb, with perhaps only a single fish making the difference between each one and the next.

During the real height of the action here it is possible to catch these fish on really crude tackle. Lines of 6lb and hook lengths of 5lb to a size 10 are not out of order. But today it isn't going to be that simple. The water is being fished a lot and regular matches have taken the edge off it just a little, so the approach will need tempering a shade too.

Fishing these sort of events means a lot of bait. Maggots are the main source and a gallon is not going

over the top. Casters catch fish, but they take longer to bait up and so any advantage they may have is soon lost. There's a ban on coloured maggots and also on cereal groundbaits, so it's going to be plain white hookers and three pints of hemp. As change baits, a small can of sweetcorn, a few cubes of luncheon meat and a ball of meat paste made from sausage meat and dry groundbait will be taken along. Practice has been impossible because the water is only let to matches and this is the first one for which I've managed to get a ticket. My plan is based upon a walk along the bank the previous weekend to watch a match, along with what has been picked up by talking to reliable sources who have fished the water several times.

It seems the lake is always thickly coloured due to the number of fish it holds. They come on quickly once the feed starts going in, but because groundbait is banned they tend to come up off the bottom and are often caught as close as eighteen inches to the surface.

Fish of 5lb are common but there are large numbers in the 1lb to 3lb bracket. I've been warned to watch out too for the big ones that go into double figures. The only other fish present are tench of a few ounces up to 2lb or so and a big head of small roach and rudd.

It seems from past results that all but the corner pegs can produce good weights. In the corners fish tend to dry up well before the end of the match, simply because these pegs offer only a limited amount of water in front of the unfortunate anglers who draw them. The real hotspot is along the dam-wall end of the lake where there's plenty of weed cover.

The wind plays an important role too, and, as so often happens on stillwaters, if its direction has been constant for a few days then the favourites draw with it in their faces.

The maggots have been given a good clean-up and will be riddled off again at the waterside, leaving only

the minimum of maize in them. This will help reduce the chance of maize blowing back into my face should I be lucky enough to draw that exposed windward bank.

Prior to the match the pole has been rigged for crunching. The usual elastic has been replaced with some really heavy stuff, around number 8. It's been given a good going over with lubricant too. Ideally, for this sort of fishing it's a good plan to have a pole with the first few sections telescopic rather than take-apart, just as a precaution against having the top sections pulled out by a big fish. My pole doesn't have that sort of joints so it will be a case of using extra care. Of course this is no place for ultra-light poles. It needs a weapon that can stand up to a lot of heavy work because a certain amount of bullying is going to be done in order to build a winning weight.

Main attack will come from the pole, but a waggler and a straight leger will also be set up just in case something goes wrong – and as a means of giving the shoal a rest if it gets a bit fickle.

That's the plan: nothing fancy, just the confidence to take on these fish with a pole.

The draw has been reasonably kind. The gentle wind is blowing into the bank, which is favourable in that it has put a slight ripple on the water. Over the other side it is completely sheltered and the water is like a mirror so that anglers will need to be careful not to scare the fish while getting them settled into feeding.

Rig for the pole is 3½lb main line with a 16 hook to 2¾lb bottom. Hook pattern is a flat-forged barbless: barbless because the fishery rules ban all forms of barbs, even micros.

Float is a small piece of balsa with a flat top, and a short needle as a stem. It's locked on the line bottom only, with its total load of four number 4s and two 10s. The two 10s are put on last so that they can be brought down the line should a faster drop be needed.

Water depth is about five feet and the total rig length four metres. The fairly long line above the float will help keep the float still if the wind gets up, and also give a bit of scope so that the swim can be searched better.

• A Mallory Park carp. This is the sort of fish that provides some spectacular action for the match angler who is prepared to change tactics and beef up his tackle. This one was caught while testing a new pole. It did that well and also put the elastic through its paces

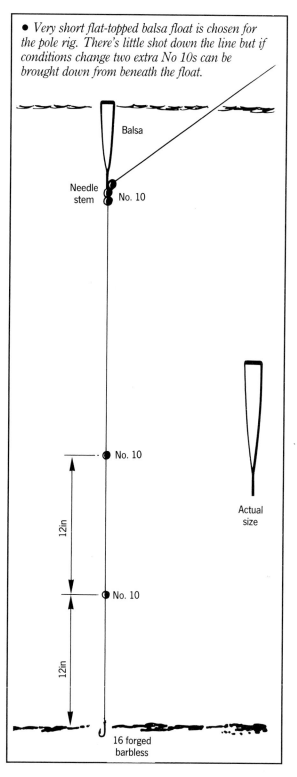

• Very short flat-topped balsa float is chosen for the pole rig. There's little shot down the line but if conditions change two extra No 10s can be brought down from beneath the float.

Balsa

Needle stem   No. 10

No. 10

12in

No. 10

12in

Actual size

16 forged barbless

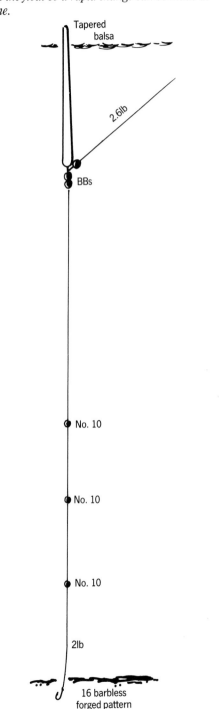

• *A carp-crunching waggler rig. An adaptor is used on the float so a rapid change can be made at any time.*

Tapered balsa

2.6lb

BBs

No. 10

No. 10

No. 10

2lb

16 barbless forged pattern

The float is a tapered balsa waggler taking 3BB and three 10s, the BBs used as lock shot and the 10s spaced down the line. The float is used with an adaptor so a rapid change can be made if required. Line on this one is a new 2.6lb and the hook a forged 16 to 2lb.

The leger is a real last-ditch standby to get a bonus fish, and with this in mind it's a 3SSG link to a 4½lb line direct to a 10 hook. The link is a free-running one stopped by a small shot so that the hook tail can be varied.

The rod is a heavy feeder model but the quivertip isn't going to be used as an indicator. The rod will be set in a rest so that it points straight at the lead. Having cast and wound up to the bomb in the usual way, a foot or so of line can be pulled off the reel and

• *A heavy feeder rod is used for legering on these carp waters. No bite indicator is used on the rod, and instead the tip points straight at the bait and a bobbin made from a piece of paste is used just in front of the reel. Make certain line can pass easily through the rod rest.*

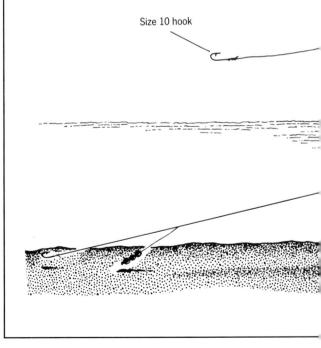

Size 10 hook

used to set a small piece of the meat paste as a butt indicator. It sounds crude, but with this simple idea there is nothing that can go wrong, and it gives the fish a chance to take the bait without feeling any undue resistance.

Setting out the other gear is done with speed in mind but the peg is tidied up so that it is uncluttered. The box is nice and level, bait easy to reach, spare hooks are sorted and laid inside their wallet where they can be got at quickly.

Two landing nets have been assembled: the usual one which will cater for most fish and a larger one just in case one of those doubles shows up. The keepnet is set so that a fish can be rolled from the landing net straight into the mouth without fear of its slipping

back. A dropped fish here can mean the loss of 5lb or more. It's worth staking the keepnet out too, so that there's no chance of it collapsing on the fish.

All set up, now time to study the peg. The water is like coffee so there must be fish in the area. Twenty metres of fairly clear water are between the bank and a solid bed of lilies that looks thick enough to walk on and covers most of the lake's centre area. Nine metres out there are two other patches of lilies, one three metres to the left, the other a bed three metres across, again at nine metres range and three metres to the right, giving a clear channel six metres wide straight out to the main bed.

Ideally the bigger patch to the left will be where the bulk of the carp will come from, but the right-hand

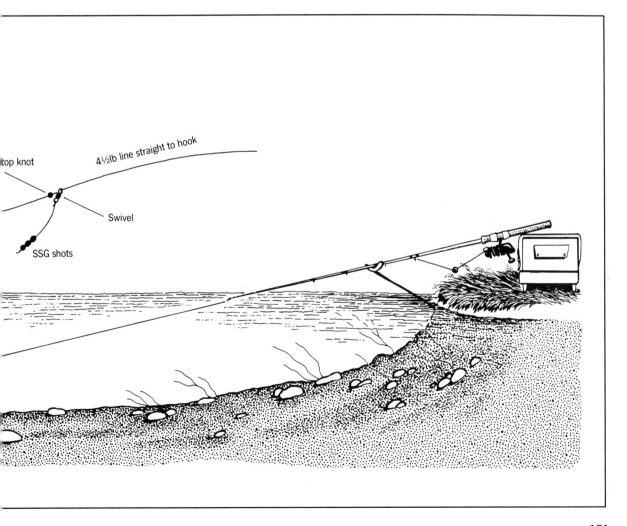

top knot

4½lb line straight to hook

Swivel

SSG shots

Carp on the pole

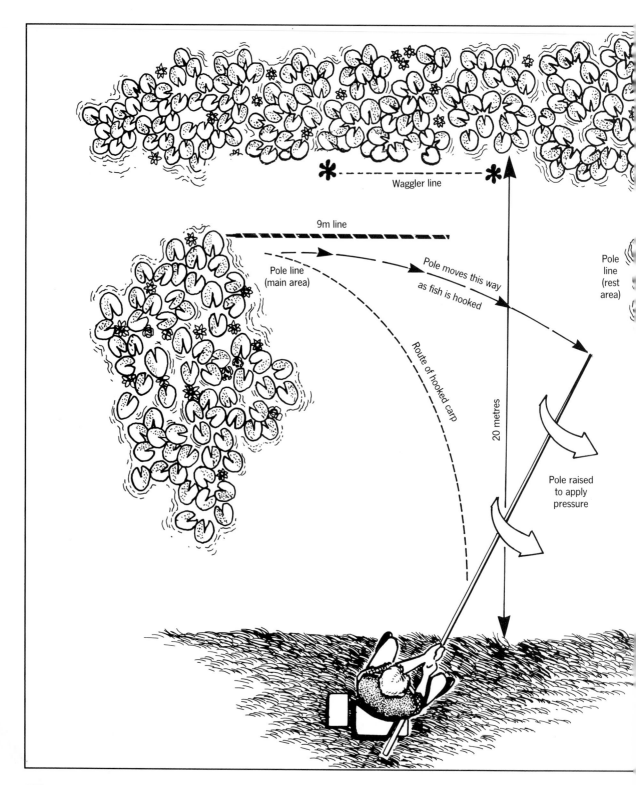

Waggler line

9m line

Pole line
(main area)

Pole moves this way

as fish is hooked

Pole line
(rest area)

Route of hooked carp

20 metres

Pole raised
to apply
pressure

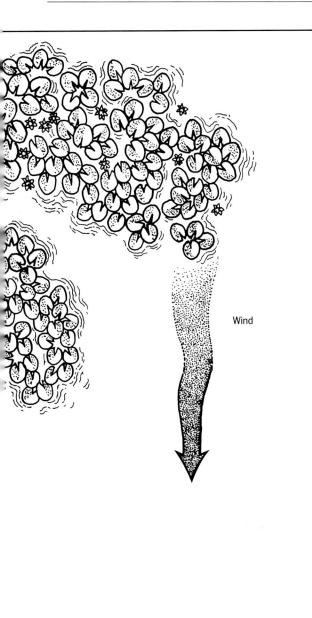

Wind

• *The swim is full of weed ... and fish. Three areas are selected so that each can be rested in turn. Note the direction in which a hooked carp is going to be steered towards the net.*

patch will serve as a good reserve area while the main swim is rested. Straight out to the main bed offers the third option, where waggler and bomb come into play.

A quick plumbing with the pole shows the expected depth at the edge of the two weed-patches, and the waggler suggests there is little difference further out. So the waggler is set to fish just on the bottom and the pole a couple of inches off it, using the two 10s spread down the line until the fish move up for the falling bait.

Time! In goes all sorts of tackle around the lake but first priority is to introduce some feed. Out go a couple of dozen maggots by hand but they fall well short of the nine-metre mark. The breeze has been underestimated so a catapult is going to be needed. That really was an oversight but maybe no harm has been done this time. Two dozen other maggots go in to the left and the same number to the right. A third pouch goes to the weeds at 20 metres. A pouch of hemp to each follows straight away. This seed bait will get fish rooting around, and might pay off as a holding bait later on.

The 16 hook on the pole takes two big hook maggots easily and the rig is pushed out to the left-hand edge of the weeds. Almost as if over-shotted it vanishes from view, and the pole is lifted into a fish that powers straight for cover and is lost. Mistake two, underestimating the opposition. Things aren't going well, so feed straight away to the area where the fish was hooked and hope no long-term damage has been done.

The rebaited hook follows the loose feed and again hardly settles before sliding away. This time I'm ready and lift the pole smartly upwards and slightly to the right. Straight away the elastic takes control and, while not giving too freely, still comes out close to a metre from the tip bush.

By keeping a good angle between the pole tip and the elastic, maximum pressure is being applied as the pole is fed backwards over the left leg. The pole is kept at an angle of about 30 degrees to the water and moved in an arc so that the fish is steered away from weeds and other fish in the feeding area. Once in front of me, the pole is unshipped and the remaining sections moved into a vertical position as the carp is netted. Close on 3lb is not a bad starter, but it is by no means the only one already in the net. All around the lake there are sounds of excited voices and splashing fish.

Now is the time to stay cool: remember to feed both

near weed-beds, and, as soon as time permits, get a little more out to the far swim.

Bubbles suggest that a lot of fish are milling around, and there are signs of the weeds moving as more carp make their way to the feed. So far, despite that shaky start, the signs are good.

Two missed bites and then a small roach is hooked, suggesting there could be a problem looming if too many of those move in. A good pouch of maybe forty maggots might feed them off but if the carp get going they should push the other species out of the way.

Another carp is hooked but it's smaller than the first and soon slips the barbless hook. Often the small ones twist their way off soon after striking, but with fish of a decent size this problem is less likely so I'm not going to worry – there's nothing that can be done.

Again the float goes straight away as it hits the water. Another carp of 3lb gets the same treatment as the first and after netting is unhooked. By gripping it with the landing-net mesh it can be held still and then rolled straight into the keepnet mouth.

Feed rate now needs to be kept up, and in order to capitalise on fish moving up in the water the 10s are pushed up to the float, which has been shallowed down to fish at two feet deep.

Straight away a fish takes, but this time a smaller one of 8oz or so. That will need watching. If the size stays low it will mean switching back to the original set-up. Sometimes the bigger fish don't come up, but I've a feeling they will today. While I'm making the adjustments a few grains of sweetcorn are fired to the waggler line and, just for good measure, a few to the main catching area to hold any big fish that may be lurking.

The wind has dropped a bit and it is now just possible to get bait to the nine-metre mark without trouble. A dozen maggots go in and the float follows. Down it goes again, and this time the fish continues to move away from the pressure of the elastic. The pole is raised to full height and the steep angle applies more pressure, causing the fish to turn for the open water. The elastic is keeping pressure on but two extra joints of the pole have to go on before any real impression is made. Thankfully the first rush has slowed and gradually the fish is turned carefully but positively back towards the bank. Danger time will be when it comes between the two weed-patches, so the pole is kept high as the extra joints come off. That panic over, the next break-down is made and the fish netted without

more trouble. Close to 6lb, but the commotion may have unsettled the peg for a while.

To settle everything down, feed again with both hemp and maggots, and for a change try the right-hand weeds after throwing a few maggots there too.

Nothing, but five fish for 12½lb in thirty minutes is looking good enough. Keep this up and 60lb for five hours is still on, and there's two-thirds of the swim still untouched. The breather has calmed my nerves, and hopefully the swim too. Another bite, and a carp, this time a small mirror, breaks the spell and suggests the smaller weed-patch can produce more.

Feed both areas again and catch a couple more small carp from the right before switching back to the left where the size immediately increases again to over 2lb. It certainly seems as if the quality fish prefer the extra cover provided by the mass of weed.

Another big fish is lost, and on checking the hook shows that the bend has been straightened slightly. No risks, off it comes and a new one goes on, this time a 14. A bite follows but it's a little tench of 6oz. That took only seconds to land on this gear but ten blank minutes follow; obviously they don't like a big hook. But before changing back to a 16 it's worth slipping on a piece of sweetcorn just to see what's happening. Two minutes and nothing. No more time to waste, off comes the hook in favour of a 16 and two maggots. The secret is to keep catching. Waste too much time and it is hard to make up when someone is catching fish of 3lb or more.

While all this hectic sport has been going on it's easy to get blinkered, so remember to keep an eye on what others are catching. If you are holding your own, carry on. If not, then look for an alternative to get you back in touch. It may be that a specimen-hunter approach with the leger and a big bait is called for; or perhaps just step up the feed rate and draw fish in from the next pegs. There are no hard and fast rules, but if in doubt do something rather than just sit it out and get further behind.

For a time there was a run of carp to the shallow rig but they seem to have stopped feeding. Maybe the

---

● *You need nerve to hit and stop a hard-fighting carp on match tackle. With the pole you are right over your fish as soon as it's hooked and usually they are landed quickly. With running tackle, like this light leger outfit, you must keep the pressure on and the rod angle constant*

hemp has pulled them down deeper. The rig is changed back to fish at five feet with the 10s spaced again at a foot and two feet from the hook.

Once again it works like magic, and three tench and two nice carp come in the space of eight casts. Then a big one is hooked and lost in the weed and all goes quiet again. This time it looks a little more serious as the anglers either side are struggling too. Time to change again.

Chances are the fish were getting a bit spooky and that lost carp was the final straw. So now the waggler must come into play, casting to within a couple of feet of the big weed-bank at 20 metres. Before casting, a pouch of two dozen maggots goes in, and at the same time both the inside lines get topped up too.

Soon bites and fish are coming again from the fresh area and because the size is averaging less than 1lb they can be hustled a bit to keep them away from the shoal and the weed. It seems that if you hook these carp and start winding they come in better than when they are given thinking-time. A couple have swum straight into the net and have taken a matter of seconds to land. This operation has been a continuous strike-and-wind movement, keeping a constant pressure to help stop them twisting their way off that barbless hook.

A good hour on the waggler has really upset the original pole plan, but it is a good example of being prepared to rethink a match as it develops. The pole wins a lot of matches on this water, but like any other it can go off and a change of approach will pay handsomely.

But now the two anglers on either side have started fishing the same waggler line as me and bites are again slowing down, possibly because the fish in my peg are being pulled away. Stepping up the feed is holding a few, but some missed bites suggest they are now less keen to have a go.

Change again, back to the original pole plan and the fish are back. Smaller they may be than at the start, but, still averaging a pound, they are building my weight nicely and can be landed quickly. What needs to be done now is to keep feeding the far waggler line to

hold some fish away from the other anglers, while concentrating on the pole for as long as the peg will keep going. There's a bit less than an hour to go and these smaller carp and tench seem to be happier now than at the start. Perhaps that lost big fish was the one bossing its way through the swim and not giving the others a chance to settle into feeding.

Something I did learn on this type of water is: never, ever, leave your tackle in the water for a moment unattended. I once saw a match rod dragged from a rest and pulled right across a lake by a carp. The angler concerned could only stand and watch in horror as he tried to spend a penny behind a tree. Apart from the obvious danger of losing tackle it also means a good peg can be ruined by a fish charging through a feeding shoal and taking them with it.

As the minutes tick away the pole continues to take a few fish, some right down to 4oz in size, which suggests that the quality carp have had enough and all that's being caught now are those fish that couldn't get a look in earlier. Still, at this stage those extra few ounces may well be vital, so fish on until the end.

At these matches there is always a certain amount of bankside pushing and shoving as anglers follow the scales along, so it's best to get as much tackle away as quickly as possible, even if it means spending time at home later to sort out the mess. A pole left on the bank is going to get stepped on so make the best use of the time between now and the scales' arrival.

The keepnet has perhaps 60lb plus in it, so be kind to both the net and its contents by lifting it carefully, getting someone to give you a lift if you think it will help. Lift carefully and slowly, and if you have to handle individual fish – as you would with the larger ones – take care not to drop them. The landing net is a good means of transferring them back to the water rather than trying to hold them in your hands.

Keep an eye on the scales too. It wouldn't be the first time a scaleman has been found to be a poor mathematician who can't add up. Check each weight yourself and then tot up multiple weights to be sure you get what's due.

14

Winning with eels

It's a sad fact of match-fishing life that many of the once-great competition rivers such as the Witham, Welland, Nene and Fen Drains have declined to the point where eels, once regarded as pests, are now often match winners.

On waters like the North Bank of the Nene near Peterborough, the eel is often the main summer target. Weights well into double figures are possible and the bonus is that they are often more predictable and evenly spread than the roach and skimmer bream that once dominated Nene results.

But catching eels fast is not easy. It takes a bit of thought, a lot of practice and a considerable amount of preparation.

For a start, the number of hooks required means a couple of evenings spent tying up perhaps four dozen or more barbless 22s to 1.1lb bottoms, plus a few to 1.7lb just in case the average size is something special. Although barbless hooks are not the normal pattern for long-pole and short-line fishing an exception is made for eel fishing, simply because as many as possible need to be caught without losing a hook.

A good pattern is one that can withstand a bit of stick. The last thing you need is a fine wire one that continually straightens. Go for a fairly long shank too, so that unhooking is quick and easy.

The match to be fished is a five-hour one and the venue is a typical match water, somewhat featureless and, because of low water levels caused by a spell of warm weather, with very little flow.

So having tied up those hooks a few rigs need to be prepared. The entire match will be fished with a pole, probably at 10 or 11 metres.

Main line will be 2.6lb and the floats varying in size from 0.5g to about 1g. There's nothing particularly fancy needed, except to make sure there is a good choice of bright-tipped floats in a range of sizes to meet the expected conditions.

The venue to be fished is so slow that a stillwater pattern can be used. A wire stem gives stability, and because few fish are likely to take on the drop there is no point in going for a cane stem.

If there was more flow then a balsa body with the bulk high up its length would enable the tackle to be held back. But no matter which pattern is the final choice, it must have a bristle tip with a bright colour that can be seen when beneath the surface.

The reason for this is that a lot of bites may well pull the float right under but striking will be delayed in order to let the eel get hold of the bait fully.

At 11 metres the depth is around eight feet and the rigs will be made up to give a five-metre breakdown point. Loading is by an olivette, except for a couple of small drop shots which are spread between hook and olivette; the lowest one, a number 10 or 8 goes a foot from the hook. There's another foot to the second shot and then fifteen inches to the olivette. A bunch of small shots can be used as an alternative to the olivette but I prefer the olivette, for no other reason than neatness.

The total length of rig is five metres, which because the float is to be fished at about 8½ feet leaves a good length between it and the tip. This ensures that any movement of the pole caused by wind will not upset the float and, ultimately, presentation.

If conditions are particularly bad and the wind is such that the pole cannot be held still enough, then a large shot – even as large as an AAA – can be pinched to the line mid-way between float and pole tip. By holding this shot out of the water an angle will be formed in the line between float and hook to act as a buffer. If this fails, then take the equivalent of a number 8 or 6 off the main shotting pattern and use it as a backshot mid-way between the float and the tip. Fish in the normal manner but with the pole tip pushed beneath the surface. The backshot will then act as a buffer to steady the effect the movement has on the float.

Final part of the pole set-up is the elastic. It must be

Winning with eels

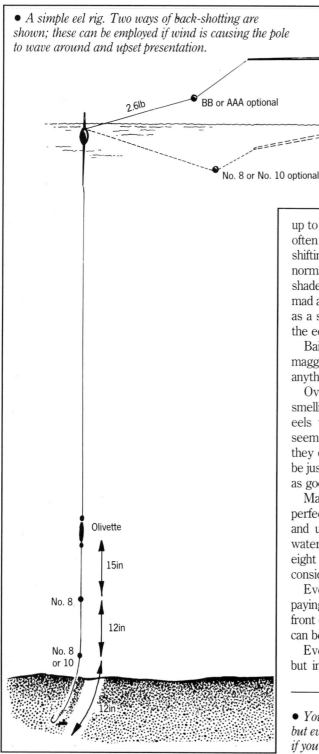

● *A simple eel rig. Two ways of back-shotting are shown; these can be employed if wind is causing the pole to wave around and upset presentation.*

2.6lb

BB or AAA optional

No. 8 or No. 10 optional

Olivette

15in

No. 8

12in

No. 8 or 10

12in

up to the job of stopping these tough little fish that can often charge off quickly or dig in and take a bit of shifting off the bottom. For this reason the more normal number 4 elastic is stepped up to a 5 and set a shade tighter than usual. Having said that, don't go mad and rig it so that it is too powerful. It must still act as a shock absorber and not simply rip the hook from the eel.

Bait is straightforward, just four pints of white maggots, cleaned up as usual. No groundbait or anything else that might distract from the main plan.

Over the seasons I have tried all sorts of foul-smelling additives on my maggots in the hope that the eels will come to the swim very quickly. Fish oils seemed the obvious choice but I cannot honestly claim they did me any good. So for this match it is going to be just good fresh maggots – which probably smell just as good to the eels as anything extra we might add.

Match morning proves to be a dull but warm day, perfect for eel fishing in fact. Eels don't like bright light and under such conditions will head for the deeper water. Today they should be at that 10 metre mark in eight feet of water, which has a good colour considering the lack of flow.

Everything is set up in the normal efficient manner paying special attention to the keepnet. Get it right in front of you, but high enough so that the actual netting can be used to grip any eels that need unhooking.

Every good match angler checks his nets regularly but in the case of eel fishing it is a vital part of the

● *You'll be lucky to catch eels of this stamp on the pole, but even the smaller ones can be built into a good weight if you get them going*

• *Pieces of sticky tape are attached to the pole to show correct depth settings for fishing at both planned fishing ranges.*

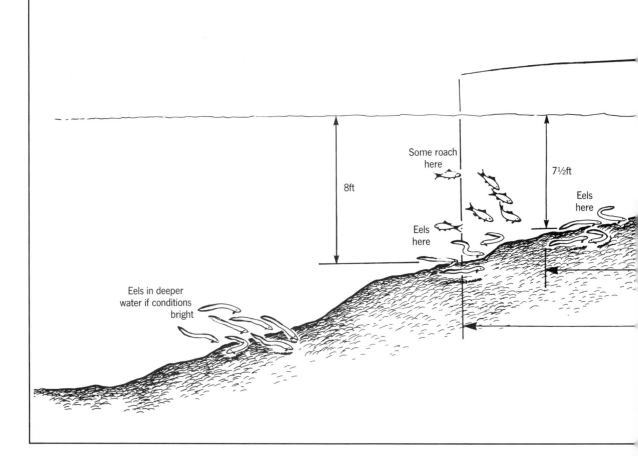

• *Plumbing shows the swim contours vary by 6in between the 8 and 10m range. If conditions are bright eels will usually move into the deeper water.*

preparation. Even the smallest damage to a keepnet is sure to result in eels escaping. A torn landing net is also going to cause trouble if an eel gets its tail through it. Search carefully and sew up any damage with a length of cobbler's thread.

Conditions are good and a 0.5g float is all that is going to be needed. These eels don't like heavy gear and will not drag around a float that offers a lot of resistance. Perhaps they are getting more crafty through being caught more often as the number of anglers fishing for them increases.

Plumbing shows the depth is, as thought, eight feet,

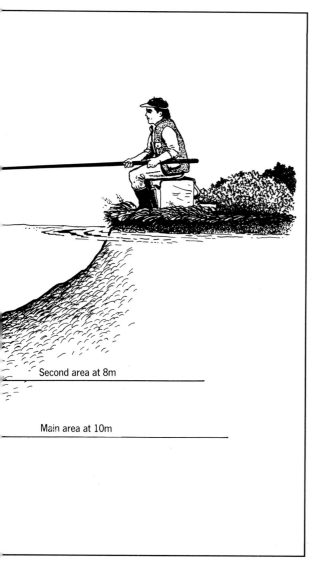

Second area at 8m

Main area at 10m

so the rig is set to fish six inches overdepth, with the tell-tale shot well off the bottom. Having got the depth set, mark it accurately on the pole with a piece of sticky tape. Do this by slipping the hook over the end of the five-metre joint and marking the float's position. Now come in to eight metres and plumb again. Here it is just six inches shallower and a second piece of tape goes on the pole that much below the first. Re-set to the deeper setting and get everything else ready for action.

Eels often take a little time to come to the bait so it may be worthwhile setting up a waggler rod, or any other method that might put a pound or so in the net during the initial period before they arrive.

In the case of this venue it is going to be a second pole-rig set with styls, to fish on the drop for the small roach which can usually be caught for a short time at 10 metres but dry up after perhaps half an hour.

Real secret of successful eel fishing is feeding correctly and being able to hit what can at times be difficult bites.

Two areas are to be fed, one at 10 metres and a second at 8. Both will get a handful of maggots as the whistle goes.

The countdown begins and the roach tackle is ready. Off we go and in goes the bait at both pre-plumbed distances. The styls rig is baited with the same white maggot and soon brings a result – a roach of maybe an ounce. Keep going on this and three more roach of the same size go into the net within fifteen minutes. But this isn't going to win anything, it's just a fill-in method. With that in mind the eel rig is tried at 10 metres, but after five minutes nothing has happened. In go another two dozen maggots at each line and the waiting begins.

Another five minutes and the orange bristle dives away. First reaction is to strike but to do so would be chancing a missed eel. Instead the orange tip can be seen still going down. Count to three and strike. The first eel is hooked and the pole quickly pushed backwards, unshipped and raised to swing in the eel. It's a fish of perhaps 2oz but at least it shows they are going to feed.

Get back in quickly but now go easy on the feeding. Try ten maggots to the 10 metre line every cast, with just half that number going to the nearer mark every third cast.

While eels continue to show the feed rate can be kept down, but if they slow it may mean they have

● *Efficient eel fishing means a well-planned layout of equipment. Get everything close to hand and the keepnet high enough so the netting can be used to hold the eels as they are unhooked*

moved off or lost interest and need to be pulled back by increasing the number of maggots going in.

Bites continue to bury the float and once or twice they have been missed through striking too quickly. Those that have been connected with have been eels to 4oz, at which stage they have been netted.

Another 4oz eel is hooked, the pole broken down and the eel pulled towards the net in a firm but smooth fashion. Safely in the net, slide the handle across the knee and grab the eel from outside the net, using the mesh to give a firm hold. The hook this time is clearly visible and can be easily removed with the fingers. Still holding the eel with the net, tip it straight into the keepnet.

Next time in the performance is repeated, but this time the hook is well down the eel. Don't poke around with a disgorger for to do so will probably damage both hook and eel. It is far kinder – and quicker – to break the hook length close to the eel's mouth and tie on one of those you tied earlier!

Now this may sound a bit unkind to the eel but in fact it is the safest means of dealing with any that are deeply hooked. Eels quickly shed the hook left in them

and appear to be none the worse for the experience.

This landing-net technique sounds slow but it is one way of stopping the eel tying itself in knots and probably breaking the rig. Swinging them in is fine as long as they can be dealt with quickly, but give them a few seconds too long and they flick their tails over and leave you with a nasty mess to sort out.

The 10 metre line is performing well so the feed rate is kept down. Now only every other cast is being fed, and with no more than ten maggots. A few eels have come to hand well and dropped straight off at the keepnet mouth, saving a lot of handling time. But this one is different and will need unhooking. Instead of using the landing net it is swung straight inside the keepnet mouth and gripped through the mesh. This is why I was so keen to get the net mouth set a bit higher than usual, so that I can easily reach the mesh without having to bend too far forward.

Another bite, but this time it has gone down a couple of inches, stopped and come back up. I do nothing until it goes off and continues to go right out of sight, at which stage the pole is lifted into an eel of perhaps 6 oz.

So far everything is going to plan, but after a few more eels the bites go really funny. The float goes down a little and then does nothing. Striking is pointless in that no fish are caught. Reason is possibly very small eels just hanging on the maggot without getting hold of it all.

Solution to this annoying situation, which has come just as the swim was building well, is to step up the feed rate and fill them up in the hope that better ones will follow.

While trying to feed off these mini-bootlaces I am coming in to the 8 metre line to see what's going on there. The float is moved down six inches to the second mark on the pole and as soon as the bait hits bottom a good bite registers and the size returns to 3oz or so. If I can keep them coming here for a time it's a good bet the final weight will be high. In any case the shorter pole is giving me a rest and ensuring that the quality of presentation stays high.

Some days eels don't seem to bother about the bait moving, but on others they want it nailed dead still. Overall the still bait seems to be the one that builds the biggest weights, so it's the one I choose whenever it's possible.

One dodge that seems to increase the percentage of hit bites when holding back hard to the float is to move the pole tip towards the float the moment a bite shows. This has the effect of reducing pressure on the float and thus lowering the resistance the eel is feeling.

Bites keep coming for a good hour and during that time fishing has been fast and furious. At times it's been almost a new hook for every eel, but there seems to be no answer to the problem. I have shallowed off three inches but that resulted in a reduction in both the number and the quality of the eels. Maybe the swim holds eels of varying sizes and that is part of the reason bites are being missed. This is nothing new and whenever I'm eel fishing I expect to miss a lot, but it doesn't bother me because everyone else suffers the same way.

As the inside swim begins to die it is time to return to the 8 metre mark – which has been fed regularly but sparingly while being rested.

The first drop in, after adding that six inches of depth taken off for the 8 metre mark, shows the better eels are back. Nothing changes, it's just a case of plugging away and keeping up the concentration and working the pole well.

The match is over but there is one more thing to watch as the scales arrive. Drop a fish from your keepnet as they are tipped into the scale pan and it is no problem picking it up again. Do the same thing with an eel and a long and often fruitless hunt through the grass begins.

If possible, get the scales to move well back from the water's edge and over an area of ground that offers no hiding place for any escapees. Watch too for weighing-nets that have large mesh sizes. These are deadly and can cost the eel angler a lot of valuable ounces. Some organising clubs provide plastic bags with which eel weights can be dealt quickly and efficiently.

This time the scales tot up a 9lb 6oz total for the effort. It has cost dearly in hooks and patience and I must admit it is not my favourite way of fishing. But as a team method it is one that must be mastered, and as a means of getting a high individual place it is a better bet than just hoping for a bream draw. That's no more than playing angling bingo.

The final point in the personal performance analysis after this match concerns bream. By fishing exclusively for eels, the area down the middle of the river had been left to the mercy of the anglers on either side. As it worked out the draw left me with no chance of catching bream, but given a better peg it might have

● *This catch of eels earned Doncaster's Sandra Halkon-Hunt the ladies' national championship in 1990. Sandra's company is responsible for much of the team clothing seen at today's matches*

been a good plan to have fed a few balls of caster-laced cereal out there, to ensure that if they showed on either side of me I would have been in with a chance of catching some.

That oversight is taken note of for the future; but the bream plan would have meant taking along a lot of extra bait that stood a good chance of remaining unused. Planning such a match is really playing the numbers game and needs a lot of thought beforehand.

Overall the eel plan was sound enough and unless the match is a very important one, with either big prizes or team honours at stake, it may be best to go with a single-minded plan and stick at it. After all, over the years it will probably emerge that the best results come from those matches where you fished the same method right through.

15

Chub and barbel on the feeder

As we saw in Chapter 13, not all match fishing is about fine lines and tiny hooks. There are many venues that demand a brave approach and tackle more suited to specimen hunting than competition.

Big, fast rivers like the Severn, Trent and Wye call for gear that can stop big chub or barbel, fish that make up terrific weights on methods that a few years ago would have been considered nothing short of fantasy.

Biggest impression on such venues has been made by those match anglers who mastered the technique of fishing big feeders to beat what at first may seem the more skilful technique of the float fisher.

Strong tackle and a lot of bait add up to a 'bag up or bust' approach to these matches. Scratching around to catch even 10lb of small fish is not going to win anything when a similar weight can be made with just three or four feeder-caught fish.

But it isn't just a case of sticking a big feeder on a hefty rod and throwing the thing into the river. That approach will result in little except missed bites and a lot of smashed tackle.

The target match in which a feeder plan is to be used is on a typical big river that pushes through very fast even during summer, when smaller venues lack flow. A run of big weights, mainly of chub, have been the talk of the angling world and it's just by chance that my regular club has had a match booked here every season for years. The trip could prove to be the highlight of the club's season. The river is in sparkling form; a few practice days have shown that it will probably need 80lb to win and that most pegs are

capable of at least half that weight if fished well and with thought.

In previous years caster and hemp have been the best baits, but of late the fish seem to have had enough of them, and all the biggest wins have been made with bronze maggots as hookbait with some hemp in with the feedered maggots.

First thing to get organised is the bait. It is no good going to these matches with all sorts of bits and pieces. Twelve pints of bronze maggots with a few reds included and three pints of hemp is what is needed. Fish can be caught on luncheon meat or sweetcorn, and still a few on caster, but all these are nothing more than second-rate alternatives and, rather than get confused, the hemp and maggot is all that's going to my peg.

The maggots are going to be cleaned up well and taken to the match in some ground maize which will be riddled off on the bank just prior to the start, removing all but a tiny amount which is left to prevent sweating. The hemp is prepared and packed into three bags and then frozen. These will be taken to the river in with the maggots to act as cool packs.

Tackle is going to reflect a total legering approach. A heavy feeder rod with a fairly steep taper that can handle a 3oz feeder and cast it well beyond the middle if required. Although the rod is powerful it does have

---

● *Jim Gear used a big feeder to catch this terrific net of barbel and chub to set a new River Trent match record. The catch came from a very fast-flowing peg below the weir at Thrumpton*

164

some 'give' in the tip section and ends with a glass-fibre quivertip, which, although thick, is not too rigid.

A second rod, still quite powerful but more in keeping with handling a 1oz bomb, is also going to be needed. Both rods have good quality reels. Throwing big feeders and playing powerful fish such as barbel require sound and very solid engineering. My own favourites are a superb Shimano and an original Abu Cardinal. Both are smooth and have gearing and bale-arms that can handle the considerable pressures inflicted by this style of fishing. Line is 6lb on the big feeder rod and 4lb on the leger so the model you choose needs to have a big spool, the wider the better to prevent line bedding in.

Turning to the feeders, the first thing to consider is the weight they will need to carry. Experience has shown that 3oz just holds bottom and both very large and medium sizes of block-ends are going to be needed during the five-hour match.

Bites will come quickly, and the feeder's contents need to be emptied fast so that bait isn't dropped all over the river every time a bite is struck and the tackle wound in. With this in mind the first task is to cut the holes into slots. This can be done by using scissors to run each hole into the one behind it. On some models, cutting diagonally across the feeder results in less strength being lost.

The end cap needs to fit well. Sort out some makes which are tight and ideally deep-fitting to prevent them from working free in the fast flow. The nylon loop that comes as a means of attachment is cut off and replaced with a short piece of twisted Power Gum. To attach the Gum, start with a piece about five times the length of the feeder and thread a small bead or swivel onto the centre of the Gum. For these big feeders that are going to be fished at long range I prefer a swivel, and if there is a possibility that the feeder will need changing I will use a small split ring on the Gum and then attach a swivel to that. This will enable the split ring to be opened and a different one attached.

Hold one end of the Gum and roll the other between finger and thumb. Now, without releasing the ends, bring them together and knot them. If you've done it correctly the Gum will now be doubled and twisted together like a rope.

Thread the knotted end through the feeder and the loose end-cap, securing it with a shot outside the fixed end-cap. Make up enough to see you through the match – maybe a dozen might be needed if the swim is snaggy. Rig some smaller sizes in the same manner.

Final step is to attach a 3oz lead to the side of the feeder. While the fold-over type are fine in the smaller sizes, I prefer to add a few spots of glue to large ones to ensure that they stay put. The same applies to ski

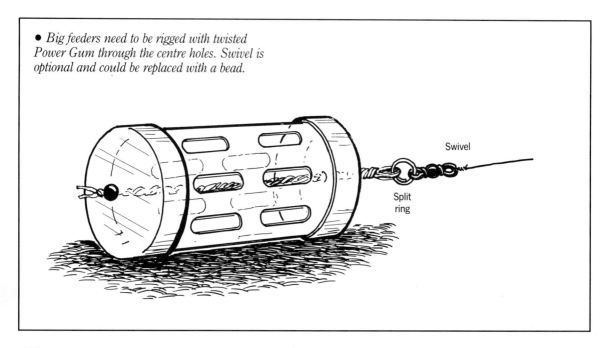

● *Big feeders need to be rigged with twisted Power Gum through the centre holes. Swivel is optional and could be replaced with a bead.*

Swivel

Split
ring

• *A long rest is essential to keep as much line as possible clear of the fast flow. Note how the angler is baiting the hook before he fills his feeder. This prevents any risk of bait spilling out of the holes*

leads: either glue them on or at least pinch down tightly with pliers the strip lead that holds them in place.

The fish on these fast rivers often move right up to the feeder and in the case of barbel may even pick the feeder up and rattle it to get at the contents. With this in mind hooks have been tied on two-foot-long lengths of nylon. A choice of sizes from 16 up to 12 will be needed and on nylon ranging from 2lb to 4lb.

Go for strong forged patterns such as the Drennan Feeder or a similar style. The main criteria are sharpness and strength.

That takes care of the bait and main tackle but something special in the way of rests will be needed too. In order to keep as much line out of the water as possible, very long bank sticks are needed. My own choice is a couple of adjustable ones that extend to

about eight feet. They need to be rigid too.

A butt cup that screws to a shorter bank stick may also be handy on some pegs but ideally I shall be looking to get the rod standing on my seat-box lid.

Actual rod-rest head can be one of your own choice but I prefer a rubber-covered flat head, some six inches wide, that has been bent slightly to form a deeper-than-usual V.

Rubber is better than plastic or nylon because it helps prevent the rod moving across the face of the rest. It's also vital to get set up neatly with no odd bits and pieces on which line can foul. Be sure, when you position the rest so the rod faces slightly downstream of you, that it isn't going to get hit during casting.

Having arrived at the peg, a few minutes is spent recovering from the walk before unpacking the trolley. This time is spent surveying the swim, which looks like most of the others in the match, which has been pegged below a weir. It's a wide river, perhaps fifty yards on average and very fast, running over a firm gravel bed. Depth is around six to seven feet and I'm planning to fish just beyond the middle.

By watching the boils and surface turbulence it is

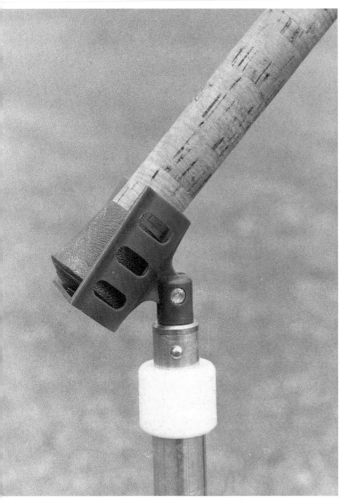

• *This special butt rest is perfect for feeder fishing when the rod needs to be high in the air*

possible to work out where any large boulders or other obstructions that could pose problems later on might be. This swim appears straightforward but there are some heavy boils about three rod lengths out which suggest there might be a rough area of bottom that will need to be avoided on the retrieve.

As always, the box is set up level. The peg is very shallow on the inside, and because the bank is broken away I'll set up a platform with the rear feet just touching the bank.

The box is going on the platform but I am planning to stand in the water alongside it, using the box and platform as stands for bait and tackle. By staying close

to the bank other tackle can be left on dry land but will still be within easy reach. The platform also avoids any danger of the box being swept away by the flow. Keepnet is also attached to the holding arm and staked out in a manner that stops it rolling around and perhaps getting in the way when a big fish is being landed.

Having set everything up to my liking the rods can be assembled. The feeder rod is threaded up and a 3oz feeder attached using the loop method described in Chapter 7. The loop on which the feeder is to run is kept at six inches for a start but if bites become difficult to hit I'll change to a fixed feeder and use the bolt-rig attack. A hook length two feet long is a good starting set-up.

For a start the hook is going to be a 14, but spares in 16 and 12 are also uncoiled and laid out in the accessory box ready for a quick change if needed.

Three maggots are to be the starting bait but if things don't go to plan that will quickly be reduced to a double. And in any case if I can get away with using two rather than three it will slightly reduce rebaiting time.

Often these large fish take a big bait without hesitation. But if they've been caught several times they get shy and may prefer a small bait – only time will tell!

Bait aprons can be useful for this type of fishing if you are forced to stand well out in the water. But today everything is to hand on the platform and I can rebait without having to bend down. The bait has been divided up so that the bulk remains to hand but safe on the bank, while enough to see me through the first hour is in a bait box that's sitting inside my groundbait tray. The tray also contains a box of hemp, a couple of disgorgers, a towel, hook wallet and some spare feeders. There's a pair of pliers too, so that running repairs can be carried out should the feeder get damaged.

Almost time; a quick check around the peg. There's nothing that can get washed away should a barge come through. Everything can be reached and the landing net is lying on the platform to act as a safety net should a fish drop off while being swung in.

The whistle goes and the hook is baited with three bronze maggots. Next the feeder cap is flicked off and the body filled. Always bait up first and fill the feeder

• *A bait apron can be an asset if you are forced to stand in the water*

last. Done this way there is less chance of bait starting to work through the feeder's holes before it can be cast.

For a start it's a half-and-half mix of hemp and maggots, but this will be changed to mainly maggots with perhaps a third of the content hemp later on. The hemp is intended to act as a holding bait but too much can get the fish obsessed with it rather than with the maggots I want to use.

Having baited and filled up, the feeder is wound to within three feet of the tip and the cast made. It's an

overhead lob, nothing hurried or jerky otherwise even 6lb line will come adrift. By casting overhead better accuracy is achieved than would be possible by casting sideways.

● *By getting a bow to form in the line bites will show as drop backs on the tip but it is essential to get the feeder weighted to just hold bottom. The rod faces downstream at about 45°, with the feeder settling directly in front of the peg. For straight legering when the going gets hard the rest is shifted so the rod faces at 60° upstream.*

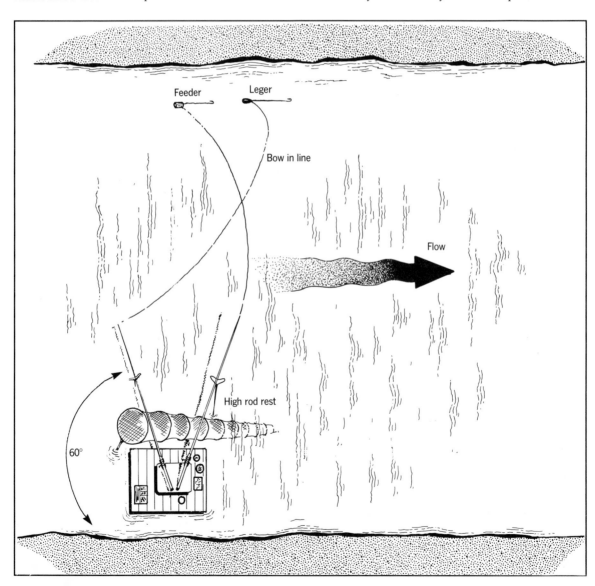

Aim to get the feeder to hit bottom directly in front of you, which may mean stealing a foot or two upstream to allow for the current. As soon as the feeder hits bottom, get the rod on the rest and wind off a couple of feet of line from the reel so that a bow forms. Now, with the rod set up high and facing downstream by around 45 degrees, bites will show as drop-backs.

To make this set-up work it is vital that the feeder just holds bottom until a fish hits the bait. This dislodges the feeder and causes the tip to straighten as pressure on it is released.

The feeder has been out there thirty seconds and now needs to be rebaited and got back quickly. By repeating this operation continually a lot of bait will be got out, and hopefully chub will begin to move in.

Cast completed, the rod goes on the rest and two feet of line are let off. The bow forms quickly and the tip begins to pull downwards with the pressure. Bump, bump: it slackens almost as if the feeder has come off. Strike: it feels as if the bite has been missed but after a few turns of the reel it's obvious there is something on the hook. Well, it's a start, a small chub of maybe 4oz. But at least it has shown that the feeder is set up right and will break away at the slightest knock.

I'll continue with the three-maggot bait for a while. Bump, the tip goes again and this time it's a better fish of perhaps 2lb. Although you can't bully these strong fish it will help if I can lead it away from the catching area as quickly as possible. Keep the pressure on and get some line back on the reel smoothly. As the chub nears netting range I'll raise the rod tip as much as possible to get the fish on the surface. By keeping a fair bit of pressure on I will be able to get its mouth out

● *You don't need many like this chub to chalk up a winning weight. Note how the hook, although large, looks minute against that rubber-lipped mouth*

of the water. Once this has been done they seem to come in much more easily. Maybe it is the air they take in or simply that with their heads half out of the water they can't see where they are going. Either way it saves a lot of time and results in easier netting.

The first half-hour has slipped past unnoticed. It's been a busy time, and while a few fish have been caught the main thing has been to keep feed going in regularly. On these prolific waters a big shoal of chub will soon wander off if it doesn't get a regular serving of bait.

Bites are still coming regularly and the fish getting bigger. The last one went well over 3lb, so I'm taking a bit of a gamble and stepping up to a 12 hook to see what happens.

A chub comes straight to it so it looks as if they are really going to have a go today. Next cast the feeder hits bottom and bang! The tip didn't drop back but the rod almost vanishes off the rest as something resembling a submarine on full power takes line off the reel. This is no chub. The anti-reverse on the reel had to be disengaged quickly and I'm thankful that for once I had remembered to set the clutch to give line at a bit below the hook length breaking-strain. The fish is still going downstream and there is no way it can be brought quickly under control. All I can do is keep up the pressure and hope it tires.

The fish turns and comes back towards me. The pressure needs keeping on and I'm winding in hard to stay in touch. This is almost certainly a barbel. They are wonderful fish but even one of 4lb will take a fair time to land. From the match point of view the chub are better because they can be dealt with so much faster.

Eventually the constant pressure is telling and the barbel is nearing the net. But they don't give up and a last-ditch attempt to escape almost caught me off guard. Thankfully the net was ready and as soon as the barbel's head was on the surface I was back in charge and the fish was landed.

The hook was right in the bottom lip and would have stayed there no matter how hard I had applied pressure. But don't underestimate these barbel, they can break even that 6lb line if they are bullied too hard.

Next bite was another drop-back and the chub that followed seemed a real weakling by comparison. But at 2½ lb a time they are building my weight nicely.

Four casts now without a bite, so off comes the 12 and the three-maggot and a 14 goes back on, this time

with just two maggots as bait. Result is a 1lb chub but the bite was hard to spot. Maybe they are getting wise to the hook or the swim is getting fished out. At best the keepnet holds 50lb and more fish are needed to get among the top placings.

At this stage the first flaw in the plan has appeared. I have neglected to feed a second line closer in as a standby. Possibly a line just below the boils that looked a problem at the start might have been worth cultivating. But the mistake has been made and there's no point in trying to build up that area at this late stage. Instead the feeder line farther downstream must be searched.

If the feeder is cast lower down the swim it will empty its contents and simply send any fish downstream after them. So the feeder is abandoned for a moment and the straight leger comes into play.

The rod rest is shifted so that the rod points just slightly upstream, and after baiting with two maggots the bomb is dropped about three yards down from where the feeder had been landing. The lighter bomb holds bottom simply because it does not have to contend with water pressure pushing against the bulk of a big feeder. Some line is again pulled off the reel to put a small bow in the set-up. This acts as a safeguard against a big fish hitting the rod hard and breaking off.

Two casts at the same spot and no bites, so out comes the bomb and it's cast another yard downstream. Response is immediate, suggesting the shoal has dropped down in search of maggots that have rolled along the bottom. After the fish, which was a chub of 1lb, the feeder is brought back into action simply to deposit more feed at the head of the swim. Because the chub seem to be dropping back after the maggots I've increased the percentage of hemp being fed, in the hope that this heavier bait will pull them back closer to the head of the swim.

At this stage the alternating between leger and feeder must continue, otherwise the already slightly unsettled shoal may decide that the food source has ceased and move away altogether.

For a while now it is a case of using the leger to search out what fish are left, gradually following them around in a trial-and-error fashion. Several are caught about mid-way down the swim but after a few more baitings with the feeder bites stop again.

The leger is abandoned now in favour of a try with the feeder, so after re-positioning the rest and scaling down to a 16 hook we'll try the original spot. First cast will be with two bronze maggots as bait but if nothing happens they will be changed for two reds, just as an alternative in case the fish have begun to feed selectively. The idea of trying bronze first is so that only one change is made at a time. The reduction in hook size may work with no other alteration. If so, that's fine. If it doesn't, then a second tactic can go into operation, and so on until the right combination is found.

Oddly enough the smaller hook has worked and a chub, although less then 1lb, shows there are still some signs of life in the peg. But it is obvious most of the fish have been caught and the rest of the match is going to be spent picking off the stragglers by constantly alternating baits and perhaps feeder and leger.

One plan that could be tried now is to reduce the size, but not the weight, of the feeder and lengthen the tail to perhaps three feet. Cutting down the feeder size will keep just enough bait going in to hold the remaining fish and the extra tail length will attract those chub that are getting wary of the feeder. From now on every fish is a bonus and it is a matter of working hard to give them something different from what they've been seeing for the past few hours.

As the final minutes tick away the fish have reduced in size and the last two have been roach, suggesting that the main body of chub have either stopped feeding or moved away. But a weight into the 70lb bracket isn't bad going.

It appears there have been some good weights and in the distance the scales have already attracted a good following. So it's a good idea to get packed up quickly to get the tackle out of harm's way before the crowd arrives.

It's obvious my catch is going to take several weighs and some time to complete, so I'll watch carefully that each batch of fish is weighed accurately, recorded and totalled up. Every season a few matches are won and lost through bad stewarding but ultimately the onus is on the angler to see that his catch is dealt with properly. If you are not happy with the way the scales are being used, then complain and get the problem put right straight away. It's too late to moan when you find you have been beaten by the odd ounce which could have been lost by sloppy weighing.

● *Not the sort of fish you really want to catch on a big feeder but often they move in before and after the main shoal feeds*

16

Roach on the stick

Watch a good stick-float angler in action and you will see poetry in motion, a constant rhythm of feed, cast, trot, strike, retrieve, re-bait and feed again. Done well it is a winning method on flowing rivers where roach, chub and dace are the main species.

Stick-float fishing is a season-long method too, and providing conditions are right it can usually be relied upon to produce its share of fish.

In the old days when caster-caught roach dominated Trent match results, stick floats were used almost to the exclusion of all other methods. The idea was to set up a rig with small shots strung out and then ease the float through, holding it back fairly hard every few inches to make the caster rise and fall attractively. Why it worked better than a bait allowed to run through unchecked I don't know. Some said it gave the fish a better chance to see the dark bait in fairly murky water, others said it was because the loose-fed casters were constantly lifted and swirled around by the current. Who was right we're not sure but the fact remains that the stick out-fished the lot.

Next came the bronze maggot revolution and the caster took a back seat, as did the holding-back technique, in favour of running the tackle through unchecked.

Now, several years down the line, a multitude of rivers still respond to the stick-float method in one or other of its many forms.

The match to be fished is a fifty-pegger along a fast-flowing river where roach and small chub dominate catches. Nets of between 12lb and 18lb are usually needed to win and a double-figure bag will get you in the frame most weekends.

The pegged bank is stone-lined and there's an average depth of between six and eight feet two rod lengths out in most pegs. A few unfortunate anglers will, however, find themselves on much shallower areas, where to find six feet they will have to resort to a waggler to throw the required distance. But these pegs can still produce fish, and have accounted for a few outstanding results.

Caster and bronze maggot seem to share the honours over a season, with the maggot having the edge during the early season. By autumn the caster begins to sort out the better fish and is usually the one to win with.

Three pints of good-quality casters and a pint of hemp, along with a pint of mixed red and bronze maggots, are all that will be needed. But this is a hard-fished water and the bait, especially the casters, needs to be of the highest quality.

As to tackle for the job, a pair of 13 foot rods with spliced tips are a good choice. The spliced tip gives the sort of action which is ideal for stick float work. A third, slightly softer rod will be needed for those

• (Right) A study in concentration. Ray Mumford watches the rod tip for the slightest movement

• (Inset) Small carp like this soon build into match-winning bags, but you need to get both tackle and attitude right to catch them quickly

waggler pegs and in any case a waggler will be worth setting up at any swim just in case the fish decide to stay away from the bank.

For stick-float fishing on this type of water the closed-face reel can be a great tool. The pick-up system allows line to run off freely but it can be engaged at any time without bumping a fish off. Only drawback is a tendency to cause line bedding, and for that reason my own choice is to be a wide-spooled fixed spool carrying some 1¾lb line. For stick floating I prefer a shiny line that will float, and if it begins to show signs of sinking I'll wipe it down with a smear of Mucilin fly leader dressing.

Prevailing wind on this river is from behind and just slightly upstream. Perfect conditions for the stick. And today is no exception.

My peg is on a straight with no cover. The bankside stones go right into the river and standing on them can be uncomfortable unless you can arrange a flat area. Sitting down is fine, but standing seems to keep you alert and is certainly better if you have to run right to the end of the swim to get bites.

Having got the peg levelled off without too much disturbance of the stones, the rest of the gear is set up. The keepnet goes in first so that the swim can settle again well before starting-time.

Landing net and all the other accessories also need placing with thought because, once the match starts, the less you move around the greater are the chances of pulling fish in close, thus reducing the time it takes to land them.

By carefully plumbing the swim it is discovered that there's a slight rise in the bottom about half-way along the peg, after which the depth resumes the average seven feet expected. The rise is nothing drastic, maybe four inches at most, but it will need some thought if a bait is to be run over it effectively.

Flow is moderate, no boils or any other deviations are obvious, so there should be no problem with using a conventional lignum stem and balsa upper-section pattern of stick.

• (Inset) A good mixed net of roach and skimmer bream, the sort that match winners are reared on

• (Left) Even a broken leg couldn't stop Denis White getting to the waterside! And by the look of that stretched pole elastic it didn't do his catch rate much harm either

• The River Trent at Gunthorpe, Notts, a match venue where many of the best stick-float anglers learned their craft. Today the feeder often dominates the same events that were once ruled by the stick

---

Because the river is wide and has open banks the water surface is bright, so the floats are to be black-tipped ones carrying the equivalent of 2½BB and 3½BB broken into size, 4s, 6s, 8s and 10s strung down the line in traditional stick-float style.

The difference in size is in case conditions change, or a more distant line is needed at some stage during the match.

Each float is fixed to the line with three pieces of silicone tubing. The bottom one, about half an inch long, overhangs the stem, while the middle piece is at the top of the cane section. The tip rubber sits very close to the float top so that line from it comes very close to the surface. Use this top rubber too far down and striking will result in a noisy splashing effect because line has to cut through the water to lift the float clear.

Hook is to be a size 22 long-shank, fine-wire pattern tied to a 1lb bottom.

The waggler rod has a 2½AAA straight peacock with a fairly thick tip locked on with 2AAA. The remaining AAA is broken down into eight number 6s. There's no point in fiddling around with minute shot on

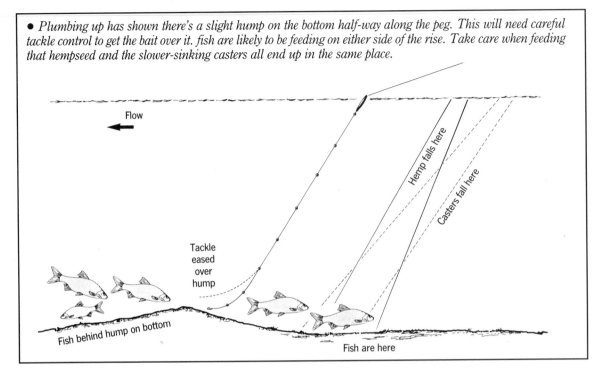

● *Plumbing up has shown there's a slight hump on the bottom half-way along the peg. This will need careful tackle control to get the bait over it. fish are likely to be feeding on either side of the rise. Take care when feeding that hempseed and the slower-sinking casters all end up in the same place.*

Flow

Hemp falls here

Casters fall here

Tackle eased over hump

Fish behind hump on bottom

Fish are here

this one because the thick quill will not register a movement on anything less than a 6. Again a 22 to 1lb finishes off the rig.

Rods ready, the seat box is positioned just to my left so that the rod butt can be rested on it and the rod laid across the keepnet mouth while rebaiting.

A bait apron is to hold enough casters to see me through the first hour. The remaining two pints are left in a water-filled bait box. Hemp is to hand on a bait tray just to the rear of the seat box.

Starting plan is to fish a rod-and-a-half length out with the possibility of going further afield if the fish get spooked.

After checking that everything is to hand there should be no reason to move from the fishing position at any time. This is close-in fishing and the fish will be easily scared by movement. As an extra precaution I have laid out my holdall and some other pieces of tackle along the bank, in the hope that this will keep spectators well back from the skyline and the water's edge.

The whistle sounds, and the stick goes in and is allowed to run through unchecked. It reached the hump on the bottom and drags under. That area will need watching if it isn't to cause a problem. But with

the bottom shot only a number 10 and set a foot from the hook, it should be possible to hold back enough to get the bait to flip over the area and down the other side.

A couple of runs through show no other obstructions are present so it is now safe to feed.

Ideally, I want to catch fairly close to where I'm standing, but just far enough down to give me room to play a hooked fish away from the main shoal.

Now fishing can start. In go a dozen casters right at the top of the swim and then, slightly below them, the same amount of hemp. This different feeding position is to take into account the faster falling-rate of the heavier hempseed.

From now on the rhythm must stay the same: feed, cast, strike, feed. By feeding first and then casting, the hookbait will arrive at the fish about the same time as the loose feed. Do it the other way around and the sequence is ruined.

For a time a bronze maggot is used on the hook but none are introduced. Idea is that the maggot will pick off a few small fish while the main caster feed is still to be accepted by the real target fish.

The early runs through are giving me a chance to search out that rise on the river bed, and after a few

Roach on the stick

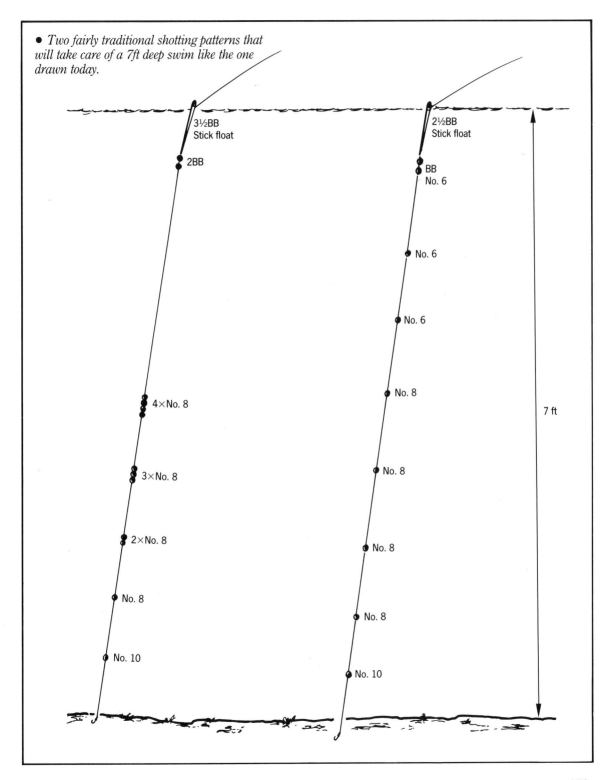

- *Two fairly traditional shotting patterns that will take care of a 7ft deep swim like the one drawn today.*

179

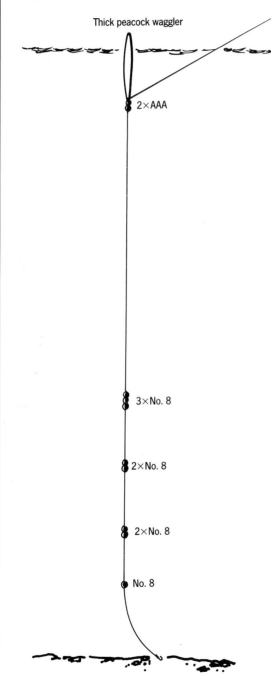

- *A waggler rig with plenty of load around the float will be an alternative should conditions change or the inside line die before the match ends.*

Thick peacock waggler

2×AAA

3×No. 8

2×No. 8

2×No. 8

No. 8

trots through I am forced to adjust the depth by shallowing off just a couple of inches. Next run down brings a roach of 2oz, followed by a chub of maybe twice that size. Both came as the float was left to trot through at the pace of the current.

The caster and hemp feed was kept at a dozen of each for the first three feeds, but has since been reduced to half that amount of casters at every cast and six grains of hemp every other cast. I have reduced the hemp because I don't want to be plagued with shot bites caused by the roach switching onto it.

After half an hour I have caught nine roach and that chub totalling maybe less than 1½lb, but it is now time to go for the caster. Immediately I hook a better fish which turns out to be a roach of 6oz, showing that the change of bait is likely to sort out the quality fish that are needed to win.

Immediately after each cast is made the rod is flicked upstream to lay all the line above the float and get it moving down under complete control. The reel bale-arm is closed and the rod moved round in an arc to follow the float's progress. Once it has run a couple of feet the float is eased back by keeping the rod still. The effect is to cause the bait to move in front of the float and rise up in the water. As the rod is again moved downstream the bait drops again and a bite registers.

This system of following the float with the rod tip keeps me in constant touch without having to concentrate on feeding line from the spool. It also means I can strike without having to close the bale-arm and risk bumping fish off.

After an hour I have caught a few more good roach, but there is no pattern. So after checking the float's depth along the rod I shorten down nine inches and run through without checking the float in any way. This works to the tune of a much smaller roach than average and then a half-pound chub. Possibly what is happening is that fish are moving up in the water to intercept the bait. But after a few more runs down it is obvious this shallower setting is not right, so depth is added again and the shotting altered by taking the first number 4 up to the float to join the BB and 4 already there. The next number 4 can now be moved up and the smaller shots spread to give a slower drop. Result is that the size of fish increases and bites come soon after the float begins its run.

Soon the catch rate slows again and it is time for another change. By constantly switching shotting and depths the fish are followed up and down in the water, but as yet the lower end of the swim has remained almost unfished.

By mid-match constant shotting and small depth-alterations have brought a reasonable return, but as bites become less frequent so the distance the float is run down is increased. The extra trotting distance means more time is spent bringing fish back, but by casting down beyond the fished-out upper limits of the peg, time-wasting is cut to a minimum.

As the lower limits of the peg get fished more it is worth hanging the bait back hard for a few seconds at the limit of each run. This tactic often results in a few bigger fish and has already picked up a couple of very good roach and a chub.

Extra depth was added a couple of casts back but this produced only a gudgeon and suggested the tackle was now not working correctly, so off came the depth and a shotting variation was tried instead.

With this type of fishing I believe in altering something every time bites aren't forthcoming. I see no point in flogging away if the bait is going over the heads of or beneath the fish it is supposed to be catching.

Another hour passes and things are getting really difficult now, so the lighter stick is discarded in favour of the second rod carrying the bigger model. A few casters go in two metres further out than the main feed line and the float follows. It's like a new world. Bites start coming again and it's soon obvious that the fish had moved out, perhaps to follow some of the casters that have been pushed out by the wash from passing boats. Alternatively, perhaps they had just got edgy and moved out into the slightly deeper water.

All goes well now for a while but the weather is changing. The wind has swung to a downstream direction, making presentation difficult.

First option as a means of coping with this new problem is to try the waggler. It works well enough and the second stick-float line continues to produce fish to this new method, even though it is a case of just letting the tackle run through unchecked. Fish are coming regularly but they are smaller than those that had been caught on the stick, probably because of the difference in presentation.

A change back to the heaviest stick rig, but this time along the nearer line, goes some way towards solving the problem but still I get the feeling things are not totally right. I need the presentation of a stick with the stability of a waggler, so a number 6 shot is added to the line a couple of feet above the float. Idea is to get the line to sink beneath the surface, and prevent a bow forming downstream of the float and spoiling presentation.

To improve the line's sinking qualities further, it can be given a wipe down with some mud. Easiest way to do this is to dip your thumb and finger into some mud and then wind in the tackle while pinching the line with your muddy fingers.

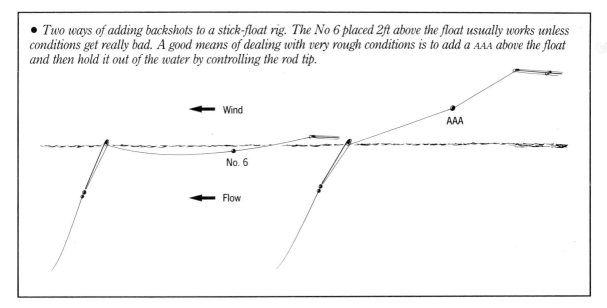

● *Two ways of adding backshots to a stick-float rig. The No 6 placed 2ft above the float usually works unless conditions get really bad. A good means of dealing with very rough conditions is to add a AAA above the float and then hold it out of the water by controlling the rod tip.*

Now, by continuing with the heavier stick and using this back-shot method, the wind is dealt with successfully and the float runs through smoothly and can be checked effectively to produce bites.

A variation of this back-shotting technique can cope with really bad winds. Try adding an AAA shot eighteen inches above the float and then holding it out of the water by keeping the rod high. By carefully controlling the shot it is possible to present a very stable bait and, at the same time, ease it through the swim. Be warned though, it takes a bit of practice and a lot of concentration to get it right.

For most of the match casters have been the bait but as it's now getting hard I have switched constantly between casters and either red or bronze maggots, to glean whatever I can from a peg that is dying rapidly.

Perhaps a small feeder or a straight leger dropped mid-way down the swim might have earned a few extra fish, but to have set them up at the start might have resulted in too many alternatives being tried too early in the match.

A case could have been made out, too, for trying a long pole. Such a rig would have coped with that change of wind direction and by using a fairly long line a lot of the swim could have been searched.

All are ideas worth storing away in the mind for next time, but it is also worth remembering that the best matches seem to be those that are started and finished on the same method. And this river is one that usually performs best to a stick, so that had to be the basis of the plan.

Something else that could have been tried during the match would have been a drop in hook length strength to, say, 12oz. Often the thinner nylon lets a bait act more naturally and will pick up some extra fish late on in a hard match. All these possibilities are now pure speculation, but around 10lb is still going to be a decent weight. If it's not enough on the day it will be worth finding out how any better weights were caught.

● *Fishing a stick float demands concentration. It helps to stand and get down close to the water*

Roach on the stick

Light stems

Although the whole idea of the stick float is to balance a buoyant upper portion with a dense stem to help prevent the float riding out of the water when held back, there are odd occasions when something different might be needed.

A very dense material such as lignum will aid casting and also do the job for which it is intended. But if fish are taking on the drop and at close range, a light stem material will show bites much better.

With a dense stem the float cocks almost straight away after casting, but with a light stem the settling process is more of a tilting nature as each shot settles. All you do to spot a bite is watch for any change in the progress of the tilt.

Suitable material for these stems would be something like model-maker's dowel or artist's paintbrush handles.

● *Boat traffic can often eliminate the middle of the river. Under such conditions a stick float run down the edge can bring rewards*

183

17

Winter on the canal

Winter has taken its toll on the local rivers. Heavy rain has put extra water into them, and fishing has been poor now for a few days. The flush through will do some long-term good, but for the time being it's going to be a case of finding somewhere different to fish. Answer is the canal, where although weights are unlikely to be anything spectacular, there is at least a sporting chance of fish at every peg.

The controlling club runs weekly Saturday open sweepstakes, which, although good matches, rarely attract more than fifty or so anglers. This water has no bait bans so bloodworm and jokers will no doubt figure somewhere in the match plan.

While the 'worm' is important, few matches are won on it here except later in the year when fishing gets really hard. For this match the target is going to be perch and roach, with the roach the fish that are going to make all the difference between success and failure.

Recent matches have been won with around 10lb, with three or four backing weights of 6lb to 7lb. But it could be harder this week. There have been a few slight frosts and the air temperature is still low. Perhaps a winning weight of 8lb, and 5lb to get in the frame, are more realistic objectives.

Best pegs are close to a factory which pumps in water that's been used for cooling machinery. Here the slight rise in the temperature of the water always attracts extra fish.

• *Canal contour shows only a slight drop off. Usually a canal that is used regularly by boat traffic has a more defined barge lane down the centre.*

General characteristics of the venue are nothing to write home about. A typical inner-city water with plenty of industrial buildings and nothing in the way of scenery.

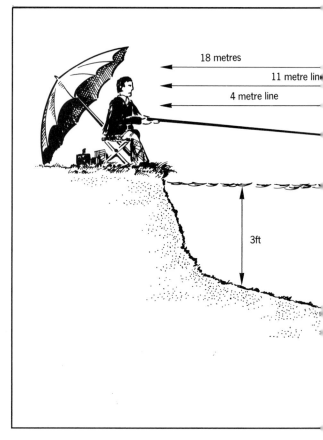

18 metres

11 metre line

4 metre line

3ft

Average width is maybe 18 metres at most and there are a few even narrower parts.

Contour of the bottom is a central boat-lane about five feet deep, with shelves from either bank sloping downwards from three feet at the edge down to the middle section. There is little in the way of a drop-off step, probably because over the years it has been eroded away.

Boat traffic at weekends is rare, although there might be the odd barge through on a Saturday, and, if the weather is good, the occasional hardy pleasure-cruiser. This lack of boats means the water is fairly clear by canal standards, but the fish don't seem to mind too much as long as the approach is right.

Caster is 'the' bait for the quality roach here, some of which can go well over 8oz and average perhaps 3oz. They are good match fish on this sort of water. There's a good head of perch, too, and leading weights will have at least a third of their total from this species.

Another good thing about these matches is the small amount of bait that's needed. A pint of jokers is ample, with just enough bloodworm for the hook. A pint of casters and that's the lot.

Collecting your own worms is possible no matter where you live, but it does take time and a bit of trouble, first to find a suitable site and then to set about scraping them. It's cold, wet work and, for the amount I use in a season, not really worth the effort. Regular canal anglers of course would do well to pursue the matter further. If you find a good bloodworm pond keep it to yourself, otherwise it won't be good for very long.

Jokers come from more polluted waters such as sewage farm outfalls, so they too can spell unpleasant work.

Thankfully far more tackle shops supply both types of worm now than a few years ago so at least they are available to everyone by one means or another. Unfortunately quality varies a lot. The bait does not travel well and in any case has a short life once

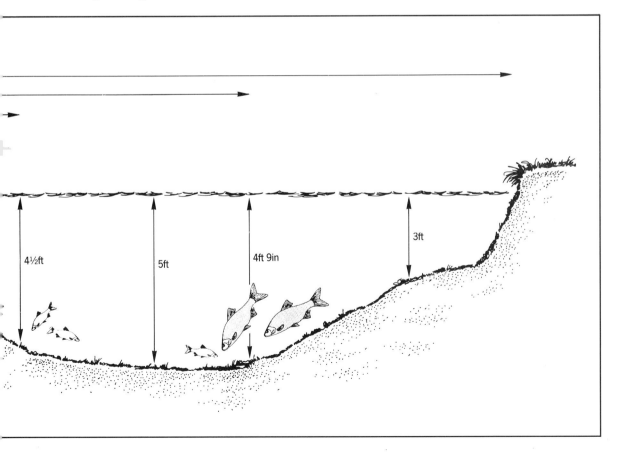

collected. Your dealer is really in the hands of his supplier and can only pass on what arrives, so don't get too angry with him if it's less than perfect.

Easiest way to ensure good worms is, if possible, to order it direct from one of the many semi-professional or professional scrapers. Both quality and price is likely to be better. But do be sure you can rely on your man, especially if you have arranged to collect it at the match.

On-the-day collection has been arranged for this match and the newspaper parcels handed over to me contain some nice bait. The bloodworm are a good size, and have a rich blood-red colour which suggests they are really fresh. The jokers too are lively, but the parcel contains a fair amount of rotted vegetation that has come from the source of supply.

This material could have been removed by running the jokers through a riddle into some water, but as it is it's a case of using the whole lot as it has arrived. It looks a bit of a mess but the extra bulk will be used to

---

● The Leeds and Liverpool canal is a busy place. Leave your tackle lying around here or on most towpaths and it's a good bet it will vanish

squeeze the jokers into small balls and then the whole lot will be thrown in. If there were not enough to hold together, a little of one of the proprietary brands of binder could have been used with it.

Casters are a much easier proposition. My pint has been produced at home and is really fresh. All are a nice light golden colour. That half-hour spent picking them over first thing this morning was really worth while and, if nothing else, has given me some extra confidence.

The draw has put me in a mid-match area, which because of the limited number of visits I have made means little. My bloodworm man reckons it's all right and that the pegs are fairly even except for those warm-water ones where the match should be won.

It's a cold morning; very dull and looking like some more rain is on the way, so the brolly can go up before the start just in case. And anyway it will provide a bit of shelter from the cold wind that is skimming along the canal.

For now I'll just get the brolly pole in place and then drop the brolly on just before the off, taking care that it doesn't obstruct the way behind when I start passing a long pole back over the towpath. A word of warning

Winter on the canal

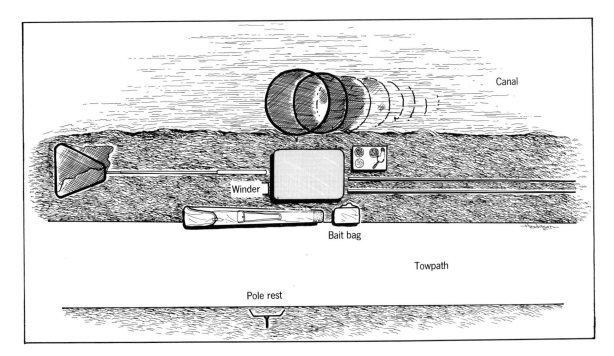

Canal

Winder

Bait bag

Towpath

Pole rest

here about these paths. They get used by all sorts of people, walkers, joggers, cyclists and more than a few of the local youngsters.

A few canals have a bad reputation for bankside theft. Youngsters wander the banks and are not averse to pocketing anything you leave lying behind your peg. So once everything is set up, this match will be one where all tackle not likely to be used will go back inside the box. Watch out too when passing a pole backwards. It's always worth checking that there's not a bike tearing along the bank. The same goes for joints not in use. Keep them parallel to the water and, ideally, where you can see them.

Well, the bank is nice and flat, so there's no need for a platform or legs to be used. The keepnet goes in first, very gently, with the mouth right at my feet and with the bottom end staked out a little way along the bank. This gives any fish I catch plenty of room to be kept safely, but prevents the possibility of the net rolling along the canal bottom and scaring any fish that may be right up on the ledge.

This net-staking is even more important in summer when gudgeon right on the shelf, maybe only a metre from the bank, are the target.

Tackle can come out now. Two poles are all I'm setting up, although a very light quivertip rig might be

● *A neat peg is essential on canals. Keep everything within reach and well clear of the towpath. Pack anything not likely to be needed back into your box before the starting whistle.*

in order sometimes. My information suggests this is not a stretch of the canal where it works so I'll pin my faith on local knowledge.

First pole is going to be a 4 metre one with a long line so that I can fish to hand. It has a softish tip but still with elastic through the first two joints. A number 3 elastic to 1lb main line. This elastic is just an insurance in case I should hook a big perch or a quality roach.

Rest of the rig is being set to fish a bloodworm and consists of a small peacock waggler with a cocktail-stick insert tip and a short wire stem. Total load, including the stem, is the equivalent of two number 1 shot at most.

The float is fixed on the line through the eye and then locked in place with a number 4 and a 6 shot. Rest of the load is made up with styl leads strung down the line. Here there is a variation, in that the first few styls beneath the float are set closer together than the smaller ones nearer the hook. This is done to provide extra stability close to the float.

Three size 10 styl go on first, followed by two 8s and then a 7 nearest the hook. Any balancing that

187

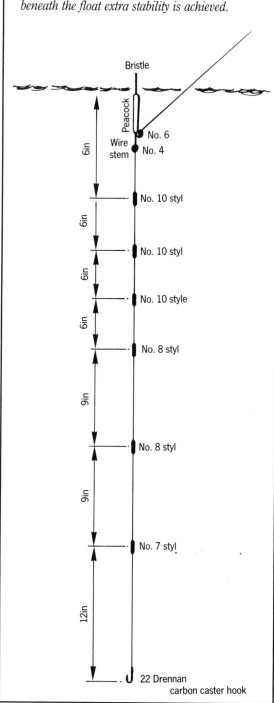

• *A rig for the bloodworm. The styls are kind to the fine line. By using three close together just beneath the float extra stability is achieved.*

Bristle

Peacock

Wire stem

No. 6

No. 4

6in

6in — No. 10 styl

6in — No. 10 styl

6in — No. 10 style

9in — No. 8 styl

9in — No. 8 styl

No. 7 styl

12in

22 Drennan carbon caster hook

• *For the 11m line a balsa-bodied float is used and the elastic stepped up to a No 4 to set the size 22 hook.*

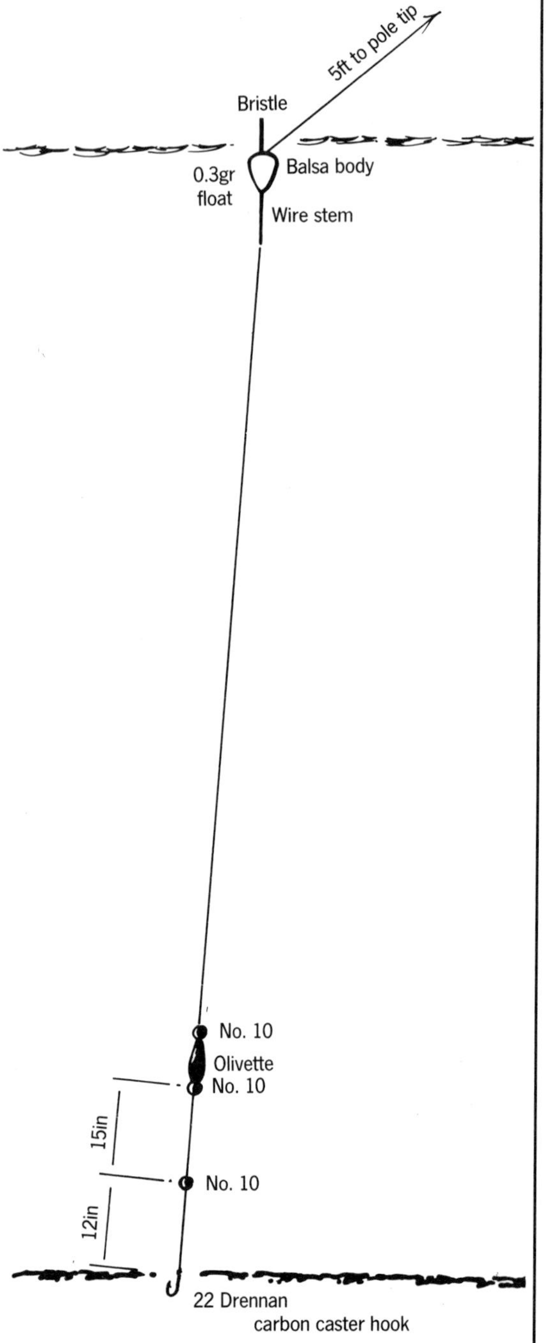

5ft to pole tip

Bristle

0.3gr float

Balsa body

Wire stem

No. 10
Olivette
No. 10

15in

No. 10

12in

22 Drennan carbon caster hook

needs to be done will be by changing the locking shots during setting-up at home prior to storing the rig on a winder.

A lighter rig could be used if conditions were favourable, but I prefer to use a float that is on the heavy side rather than risk losing anything in the way of stability. A bit of weight also makes handling the tackle in the air easier.

I have gone for styls rather than small shot because they are kinder to the fine line and can be moved around much more easily.

Hook is a fine-wire size 26 Drennan carbon caster but that's just my choice. The important thing is to use a lightweight hook that's sharp. Hook length is a six-inch piece of 8oz.

That's the rig for the inside line with bloodworm and joker. Now the other pole can be tackled. This one is 11 metres and has a number 4 elastic through the top two sections. Float is a wire-stem brittle-tipped one, with a small balsa body that's almost round but with slightly more bulk near the top.

Loading (again done at home): this time it's an

● The bushes behind this match stretch make long-pole work difficult. Before pushing pole sections through the undergrowth check to see that they are not hiding power cables. Often these wires can be at shoulder height if the canal is raised above the surrounding countryside

olivette with just a single tell-tale below it. Total load is 0.3g. Again a 1lb main line and 8oz bottom but with a size 22 hook of the same pattern as used on the other pole. It's this slightly larger hook that demands a 4 elastic, so that it can be hit home firmly on the strike and any bigger fish are dealt with positively.

Line length from float to pole is about five feet, and I have used a yellow rubber band slipped over the fourth section to anchor the tackle when not in use. The band also acts as a marker so that I know where the pole is to be broken down.

Plumbing is kept to a minimum so as not to disturb the swim. All I want on the long pole is to find where the deepest water just begins to shallow up. A drop at a full 11 metres shows five feet and by the time I am holding the pole correctly it is just three inches

189

• *A rubber band or one of these special yellow-coloured anchor loops can be used to retain the hook neatly alongside the pole when not in use. They are also perfect for marking the section which is to be broken down when landing a fish*

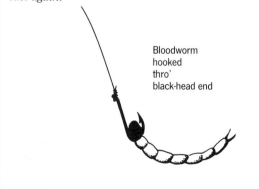

• *Bloodworm is a very natural but delicate bait. Hook it gently with a fine hook through the extreme black-coloured head end. Often if a bite is missed the worm remains undamaged and can be cast again.*

Bloodworm
hooked
thro'
black-head end

shallower, so that will be the spot on which to concentrate.

The 4 metre rig gets the same quick plumbing and is set to fish at a little less than 4½ feet.

Not long to go now, but just before putting up the brolly I've filled the caster box with water and run off a few floaters for the hook.

The short pole is first to go into action so that is made ready, and, as the starting-whistle sounds, on goes a nice big bloodworm hooked carefully through the head end. The right end to hook is the one which has a black segment at the very end.

Out it goes, followed by two walnut-sized balls of joker and debris.

That's got the line sorted out, so lift out the tackle and the long pole goes into action with a small feeding cup on the end. The cup is slipped over the pole near the tip and pulled back until it locks about a foot down the first section.

Once the cup is half full of joker, the whole pole is carefully fed out and the joker emptied right on top of where the float will be fished. This is the caster line and, while a ball of joker could have been thrown that far, a cup – assuming you keep the pole right way up – ensures pinpoint accuracy. Some anglers don't even bother with this approach, pinning their faith instead on caster alone. But a few jokers for a start seem to get some fish interested in the area. I suspect the movement of small fish feeding encourages the bigger roach to follow to see what is going on, then they find the casters and decide to stay.

Now a small canal catapult is used to fire in two pouches of casters, maybe a dozen or so in each pouch.

That's the feeding over, so back to the 4 metre pole and the bloodworm. I'll give this inside line and the bloodworm twenty to thirty minutes while the main caster swim gets going. During this opening period I want to catch a few perch to boost whatever might come from the casters later on. If all goes well I should get a pound or so as a starter.

The cast is made and the pole given a quick pull back towards me so that all the line is sunk beneath the skim. It's a case now of concentrating until the bites come. There it goes! A little perch of maybe 1oz, but it's a start and they may well get bigger as the jokers being working.

Down goes the float tip again but the bite is missed. Out it comes and a new worm goes on. Do this every time a bite is missed otherwise you can well be fishing with a damaged bait and more bites will be missed, or worse still, no more will follow.

A new worm goes on, and for the next few minutes there's the odd bite and two more perch go into the net.

The joker is used sparingly but another walnut-sized lump goes in on the same line after four fish have been caught, along with another six casters to the other swim at nearly 11 metres.

The last ball of jokers brought a response and a 4oz perch is netted. I've brought along a very small net for this match because nothing above 1lb is likely and the smaller net makes less disturbance.

So far all is going well, but then a run of missed bites suggests a change is called for. This is done by shallowing up a couple of inches to put the bait just off the bottom where perhaps the perch are intercepting those jokers. Result this time is a 2oz roach, followed next cast by another of the same size.

During this flurry of action a further six casters have gone in on the long line to keep the area topped up, and with thirty minutes gone it will soon be time for a

test with the other pole. Meanwhile, it is best to cash in on the inside while it is producing.

I'm finding that bites seem to come a few seconds after I've given the float a little twitch. Maybe the slight flutter this gives to the bait is all the extra attraction it needs. Down goes the float again and another perch of 4oz is netted. That's close to 1½lb from the inside, but it is getting harder, so before it dries up totally I'm leaving it to try the caster line.

The caster – one of those floaters I set aside – has the hook completely buried in it and out goes the tackle. The breeze makes holding the long pole steady a bit of a problem, and if it gets too bad I shall have to lengthen the line from pole to float by another two feet or so, to prevent the pole tip's movement from upsetting the float.

If the caster is working a bite should register quickly. If nothing has happened after two casts I'll go back on the inside for another fifteen minutes and then try again. We're in luck, the float slides away and a fish, a roach of maybe 1oz, is swung in. It's small but a start, so try again with another floater and this time it's a perch of 3oz. That's pretty good, 4oz in two casts. Keep that up and it will be a good result.

Another roach and a perch but it isn't really going mad. Six more casters go in and try again.

The wait was worth it. The elastic is pulled out a foot by a much better fish, and the pole is carefully and smoothly moved round to the left to steer the fish away from others that may be down there. Yes, that's the sort of roach we want, around 7oz, or maybe more.

If at this stage things die off, there is still the chance of a few extra ounces from the inside swim; so a small lump of joker can go in from time to time, while the six-casters-at-a-time treatment continues on the main line of attack.

Time is ticking away now but the fish are coming fairly regularly. It seems the swim holds even numbers of both roach and perch, and in a variety of sizes, so each fish needs to be struck and played carefully until I'm sure of what's on.

Part of the skill of fishing these canals successfully is keeping the swim going, by careful feeding and then by playing and landing each fish with the minimum amount of fuss.

The brolly plan has also helped, in that it has provided a nice bit of cover behind so that my movements are hidden from the fish. It's also been something of a deterrent to bank wanderers, who always seem to appear after the first couple of hours. With the brolly up they can see little and tend to roam off in search of someone else to distract. Having people behind is fine and everyone has to learn. But when it's hard, the water is shallow and you're fishing close in, the less disturbance the better.

Well, two more small perch and the whistle goes to end the match. Maybe close to 5lb in the net. Perhaps enough to make a low place in the pay-out. But from the bank telegraph it seems the warm-water pegs

have dominated the proceedings. Two anglers either side of the outfall are rumoured to have double figures and a few more around them are thought to have had some good roach. Well, if nothing else the operation has sharpened the pole-fishing technique a little and it's been a change from the usual winter tactics of the river – which hopefully will be back in condition before long.

● *This special, home-made plummet will cope with deep bottom silt and ensure a correct reading*

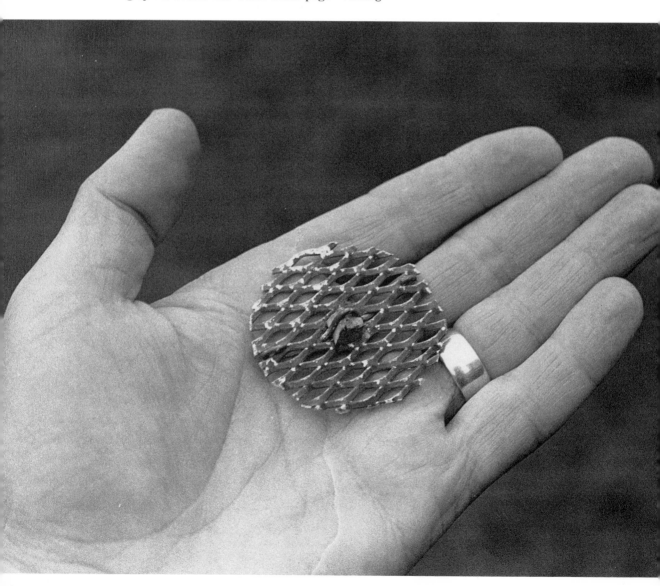

That sinking feeling

Many canals and slow-moving waterways suffer from a silt problem that can make accurate depth-finding extremely difficult.

If the bottom is covered with a soft layer of silt, a conventional plummet will sink deeply into it and a false reading of up to a foot or more out can result.

A trick I picked up from the Yorkshire-based Smithies team, while practising for a national championship on the Oxford Canal, was to use a very special plummet that works on the snow-shoe principle.

Instead of a small, dense weight, the idea is to produce a plummet that is just heavy enough to sink through the water and large enough in area to sit on the soft silt without getting buried.

To make one of these very special tools you will need a piece of perforated zinc plate – the sort that might be used for making a maggot riddle.

Cut a circular piece about 1½ inches in diameter.

Next, find the exact centre and glue on a small piece of wine-bottle cork. A short length of lead wire can be folded over the cork, forming an eye, and through the holes of the plate, folding out the ends underneath to prevent it slipping.

Leave the folded ends of the wire fairly long for a start, as these will be used later to get the correct balance.

To use this plummet, pass the hook through the lead wire and insert in the side of the cork in much the same fashion as usual. Lower the rig into the water and then set your float as normal.

By trimming the lead wire it is possible to balance the cork and zinc plate until it sinks at a slow rate. Because the plate is so large in diameter it rests easily on the silt and yet can be felt easily as the pole is raised.

These plummets are perfect for use on light gudgeon-fishing rigs where accurate depth setting is essential for good bite detection.

• *A normal plummet can easily provide a false reading by sinking into soft silt. The home-made zinc plate type will ride on the softest bottom and allow an accurate setting to be achieved.*

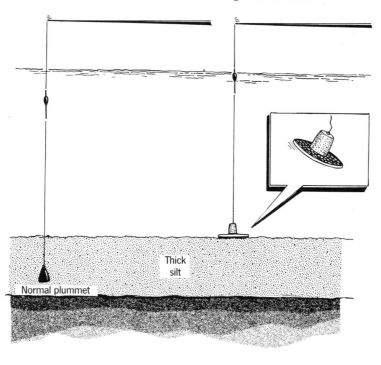

18

Team fishing

Team fishing brings out the best in a match angler. It encourages thought, planning and dedication, and above all gives you something to fish for no matter how badly you draw.

Being a part of a good squad means that a pool of information is available for the mutual benefit of the members. But team fishing will also bring disappointments. Sooner or later most people get dropped from the team, if only for one event on a water that's not suited to their style. If it happens, then you should take it well and fish all the harder to win back your place. And even though the captain or manager has overlooked you, chances are you'll be expected to go along and act as bank runner for the rest of the team.

Also on the negative side there will be times when you fancy gambling on a long shot, perhaps trying for bream in a peg where there's only an even chance that

they will show. But as a team angler you may be forced to fish to a set plan that means you must ignore them and fish for a guaranteed net of roach, or some other species that isn't going to bring individual glory but can earn vital points for the team.

Cost may also come into the equation of whether or not you join a squad. There may be club subscriptions and hefty match-entry fees to meet. The expense and time involved to attend practice sessions should also be considered.

Many match groups who take part in the National Federation of Anglers' annual national championship get no support from their parent association and have to foot the bill totally from their own pockets.

Add to this the fact that you may be needed for matches that don't inspire you. There may be a team event at a poor water on the same day as an open match on your favourite venue. All these possibilities add up to big sacrifices, yet being a part of a successful and happy group can be a tremendous experience.

There are of course good squads and bad ones. The good ones are completely open with their information and hold regular meetings at which tactics can be discussed and plans laid for forthcoming campaigns. Avoid like the plague any outfit that has a prima donna who rules the roost and is not prepared to listen to, or help, the rest. A good team works as one unit, and does not tolerate factions that sit on the fringe and pick the bones clean without contributing.

Sharing the spoils as well as the disappointments is

● *Frank Barlow knows all about the pressures of team fishing. He's been a member of the successful Shakespeare Superteam and a consisent performer with Nottingham Federation and the Trentmen. Here he plays a big fish caught as a result of gambling a long shot, something that team plans don't always permit*

the only way to work, and if you join a team and ever feel that all is not as it should be, then speak up. If the problem is solved, that's fine. If it continues as before, get out. Fishing is too valuable not to be enjoyed.

If there is no suitable group close by that will take you on, it may be worth forming one of your own. It can be a group from within your main club, or maybe your tackle dealer would be happy to support a small squad selected from among his clientele. Ideally, such a group will be hand-picked on an invitation basis so that only the right type of angler gets involved. Go for a sensible number of say fourteen anglers so there are enough for matches: fourteen anglers for instance, will mean you can field two teams of six, or one of twelve, and have reserves. That way there will always be a fight for places and everyone keeps sharp.

Some teams operating this system get the reserves to act as bank runners and, in return, count them in on the winnings, splitting everything equally among competitors and runners. The bonus from such a plan is obvious enough: the runners work very hard to provide the right information so as to stand the best chance of a reward.

Practice is vital to team success, and after each session a de-briefing meeting should be called, to talk over what has been learned in order that some new plan can be formulated for the match. It's also a good idea to elect a team captain or, better still, get a non-fishing manager who can handle affairs such as reserving tickets and entries. The captain and manager may also be given the task of selecting teams.

Much has been said and written about team selection, especially for really big events such as national championships. But there is nothing to beat straight selection done fairly and without any favouritism.

Fishing eliminators and awarding places to the best performers sounds fair, and perhaps it is, in terms of giving places to those who have won them fairly. Yet few successful clubs operate this system, usually because it is impossible to fish enough qualifiers on the match venue at a time of year close enough to the match to give a true picture.

A combination of points and selection was operated by a team I once fished for. This method involved a series of points matches, after which the top twenty-four scorers were brought together and each asked to select a team of twelve for the match. It worked well for a few seasons, but too much depended on each

angler's personality, so thankfully the system was changed and straight selection came back into operation.

One very practical way to pick a team is to have a small group of three or four anglers who are automatic choices on pure ability. These then meet, and fill the remaining places from the squad. But all these selection methods need to be done in a ruthless, but fair, manner. There can be no room for sentiment, otherwise the whole network and team spirit is destroyed.

Practice sessions for the squad should be planned almost as well as the match itself. It is no good just going along to a water and fishing it blindly in the hope that a plan will unfold.

Find out from the beginning, perhaps by recruiting some local expert help, what the possible methods will be, and then work around them.

Take each section of the match in turn and fish it in blocks, lining the whole squad up over a set of pegs. Allocate each member a method to fish for say three hours. Then pack up, re-draw for swims and swap methods for another three hours. Afterwards the team meeting can agree a tactic from what has been caught.

Get the local expert to agree to coach you all, in return for a fee, plus a bonus if you win. The bonus can be paid for by each member contributing a small amount extra towards a team bet. If the side wins then the coach gets paid out of the winnings without hitting the main prize.

Also worthwhile is a walk along the entire match length, accompanied by the coach who can then discuss individual pegs and their potential. This is a great close season pastime with teams planning a national championship campaign.

One of the worst ways to organise a team practice session is to line up and fish a sweepstake match against each other. All that does is encourage each person to stick at a method which is catching, rather than experiment to see what else can be learned.

By all means use open matches as practice, but as the real event gets close don't expect to see the top teams fishing to their true plan. It is better to fish these matches as individuals, and use them as a way to get the feel of the water rather than as a means of trying out your plans. Give a plan a go, but don't risk showing your hand too much, and above all take press reports with a pinch of salt. As an angling journalist, I've more than once been told a set of tactics totally

● *The spoils of finding a good sponsor. This is the Barnsley national squad just after signing its first big deal with Daiwa a few seasons ago*

different to the ones that were actually used by the winning angler.

If the big event is a long way from your home and only a few visits to it can be made, try sharing the fishing by perhaps having half the squad fish one event while the rest walk the banks, swapping roles on the next visit. At least that way each member gets a chance to see a fair number of swims, and also fishes to get the feel of the water.

It has to be understood that practice is not all about catching lots of fish. It's about sorting out the water into section-by-section classifications, about being sure you have floats with the right tip colours and of the required patterns, and about all the other little things that go towards being well prepared on the day.

Sponsorship

Having formed a squad and perhaps spent a season or two proving your combined abilities, it may be time to begin thinking in terms of sponsorship.

There is a fair amount of support to be had, both from tackle dealers and manufacturers and from companies and firms in your area looking to get more exposure for their name or product. But don't expect free handouts. A sponsor wants a return for the investment, and it is here that a fair number of sides quickly fall short of the mark and lose their backer after only a short time.

Finding a good sponsor can be hard work but start in a small way, perhaps with your local dealer, who may be prepared to kit you out in some sort of team clothing and maybe subsidise bait for important matches. Such deals usually mean incorporating the shop name into the team's title. For example, if Smith's Tackle Centre agrees to support your Wanderers Match Group side it could become Smith's Wanderers Tackle Team. That's fine until you try to get that mouthful into print. Few newspapers will be prepared to use long names, so work out something between you. Perhaps simply drop the Wanderers and go for Smith's Tackle Team. Dropping the team name in favour of a sponsor's is of course fine until you lose the sponsor. Smith's Wanderers is short and would be better for all concerned. And if after a season Smith drops you and along comes a bigger fish, such as a tackle company, you switch to Daiwa Wanderers or Wanderers Team Shimano.

● *Sponsorship is also available for individuals. This enterprising soul seems to have his own ideas on how to find a backer*

Having found a sponsor, find out what is on the table and what is required in terms of input from your team and, of course, results. A sliding scale of increased support in return for agreed performances is a good motivator on both sides.

Members of the team must be made aware of their commitments too. Get them thinking sponsorship, and impress on them the importance of reporting their results to the press, ensuring that the team sponsor is included in the report. 'Joe Bloggs, Wanderers Team Shimano, 10lb 3oz.' is a classic way of getting publicity.

Some sponsored teams have fallen foul of their backers by not registering their new name with organisations such as the National Federation of Anglers. If Wanderers AC is registered as such with the NFA, that's how they will appear in the national programme and press. It also pays to advise local newspapers and the national angling press of any link-

up, asking that the correct name be used in their reports.

If tackle companies come forward with support they will expect loyalty. If they provide tackle they want it used, and perhaps will ask for some development work to be done by the team.

Team clothing bearing a sponsor's name needs to look smart. No one wants to be associated with a bunch of filthy, mud-covered anglers. The captain or manager must crack the whip and get the lads out looking good.

Work hard for your sponsorship, be a credit to the company name, and chances are you will enjoy help for a long time to come.

When success comes, make sure the team can cope with it. Work out in advance who is to get what from any cash that comes in, by agreeing percentages that are to go to runners, manager and anyone else involved. Perhaps there is also a case to be made for a small amount to be deducted to go into team funds that can then be used towards future expenses.

Finally, don't forget that inquest to talk over the match and what went right and what went wrong. Don't make these a witch hunt to humiliate anyone who didn't do well, but openly discuss how things can be further improved if the same venue is fished again.

Social meetings are also a good thing, and there's a lot to be said for regular get-togethers over a pint where team members can get to know each other. Talk will probably turn towards fishing but it's not essential. Even a game of darts among the squad has value. It's all about team work.

Looking back on my own team experiences, I have seen both good and bad. There were teams which did well on the bank but didn't really see eye to eye or mix as friends off it. Those sides didn't last and soon the drift began towards other outfits in the area.

A number, myself included, went to pastures new. In my case it was to a much smaller club which went on to climb through the NFA divisions very rapidly. This group was friendly and worked well together. We shared a lot of information and worked hard in preparation for important events. Soon sponsors came forward and the team was kitted out with jackets. On the eve of the national we agreed to meet up for a relaxing drink. Without prompting, everyone turned up wearing a team jacket. From that moment I knew this was a real team. And the following evening the national results showed us in the promotion bracket!

The national

Former world champion Kevin Ashurst once said that the way to fish a national is just like any other match.

In many ways he was correct, but I believe that when you no longer get nervous the night before, it is time to call it a day. A championship of such importance should be the highlight of a match fishing year and as such deserves some respect.

Kevin's statement holds true, however, in terms of how you prepare and what you take to the bankside. It's obvious that every item of kit must be in perfect order and there can be no excuse for having anything but the best in terms of bait. But a national is no place to start using new gear or trying unproven methods.

Fishing a good national is all about knowing what you're going to do and then going out and doing it well.

● *Kevin Ashurst reckons a national is just another match. But with catches like this and a world championship under your belt it must be easy to take any match in your stride*

● *A national underway on the River Trent. Stewards should keep the crowds back – but don't rely on it. Tackle laid behind you can serve as a barrier*

You should know what bait is needed and that's what you take to the match, nothing more, nothing less. The national is a five-hour event and that's all you need to cater for.

By match morning all the planning should have been done. You will know the sections, and what your target weight is from the one you draw. But do you know the rules – all of them? If you don't then you could well land yourself, and the team, in a lot of trouble, even to the point of throwing months of effort out of the window by getting yourself disqualified.

From the time you arrive at match headquarters everything needs to be done by the rules. Stewards must be booked in and team changes made before the draw begins. The captain, or, better still, the manager, should see to all these formalities. The captain can then join the draw queue and have nothing else to worry about.

● *(Above) Time to weigh in. There will be a litter steward to collect any debris but it is your responsibility to clean up. Fail to do this and you risk disqualification*

● *(Below) The right way to do it. The scales are supported by the central top ring – or better still hung on a tripod. The angler should now be watching the dial to see that his catch is correctly registered*

● *(Below) Not all stewards know how to handle scales correctly, and used like this the reading will be inaccurate. Don't accept the weight until you are satisfied it is correct*

● *Dave Thomas shows the crowd his world championship trophy, the first to be won by an Englishman on home territory. Victory in prestigious events like world and national championships are almost guaranteed to attract sponsors*

It's a good plan to have a pre-arranged meeting point to which everyone goes as soon as the team's draw is announced over the public address system. From now on time is valuable. The captain will hand out the section cards and this is a good time for a last-minute check that each team member knows what is in store. If you have had a local angler as adviser he may be able to run a final check over what is expected from each swim, bearing in mind any changes in conditions that may have occurred.

Now gather your tackle and get on the coach which will take you to your section. You must travel on this transport, otherwise disqualification looms. You carry all your own kit too, unless you have a doctor's certificate and have sought official permission in advance.

Load your tackle yourself. Don't leave it to someone else, that's a sure way of getting it either left behind or put on the wrong coach. Get this done early on and you run less risk of getting something smashed in the rush that always seems to occur just before leaving time.

Use the journey to the section wisely. Sit down and relax. Think over all you have learned in practice, and don't get into deep conversations that may lead you up false trails or, even worse, end up with you giving away something the others don't know about. This is a tough game and you must play the cards close to your chest.

Once at the section, get away as fast as you can so that you arrive at your peg as soon as possible. This not only gives you maximum preparation time, it also ensures that the peg is not disturbed by other anglers walking too close to the water's edge. If possible, spread some kit so that they are forced to walk well back. A brolly is a good means of achieving this, even if you have no intention of using it during the match.

In a championship such as this you may find yourself next to a superstar. If you do, then don't get all panicky. Let him do the worrying. If an international gets hammered off the next peg by an unknown it's big news. If you get the hammering it will be accepted as something to be expected. Go into the match as the underdog and fish the way you know best, and chances are you'll find you do better than you expected.

The match over, get cleared up, so that by the time the scales arrive you can concentrate on having your fish weighed without fear of tackle getting broken or stolen.

The rules state that the peg must be clean, so check it carefully and pick up all litter, yours and the stuff that was there when you arrived. A member of the weighing party will be assigned the job of litter steward and will take away any debris you have collected.

Watch that your catch is weighed accurately and recorded in the book correctly – it's too late to argue when the fish have gone back.

Now get back to the coach, which again the rules say you must use, to return to headquarters. Once there, find your team and report to the captain or manager, who will want to know what you've caught and how many points you reckon it's worth.

In recent years the national result has been calculated very quickly and efficiently so the agony is soon over. In a full division of eighty teams the top ten teams get automatic promotion. At the bottom end, ten get the big drop to a lower division. Either way it all starts again, with another full year to plan the next campaign.

Acknowledgements

There are two sorts of coarse fishing. One is commonly called pleasure fishing, the other match fishing. Why we differentiate, I do not know; after all, match anglers fish for pleasure too. Think about it. How many other sports permit the average competitor to rub shoulders and compete against a world champion?

I have been in that situation many times and each occasion has given me tremendous pleasure. I can now consider some of the sport's greatest names as friends. It is those same fine anglers who continually help, teach and encourage the less-gifted in an unselfish fashion that few sports could match.

Such people certainly made my match fishing an even greater pleasure. I would like to mention them by name, but space is far too limited. Hopefully this book will help me put a little of what I have learned from them back into the sport and perhaps enable many more anglers to share the pleasures of match fishing.

Finally a special thank you to Mac Campbell for helping out with photographs, and to Colin Hodgson for creating the line drawings.

ALLAN HAINES

Index

Page numbers in *italics* indicate illustrations

Index

Index